Model Witness Examinations

ECOND EDITION

S0-BEC-975

Paul Mark Sandler
James K. Archibald

Section of Litigation

ABA

Defending Liberty
Pursuing Justice

Cover design by Lisa Empleo

07 06 05 04 03 5 4 3 2 1

Library of Congress Cataloging-in-Publication Data

Sandler, Paul Mark.
Model witness examinations / by Paul M. Sandler and James K. Archibald.— 2nd ed.
    p. cm.
Includes index.
   ISBN 1-59031-039-X (pbk.)
    1. Examination of witnesses—United States. I. Archibald, James K.
(James Kenway), 1949- II. Title.

KF8900.S26 2003
347.73'75—dc21   2003011904

This book is based on the publication *Pattern Examinations of Witnesses for the Maryland Lawyer* by Paul Mark Sandler and David Freishtat, Copyright 1979, 1987, Maryland Institute for Continuing Professional Education of Lawyers, Inc., Suite 830, Candler Building, 111 Market Place, Baltimore, MD 21202.

Back cover testimonial by Scott C. Speier reprinted with permission of TRIAL (February 1998), Copyright the Association of Trial Lawyers of America.

Discounts are available for books ordered in bulk. Special consideration is given to state bars, CLE programs, and other bar-related organizations. Inquire at Book Publishing, ABA Publishing, American Bar Association, 750 North Lake Shore Drive, Chicago, Illinois 60611.

www.ababooks.org

Contents

Foreword

Some trial lawyers look for every advantage over their competitors. These lawyers keep close to the vest their techniques for handling witnesses and offering and objecting to evidence. They do not share the jewels that they have garnered over many years of experience.

Other trial lawyers love the concept of trials, admire their comrades in the trenches, understand that their own skills and talents benefited from the guidance they received from their predecessors at the bar, and want to give something back to the profession in which they take pride. Paul Mark Sandler and James K. Archibald of Baltimore, Maryland, are two of the best examples of such trial veterans. They are confident, experienced, talented lawyers who take time from busy trial schedules and demanding practices to offer to young lawyers the wisdom they have learned from years of trying cases.

Model Witness Examinations is a gift to young lawyers and to older lawyers who are called in mid or late career to try cases. The book demonstrates how to offer testimony on direct examination, how to cross-examine and impeach various types of witnesses, and how to use discovery in the examination of witnesses. Sandler and Archibald not only illustrate model examinations, they also offer citations to rules and cases that can be relied upon by an advocate preparing an examination on an important point.

The illustrations are authentic. Sandler and Archibald know what issues arise at real trials, and their experience enables them to offer examples that are genuinely useful. They also know the danger in lawyers trying to use the exact same words and phrases over and over and advise their readers that the model examinations are starting, not ending, points. They are not a substitute for strategic thinking and are not meant to be the last word on effective advocacy.

In short, *Model Witness Examinations* is a wonderful gift from two lawyers who love the trial process to all those who will follow them.

Stephen A. Saltzburg
Washington, D.C.

Introduction to the Second Edition

Six years have elapsed since the First Edition. Still, a core skill of the trial lawyer remains that of posing the right question or series of questions. This skill also remains one of the hardest to master.

The patterns in this Second Edition have been modified to reflect continuing changes in the law. One significant change involves the amendments to Evidence Rules 103, 404, 701, 702, 703, 803(6), and 902 of the Federal Rules of Evidence, which became effective in December 2000. New case law and statutory enactments are reflected as well. We have added nine new patterns in this Second Edition. They include: Immunizing the Witness; Present Sense Impressions; Excited Utterances; Dying Declarations; Subsequent Remedial Measures; Initial Examination of a Child; Lift Stay Examination; Tangible Objects; and Lay Witness Opinions—Intoxication.

Last, but not least in importance, we express our gratitude to Robert B. Levin, Eric R. Harlan, and Richard M. Goldberg, all of Shapiro, Sher, Guinot & Sandler, and to Marta A. Markowska of Venable, Baetjer, Howard & Civiletti, LLP for their assistance. We also extend special thanks to Christopher P. Lutz of Steptoe and Johnson, LLP, for his guidance.

Paul Mark Sandler
James K. Archibald
April 2, 2003

Introduction to the First Edition

One of the hardest tasks of a trial lawyer is to ask the right question, and ask it well. The most difficult task of all is to ask a series of good questions, and to conduct an effective examination in the stress of the courtroom.

This book presents the mechanics of conducting certain types of examinations of witnesses, correlating those examinations to the Rules of Evidence and applicable case law. The examinations consist of "model examinations"—a series of questions utilized to solicit facts and opinions from the witnesses in situations that recur, regardless of the type of trial, and that require little creativity, but must be reasonably adhered to in order for counsel to obtain the needed evidence. Each model examination is preceded by a contextual outline, followed by a comment annotated to the cases, statutes, and the Federal Rules of Evidence.

A word of caution: the model examinations cannot be simply lifted from the page and applied during the course of a trial. The models are simply suggested organizational structures, which contain the basic questions designed to elicit an answer necessary to obtain a desired result. The trial of the lawsuit is more art than science; different approaches can be used to the same end. The model examinations appearing in this work are the threads from which the trial lawyer can weave his or her own cloth.

Although our comments following the model examinations include tactics and practice points on the conduct of the examination, as well as a presentation of evidentiary discussions, we are not attempting to teach advanced trial tactics. There are almost as many effective courtroom styles and strategies as there are effective advocates. Styles and strategies are, for the most part, beyond the scope of the book. For example, consider the cross-examination of a witness utilizing a transcript to impeach. *See* chapter 11A, *infra*. One approach consists of soliciting facts from the witness that contradict the deposition. Then counsel reminds the witness that she was deposed; elicits facts that she was deposed in her lawyer's office; that she took an oath; that her recollection of the events was fresher in her mind at the time of the deposition than at trial; and finally, a reminder that when counsel took the deposition, the witness testified one way in the deposition and another way at trial.

Another approach to impeachment using a transcript is to simply remind the witness that she just testified that the accident occurred at 7:00 a.m., but that in her deposition at a certain page and line she swore that the accident occurred at noon. See, for example, Herbert J. Stern, *Trying Cases to Win, Cross-Examination*, Wiley Law Publications, John Wiley & Sons, Inc. (1993).

Whether focusing on direct examination or cross-examination, there are many ways to accomplish the goal of eliciting facts. Before we can run, however, we must walk. It is our hope that the material in this book will enable the advocate to grasp the fundamental requirements in selected types of examinations of witnesses, thereby freeing him or her to focus on the refinement of courtroom style.

We express our gratitude to the following attorneys who have given us assistance: Joseph J. Coppola; Jeffrey S. Rosenfeld of Freishtat & Sandler; Randy V. Sabett of Venable, Baetjer, Howard & Civiletti, LLP; summer associate James P. Dvorak, Jr., University of Virginia Law School; law clerks Baron Franc Bond, Columbia University Law School, and Raghav Kotval, University of Maryland Law School; and to Patricia A. Augustyniak of Shapiro Sher Guinot & Sandler.

Paul Mark Sandler
James K. Archibald

About the Authors

Paul Mark Sandler co-chairs the litigation department of the Baltimore firm of Shapiro Sher Guinot & Sandler, and is an active trial lawyer representing many notable clients in a wide variety of cases in state and federal courts. He is the co-author of *The Winning Argument* (also published by the ABA Litigation Section) and *Pleading Causes of Action in Maryland*, and co-editor of *Appellate Practice for the Maryland Lawyer: State and Federal*. Mr. Sandler is a graduate of Hobart College and Georgetown University Center of Law. He is a former chair of the Litigation Section of the Maryland Bar Association, a former member of the Council of the ABA Litigation Section, and remains active in bar association and community affairs.

James K. Archibald is a litigation partner in the Baltimore and Washington, D.C., offices of Venable, Baetjer, Howard & Civiletti, LLP, where he has maintained a varied litigation practice for many years. Mr. Archibald is a former president of the Maryland Association of Defense Trial Counsel and is active in the Litigation Section of the ABA, the Defense Research Institute, and the International Association of Defense Counsel. He is also the co-author of *Pleading Causes of Action in Maryland*. He has written numerous articles on litigation issues and has lectured widely on litigation topics and techniques. He received his law degree from the University of Maryland in 1975, after completing his undergraduate education at Johns Hopkins University.

Part 1

Direct Examination

Recollection 1

A. PRESENT RECOLLECTION REVIVED

During the course of a criminal trial, a police officer is on the witness stand. The officer has no present recollection of the description of the alleged assailant, which was related to him by an eyewitness. Another police officer, however, now deceased, recorded the eyewitness's description in a police offense report. Defense counsel desires to use that offense report to refresh the recollection of the witness on the stand. The defense rests upon the discrepancy between the eyewitness's description of the height of the assailant and the height of the defendant, which is 5 feet 4 inches.

Defense Counsel:

Q. Officer, what time did you arrive at the scene on the day of the incident?

A. Around 10:30 a.m., five minutes after the robbery.

Q. What, if anything, did you do upon arriving at the scene?

A. I conducted a routine investigation.

Q. What did that investigation consist of?

A. Interviewing witnesses, inspecting the crime scene to see if there was any evidence left by the robber, and calling for the crime lab.

Q. Did any of the witnesses furnish you a description of the assailant?

A. Yes, one witness did.

Q. Tell us, please, what description did that witness give of the robber?

A. I don't remember.

Q. Is there anything that could refresh your recollection as to the description given?

A. Officer Smith, who is now deceased, accompanied me to the scene and recorded the statements of all witnesses. His report might help me remember.

Q. Did Officer Smith also record in his offense report the description of the one witness you referred to?

A. I believe he did, yes.

Q. I show you what purports to be a police report and ask you if you can identify it.

A. This is Officer Smith's report.

Q. Please read the report to yourself, officer.

(Officer reads the report.)

Q. Is your recollection refreshed?

A. Yes, it is.

Q. Now, sir, tell us what description was given of the robber by the one witness who offered a description?

A. John Peabody described the robber as a tall thin man approximately 6 feet in height with a mustache and long curly hair.

Comment

Although not absolute prerequisites, the key circumstances enabling a witness to refer to his or her notes for purposes of refreshing recollection are: (1) that the witness cannot recall particular facts; (2) that a particular document or memory aid, prepared by either the witness or someone else, might help the witness recall the particular facts; and (3) that after reviewing the document or memory aid, his or her memory is refreshed. United States v. Humphrey, 279 F.3d 372 (6th Cir. 2002); United States v. Frederick, 78 F.3d 1370, 1376-77 (9th Cir. 1996); Hall v. American Bakeries Co., 873 F.2d 1133, 1136 (8th Cir. 1989); United States v. Rinke, 778 F.2d 581, 587-88 (10th Cir. 1985); Sporck v. Peil, 759 F.2d 312, 317 (3d Cir.), *cert. denied*, 474 U.S. 903 (1985); 20th Century Wear, Inc. v. Sanmark-Stardust, Inc., 747 F.2d 81, 93 n.17 (2d Cir. 1984), *cert. denied*, 470 U.S. 1052 (1985); United States v. Scott, 701 F.2d 1340, 1346 (11th Cir.), *cert. denied*, 464 U.S. 856 (1983); United States v. Shoupe, 548 F.2d 636, 642 (6th Cir. 1977); United States v. Morlang, 531 F.2d 183, 191 (4th Cir. 1975); United States v. Wright, 489 F.2d 1181, 1188-89 (D.C. Cir. 1973); Thompson v. United States, 342 F.2d 137, 139 (5th Cir.), *cert. denied*, 381 U.S. 926 (1965); NLRB v. Fed. Dairy Co., 297 F.2d 487, 488-89 (1st Cir. 1962). In *United States v. Mkhsian*, 5 F.3d 1306, 1313 (9th Cir. 1993), however, the Ninth Circuit Court of Appeals held that "it is not essential that the prosecutor first establish that the witness has exhausted his present recollection before [the prosecutor] can refresh his memory." The court further observed that "[t]he trial court has 'wide limits of discretion' in its decisions to permit the prosecution to refresh the memory of a witness." *Id.* at 1312 (citation omitted). Examples of when the foundational requirement of showing exhausted memory is relaxed include efforts to expedite or better organize the thoughts of a witness, and efforts to refresh the recollection of a witness who does not realize that he or she has forgotten important details. *See* Doty v. Elias, 733 F.2d 720, 725 (10th Cir. 1984); United States v. Thompson, 708 F.2d 1294, 1300-01 (8th Cir. 1983).

The witness in this case is not required to state that he prepared the report, knew of the report at the time it was prepared, or even that the report was or is correct. However, from a tactical point of view, the more detailed facts that the witness can offer to demonstrate the trustworthiness of the document or memory aid he utilizes to refresh his recollection, the greater the impact will be upon the trier of fact.

It is the testimony of the witness that is admitted in evidence. The memory aid used to refresh recollection is merely the stimulus for triggering recollection and is not evidence itself. Moreover, the memory aid need not be a document or a writing. It may be anything that triggers the memory, e.g., "[t]he creaking of a hinge, the whistling of a tune, the smell of seaweed . . . ." Fanelli v. United States Gypsum Co., 141 F.2d 216, 217 (2d Cir. 1944), and United States v. Rappy, 157 F.2d 964, 967-68 (2d Cir.), *cert. denied*, 329 U.S. 806 (1946) ("anything may in fact revive a memory: a song, a scent, a photograph, an allusion, even a past statement known to be false").

Opposing counsel may examine the memory aid, show it to the jury and attempt by questioning the witness to show that the memory aid did not refresh recollection or that refreshed recollection is unreliable. "When a witness declares that [something] has evoked a memory, the opposite party may show, either that it has not evoked what appears to the witness as a memory, or that, although it may so appear to him, the memory is a phantom and not a reliable record of its content." United States v. Riccardi, 174 F.2d 883, 888 (3d Cir.), *cert. denied*, 337 U.S. 941 (1949). *Accord* 20th Century Wear, Inc. v. Sanmark-Stardust Inc., 747 F.2d 81, 93 (2d Cir. 1984), *cert. denied*, 470 U.S. 1052 (1985); United States v. Wright, 489 F.2d 1181, 1188-89 (D.C. Cir. 1973); United States v. DiMauro, 614 F. Supp. 461, 466 (D. Maine 1985). Opposing counsel may use the memory aid to impeach the witness. Since the memory aid is not evidence, use of the memory aid or cross-examination relating to the memory aid is for the purpose of testing whether the witness's memory has been refreshed. *See also* Fed. R. Evid. 612; John W. Strong et al., McCormick on Evidence § 9 at 32 (4th ed. 1992).

Whether the police officer in this pattern can testify to a hearsay declaration by an absent witness might present a problem. *See, e.g.*, United States v. Smith, 521 F.2d 957 (D.C. Cir. 1975); John W. Strong et al., McCormick on Evidence 501 (4th ed. 1992). However, assume that an appropriate hearsay exception such as "excited utterance," or res gestae in state court proceedings, would be recognized, or that the out-of-court description of the witness is not offered to prove the truth of the matter asserted but for the purpose of impeaching the previous trial testimony of the eyewitness. *See infra* pp. 10-12 for discussion of hearsay contained within past recollection recorded and *infra* chapter 2.B, 2.F, and 2.G for discussions of hearsay contained within business records, police accident reports, and public records, respectively.

For a discussion concerning the difference between present recollection revived and past recollection recorded, see United States v. Riccardi, 174 F.2d 883, 886 (3d Cir.), *cert. denied*, 337 U.S. 941 (1949). *Accord* United States v. Rinke, 778 F.2d 581, 588 (10th Cir. 1985). *See also* Fed. R. Evid. 612; JOHN W. STRONG ET AL., MCCORMICK ON EVIDENCE § 9 at 29 (4th ed. 1992).

This pattern has been cited with approval in the following texts: MICHAEL H. GRAHAM, EVIDENCE: TEXT, RULES, ILLUSTRATIONS & PROBLEMS 51-52 (2d ed. 1988); LYNN MCLAIN, MARYLAND EVIDENCE: STATE AND FEDERAL § 612.1 n.1 (1987 & Supp. 1995).

B. PAST RECOLLECTION RECORDED

During a criminal trial, a police officer is on the witness stand. She has some recollection of the description of the assailant given to her by an eyewitness to a murder. She does not, however, recall the details of the eyewitness's description. Defense counsel wants to introduce the police officer's personal notes, which contain the statement given by the eyewitness, to demonstrate that his client was not the assailant, since the assailant was 6 feet tall and the defendant's height is 5 feet 4 inches.

Defense Counsel:

Q. What time did you arrive at the scene on the day of the incident?
A. Around 10:30 a.m., five minutes after the robbery.
Q. What, if anything, did you do upon arriving at the scene?
A. I conducted a routine investigation.
Q. What did that investigation consist of?
A. Interviewing witnesses, inspecting the crime scene to see if there was any physical evidence left by the robber, and calling for the crime lab.
Q. Did any of the witnesses furnish descriptions of the assailants?

A. Yes.

Q. How many witnesses furnished descriptions?

A. I cannot remember. I believe one.

Q. Tell us what description that witness gave of the robber.

A. I can't remember the details of the description, although I remember generally that the witness described the robber as being rather tall.

Q. Did you take any notes while you interviewed the witnesses to the incident?

A. Yes.

Q. Did you record in those notes the one eyewitness description of the assailant to which you previously referred?

A. Yes.

Q. Do you have your notes with you?

A. Yes.

Q. May I see them?

A. Yes.

Q. If the court please, I would ask that the police officer's notes be marked as the next exhibit in order for identification.[1] In whose handwriting are these notes?

A. Mine.

Q. When were the notes prepared?

A. About 5 minutes after the incident occurred.

Q. Where were the notes prepared?

A. At Hansen's Grocery, the scene of the incident.

Q. Were the facts recorded in your report when they were fresh in your mind?

A. Yes.

Q. Did these notes accurately reflect the facts as you obtained them and recorded them?

A. Yes.

Q. Are you satisfied now that the notes are accurate?

A. Yes.

Q. Do you have sufficient recollection about the matters contained in your notes to testify fully and accurately concerning those matters?

---

1. The practice for marking and introducing exhibits varies from court to court. Consult the local rules.

A. No.

Q. Would your notes refresh your recollection?

A. Not fully, no.

Defense Counsel: We offer the notes in evidence.

U.S. Attorney: Objection. The witness indicated that he had some recollection of the description he obtained from the witness. Since the witness has some recollection of what occurred with regard to his interviews, the notes are inadmissible in evidence under the doctrine of past recollection recorded. The witness's memory is not exhausted.

The Court: Rule 803(5) provides that it is not necessary that the witness lack all recollection of the event. The Federal Rules provide that the witness need only testify that he has insufficient recollection to enable him to testify fully and accurately. However, I shall sustain your objection in part on the grounds that Rule 803(5) of the Federal Rules of Evidence does not allow defense counsel to introduce this writing in evidence unless the government requests that it be introduced. The federal rule, however, does permit the witness to read the document in evidence. Therefore, I shall allow the officer to read portions of her report in evidence. (Officer reads eyewitness description reflecting that assailant was described as 6 feet in height.)

Comment

The foundation necessary in federal court to introduce a document considered to be a prior hearsay statement pursuant to the doctrine of past recollection recorded requires the following testimony: (1) that the writing was made by, or adopted by, the witness at a time when the witness had a clear recollection of the event; (2) that the document was accurate at the time of the writing or at the time the witness adopted the writing; (3) that the witness presently vouches for the accuracy of the writing; and (4) that the witness lacks sufficient recollection to testify fully and accurately about the events contained in the document. *See* Fed. R. Evid. 803(5); United States v. Porter, 986 F.2d 1014, 1016-17 (6th Cir.) (citation omitted), *cert. denied*, 510 U.S. 933 (1993); United States v. Schoenborn, 4 F.3d 1424, 1427 (7th Cir. 1993) (citations omitted); United States v. Ray, 768 F.2d 991, 994-95 (8th Cir.) (citation omitted), *appeal decided by* 777 F.2d 423 (8th Cir. 1985); United States v. Patterson, 678 F.2d 774, 778 (9th Cir.), *cert. denied*, 459 U.S. 911 (1982). *See also* United States v. Green, 258 F.3d 683

(7th Cir. 2001); United States v. Smith, 197 F.3d 225, 231 (6th Cir. 1999); United States v. Shorter, 1999 U.S. App. LEXIS 19670, at *4 (4th Cir.), *cert. denied*, 528 U.S. 1011 (1999), *subsequent appeal*, 2002 U.S. App. LEXIS 5347 (4th Cir. Mar. 29, 2002)[2]; Wilson v. Pope, 1997 U.S. Dist. LEXIS 10228, at *17 (N.D. Ill. July 9, 1997); United States v. Picciandra, 788 F.2d 39, 44 (1st Cir.), *cert. denied*, 479 U.S. 847 (1986); United States v. Morlang, 531 F.2d 183, 190-91 (4th Cir. 1975); Solino v. United States, 387 F.2d 354 (5th Cir. 1968); Tatum v. United States, 249 F.2d 129, 131-32 (D.C. Cir. 1957), *cert. denied*, 356 U.S. 943 (1958); United States v. Riccardi, 174 F.2d 883 (3d Cir.), *cert. denied*, 337 U.S. 941 (1949); *In re* Messenger, 32 F. Supp. 490 (E.D. Pa. 1940); United States v. Giovanelli, 747 F. Supp. 915 (S.D.N.Y. 1989); MICHAEL H. GRAHAM, HANDBOOK OF FEDERAL EVIDENCE § 803(5) (3d ed. 1991 & Supp. 1994).

The most important consideration involving the doctrine of past recollection recorded is the requisite degree of impaired memory to establish a proper foundation to have the document admitted in evidence. Federal Rule of Evidence 803(5) requires that the witness demonstrate insufficient recollection to enable him to testify fully and accurately. This standard offers a compromise approach between two schools of thought: (1) the traditional approach, which requires that total failure of memory be established before invoking the doctrine; and (2) the minority approach, which recognizes the doctrine of past recollection recorded on the basis of the trustworthiness of the writing rather than the state of mind of the witness at the time of his testimony. The federal rule's compromise is that a somewhat faded memory will suffice. *See generally* JOHN W. STRONG ET AL., MCCORMICK ON EVIDENCE § 282 (4th ed. 1992); Fed. R. Evid. 803(5) Advisory Committee's note and practice comment for cases construing the rule.

The Advisory Committee on the proposed Rules deemed the compromise approach desirable, because a total absence of the requirement of memory impairment "would encourage the use of statements carefully prepared for purposes of litigation under the supervision of attorneys, investigators, or claim adjusters." *See* United States v. Judon, 567 F.2d 1289, 1294 (5th Cir.) (quotation omitted), *appeal after remand*, 581 F.2d 553 (5th Cir. 1978).

The proponent of the past recollection recorded cannot introduce the

---

2. Throughout this book, we have included citations to unpublished decisions. Some jurisdictions allow unpublished decisions to be cited in court papers; other jurisdictions do not.

document in evidence, although the witness is permitted to read from the document. On the other hand, the adverse party may offer the document as an exhibit. Even if the adverse party does not offer the document into evidence, the document should be marked for identification and made part of the record. *See id.*

The witness testifying under the doctrine of past recollection recorded must have personal knowledge of the underlying events. If the writing contains information which itself is hearsay, that hearsay can only be admitted over objection pursuant to a hearsay exception. *See, e.g.*, United States v. Smith, 521 F.2d 957 (D.C. Cir. 1975); JOHN W. STRONG ET AL., MCCORMICK ON EVIDENCE 501 (4th ed. 1992). For example, in the present pattern, "excited utterance" might qualify as an exception, depending on the factual circumstances. If no exception to the hearsay rule is applicable, the witness who offered the description of the assailant to the police officer must testify. The police report would then be admissible through the officer as the past recollection of the observer, not of the police officer. *See* Swart v. United States, 394 F.2d 5, 6 (9th Cir. 1968).

Moreover, the examination of the police officer to elicit testimony concerning the witness's description of the assailant can be construed as nonhearsay if the examination is designed for impeachment purposes rather than for the truth of the matter asserted. *See supra* chapter 1.A for discussion of hearsay problem with present recollection revived and *infra* chapters 2.B, 2.F, and 2.G for discussion of hearsay contained within business records, police accident reports, and public records.

Finally, the trial judge has discretion to determine whether the witness actually satisfies the requirements of the rule. For example, if a witness was intoxicated when he recorded a statement, he may not have accurately understood the facts at the time of the recording. *See* United States v. Edwards, 539 F.2d 689, 692 (9th Cir.), *cert. denied*, 429 U.S. 984 (1976); United States v. Riccardi, 174 F.2d 883 (3d Cir.), *cert. denied*, 337 U.S. 941 (1949). *But see* United States v. Porter, 986 F.2d 1014, 1017 (6th Cir.), *cert. denied*, 510 U.S. 933 (1993), where the witness stated that because of drug use she could not be sure that her past statement was truthful, and the court permitted the doctrine to be invoked based on the trustworthiness of the document.

C. IDENTIFICATIONS, JUDICIAL AND EXTRAJUDICIAL

Joan Tisdale is the victim of rape. As a witness for the prosecution, she is asked to identify the defendant as her assailant.

Prosecutor:

Q. Ms. Tisdale, what opportunity, if any, did you have to observe your assailant?

A. During the entire rape his face was only inches away from mine.

Q. Did you have an opportunity to closely observe his face?

A. Yes.

Q. How long a period of time did you observe his face?

A. For at least five minutes.

Q. What were the lighting conditions at the time of the incident?

A. Although there were no lights in the car, it was stopped about 15 feet from a street light, and the car light went on when he opened the car and pushed me out.

Q. Did you observe anything unusual about your assailant's appearance?

A. He was missing both front teeth and had a two-inch scar over his left eye.

Q. Would you please indicate the location of the scar? (Witness indicates.) Let the record reflect that Ms. Tisdale indicated a scar at approximately a 45-degree angle starting approximately one-half inch above the left eyebrow on the forehead.

Q. Can you identify the person who raped you?

A. Yes.

Q. Is he in this courtroom today?

A. Yes.

Q. Would you point to him, please?

A. (Witness points to the defendant.)

Q. How is the defendant dressed today?

A. He is wearing brown pants and a gray sweatshirt.

Q. Do you observe any marks on his face?

A. Yes, I see a scar over his left eye.

Prosecutor: Let the record reflect that the witness has identified the defendant.

Q. Ms. Tisdale, after the incident, did you have occasion to identify your assailant.

A. Yes.

Q. When?

A. Two days later. Officer Johnson brought me twelve photographs to examine.

Q. Ms. Tisdale, I show you State's Exhibit 31, (A) through (L), and ask if you can identify the exhibit for us?

A. Yes, this is the group of photographs which Officer Johnson brought to me. (These photographs were previously introduced through Officer Johnson, the officer conducting the photo identification. The officer also identified Exhibit 31(B) as a photograph of the defendant and the photograph identified by the witness.)

Q. What instructions, if any, did you receive from the police officer who showed you the photographs?

A. I was told to look at the photographs and to state whether I could identify the individual who raped me.

Q. Were you able to identify the individual?

A. Yes.

Q. Who did you identify from the photographs?

A. The same man I just identified in this court.

Q. Would you please identify that picture for us.

A. (Witness points to the photograph she had identified before Officer Johnson.)

Prosecutor: Let the record reflect that Ms. Tisdale has identified Exhibit 31(B) as the photograph she had identified as that of her assailant when Officer Johnson brought the twelve photographs to her to examine.

Q. Ms. Tisdale, have you had any other occasions to see the defendant?

A. Yes.

Q. Can you tell us when and under what circumstances?

A. Yes.

Q. Please do so.

A. I came to the police station about two weeks after the rape and was asked to look at five men.

Q. Where were these men?

A. They were standing in a lineup in a room, through which I could see, and I understand that they could not see me.

Q. Did you have any trouble in observing the individuals in the lineup?

A. No.

Q. How far away from the individuals in the lineup were you?

A. Less than 12 feet.

Q. How much time did you spend at this lineup?

A. I spent about 5 minutes, but I identified my assailant within 1 minute of looking at the individuals in the lineup.

Q. Describe what the men in the lineup were doing while you were looking at them?

A. They were standing in a line facing forward.

Q. What instructions, if any, did you receive from the police who conducted the lineup?

A. I was told to look at the people and to state whether I could identify the individual who raped me.

Q. Were you able to identify the individual who raped you?

A. Yes.

Q. Ms. Tisdale, I show you Exhibit 34 for identification and ask if you can identify it?

A. Yes, this is a photograph of the group of men I viewed at the police station and from which I identified my assailant. (This photograph of the lineup was previously introduced through the police officer conducting the lineup.)

Q. Can you identify in Exhibit 34 the individual whom you identified at the lineup?

A. Yes.

Q. Would you please take this pencil and mark with a check mark above the individual you identified?

A. Yes.

Q. Do you see the person in this courtroom whom you identified at the lineup?

A. Yes.

Q. Would you point to him, please?

A. (Witness points to the defendant.)

Comment

The identification of a defendant in the courtroom is referred to as a judicial or in-court identification. An identification made prior to trial, either by photograph or lineup, is known as an extrajudicial or out-of-court identification. Principles governing the admissibility of photographic identifications and lineup identifications are the same. *See* United States v. Marchand, 564 F.2d 983 (2d Cir. 1977), *cert. denied*, 434 U.S. 1015 (1978) (photographic identification); United States v. Fabio, 394 F.2d 132 (4th Cir. 1968) (pre-indictment lineup). The federal rule generally considers the testimony of identification as non-hearsay. *See* Fed. R. Evid. 801(d)(1)(C).

There are three elements composing the proper foundation for a judicial or in-court identification: (1) the witness must be present at trial and testify about the event in question; (2) the witness must have the ability to reconstruct the occurrence and identify the defendant from the witness's observation of him at the time of the event; and (3) the defendant must be present in the courtroom to enable the witness to observe him and compare his appearance to that of the perpetrator. United States v. Foppe, 993 F.2d 1444, 1450 (9th Cir.), *cert. denied*, 510 U.S. 1017 (1993); United States v. Crews, 445 U.S. 463, 471 (1980).

Evidence of an extrajudicial or out-of-court identification is admissible to corroborate a judicial or in-court identification. A proper foundation requires: (1) a showing of circumstances precluding unfairness; (2) testimony demonstrating the reliability of the identification; and (3) an in-court identification serving as a predicate for the corroboration. *See* Manson v. Brathwaite, 432 U.S. 98 (1977); Neil v. Biggers, 409 U.S. 188 (1972); United States v. Donaldson, 978 F.2d 381 (7th Cir. 1992); United States v. Edwards, 816 F. Supp. 272 (D. Del. 1993).

In the federal courts, evidence of an extrajudicial identification may be offered as independent substantive evidence of identity, even if the witness is unable to make an in-court identification. The rationale for this rule rests upon the notion that the earlier identification has greater probative value than the subsequent in-court identification with the pressures and suggestions surrounding the trial. *See* Gilbert v. California, 388 U.S. 263, 272 n.3 (1967); Samuels v. Mann, 13 F.3d 522, 527 (2d Cir. 1993), *cert. denied*, 513 U.S. 849 (1994); Jamison v. Grier, 2002 U.S. Dist. LEXIS 1160, at *38 (S.D.N.Y. Jan. 25, 2002). *See* Fed. R. Evid. 801(d)(1)(C).

However, the federal rules specifically require the presence of the declarant and that he or she be subject to cross-examination as a prerequisite to admissibility of extrajudicial identifications.

The federal rules do not limit testimony establishing the statement of identification solely to the identifying witness. The rationale for the rule remains fully applicable when the person who testifies to the statement of identification is not the person who uttered it, as long as the latter also testifies and is available for cross-examination. *See* United States v. Lopez, 271 F.3d 472, 485 (3d Cir. 2001), *cert. denied,* 122 S. Ct. 1211 (2002); United States v. O'Malley, 796 F.2d 891, 899 (7th Cir. 1986); United States v. Elemy, 656 F.2d 507, 508-509 (9th Cir. 1981); United States v. Irby, 517 F.2d 506 (4th Cir. 1975), *cert. denied sub nom.* Smith v. United States, 424 U.S. 973 (1976).

This pattern illustrates an in-court identification and an extrajudicial identification, which corroborates the in-court identification. Notice the way the witness linked the photograph identification to "the same man I just identified in this court." This out-of-court identification can also be used as substantive evidence. If, for example, the witness is unable to identify the defendant at trial, and the prior extrajudicial identifications are the only evidence linking the defendant to the commission of the crime, those identifications would be treated as substantive evidence in the case.

Constitutional considerations play a significant role in the admissibility of extrajudicial identifications in criminal cases. These considerations are discussed in such cases as *Manson v. Brathwaite,* 432 U.S. 98 (1977), *Kirby v. Illinois,* 406 U.S. 682 (1972), and *Webster v. State,* 474 A.2d 1305 (Md. 1984). *See also* United States v. Moody, 206 F.3d 609 (6th Cir.), *cert. denied,* 531 U.S. 925 (2000); Hanks v. Jackson, 123 F. Supp. 2d 1061 (E.D. Mich. 2000). Under federal law, a defendant wishing to challenge the legality of an identification in a criminal case must exercise his rights by filing a motion to suppress. *See* Fed. R. Crim. P. 12.

Documents 2

A. PRIVATE WRITINGS

Plaintiff Boady, claiming to be the owner of 3245 Walnut Hill Road, institutes suit against Defendant Butterball claiming damages for failure to pay rent. Defendant claims that the property is not owned by Plaintiff, but by Plaintiff's mother. Plaintiff's counsel seeks to introduce in evidence the deed to the property and a lease.

Plaintiff's Counsel:

Q. Mr. Boady, who is the owner of the premises known as 3245 Walnut Hill Road?

A. I am, sir.

Q. And when did you acquire ownership of the property?

A. Ten years ago, in 1986.

Q. From whom did you purchase the property?

A. Ronald Hall.

Plaintiff's Counsel: Your Honor, we would like to mark this document as Exhibit No. 1 for identification. (The exhibit is marked.)

Q. Can you identify Exhibit No. 1 for identification?

A. Yes, this is the deed to 3245 Walnut Hill Road, which I acquired ten years ago.

Q. Did you subsequently have this deed recorded?

A. Yes.

Q. When?

A. Immediately after the settlement for the property.

Q. Where was the deed recorded?

A. In the Circuit Court for Baltimore County.

Q. Directing your attention to the last page, can you identify the signature appearing above the word grantor?

A. Yes.

Q. Whose signature is it?

A. It is the signature of the person who sold me the house, Mr. Ronald Hall.

Q. Let the record reflect that the witness is pointing to the signature written in the space above the name Ronald Hall.

Q. Did Mr. Hall execute this deed in your presence?

A. Yes, he did.

Plaintiff's Counsel: Exhibit No. 1 for identification is offered in evidence. The deed bears liber and folio number BLW 2601/131.

Q. Mr. Boady, what use, if any, do you make of the premises 3245 Walnut Avenue?

A. I rented it to Henry Butterball.

Q. Do you have a lease with Mr. Butterball?

A. Yes.

Plaintiff's Counsel: Please mark this document as Plaintiff's Exhibit No. 2 for identification. (The exhibit is marked.)

Q. Mr. Boady, I show you Plaintiff's Exhibit No. 2 for identification. Can you identify this document?

A. This is the lease agreement which Mr. Butterball and I entered into.

Q. Directing your attention to page 3, can you identify any of the signatures as your own?

A. Yes.

Q. Do you see the signature of Mr. Butterball on that page?

A. I do.

Q. Did Mr. Butterball sign this lease in your presence?

A. Yes, he did.

Q. When and where?

A. On October 1, 1995, in my office in downtown Baltimore.

Q. What were the rental terms under the lease?

A. The lease is a year-to-year lease with the monthly rental of $450.

Plaintiff's Counsel: I offer Plaintiff's Exhibit No. 2 for identification in evidence.

Comment

There are various requirements and techniques for authenticating documents that constitute private writings. *See* United States v. McMahon, 938 F.2d 1501, 1508-09 (1st Cir. 1991) (authenticity of unsigned note was based on circumstantial indicia of ownership); United States v. Coughman, 1997 U.S. App. LEXIS 15392, at *6 (2d Cir. June 25, 1997), *appeal after remand*, United States v. McCoy, 210 F.3d 356 (2d Cir. 2000); United States v. Bello-Perez, 977 F.2d 664, 671-72 (1st Cir. 1992); United States v. Natale, 526 F.2d 1160, 1173 (2d Cir. 1975), *cert. denied*, 425 U.S.

950 (1976); United States v. Brown, 688 F.2d 1112, 1116 (7th Cir. 1982); John Paul Mitchell Sys. v. Quality King Distribs., Inc., 106 F. Supp. 2d 462, 471-72 (S.D.N.Y. 2000), *summ. j. granted, summ. j. denied*, 2001 U.S. Dist. LEXIS 11587 (S.D.N.Y. Aug. 10, 2001). Authentication "is satisfied by evidence sufficient to support a finding that the matter in question is what the proponent claims." Fed. R. Evid. 901(a). *See* Wells v. Liddy, 2002 U.S. App. LEXIS 3356, at *22 (4th Cir. Mar. 1, 2002); United States v. Dhinsa, 243 F.3d 635, 658-59 (2d Cir.), *cert. denied*, 122 S. Ct. 219 (2001); Smith v. City of Chicago, 242 F.3d 737, 741-42 (7th Cir. 2001); United States v. Szehinskyj, 104 F. Supp. 2d 480, 488-89 (E.D. Pa. 2000), *aff'd*, 277 F.3d 331 (3d Cir. 2002); Kalamazoo River Study Group v. Menasha Corp., 228 F.3d 648, 661 (6th Cir. 2000), *appeal after remand*, 274 F.3d 1043 (6th Cir. 2001); United States v. Skipper, 74 F.3d 608, 612 (5th Cir. 1996); United States v. Manning, 56 F.3d 1188, 1199 (9th Cir. 1995); United States v. Holmquist, 36 F.3d 154, 167 (1st Cir. 1994), *cert. denied*, 514 U.S. 1064 (1995); Downes v. Volkswagen of Am., Inc., 41 F.3d 1132, 1143 (7th Cir. 1994); United States v. Coohey, 11 F.3d 97, 99 (8th Cir. 1993); United States v. Thorne, 997 F.2d 1504, 1508 (D.C. Cir.), *cert. denied*, 510 U.S. 999 (1993); United States v. Branch, 970 F.2d 1368, 1370 (4th Cir. 1992); United States v. Ruggiero, 928 F.2d 1289, 1303 (2d Cir.), *cert. denied*, 502 U.S. 938 (1991); Threadgill v. Armstrong World Indus., Inc., 928 F.2d 1366, 1375 (3d Cir. 1991); *In re* Grey, 902 F.2d 1479, 1482 (10th Cir. 1990); Stuckey v. N. Propane Gas Co., 874 F.2d 1563, 1574 (11th Cir. 1989); United States v. Carriger, 592 F.2d 312, 315-16 (6th Cir. 1979); United States v. Bin Laden, 2001 U.S. Dist. LEXIS 2897, at *2 (S.D.N.Y. Mar. 20, 2001); United States v. Demjanjuk, 2002 U.S. Dist. LEXIS 6999, at *54 (N.D. Ohio Apr. 22, 2002); Renaldi v. Sears Roebuck & Co., 2001 U.S. Dist. LEXIS 3523, at *24 (N.D. Ill. Mar. 20, 2001), *summ. j. granted*, 2001 U.S. Dist. LEXIS 3536 (N.D. Ill. Mar. 20, 2001); Ragan v. Jeffboat LLC, 149 F. Supp. 2d 1053, 1062 (S.D. Ind. 2001). Compare with self-authentication requirements and techniques associated with certain documents, such as public records. *See infra* chapter 2.G; Fed. R. Evid. 902(3).

The introduction of deeds, leases, letters, and related documents follows a similar pattern. This pattern illustrates the method of authentication through testimony based on direct observation that establishes the following facts: (1) time and place the witness observed the execution of the document; (2) the circumstances under which the document was executed; and (3) that the witness recognizes the document that is being offered in evidence. *See* United States v. Scurlock, 52 F.3d 531, 538-39

(5th Cir. 1995); United States v. Reilly, 33 F.3d 1396, 1404 (3d Cir. 1994); United States v. Chu Kong Yin, 935 F.2d 990, 995 (9th Cir. 1991), *cert. denied*, 511 U.S. 1035 (1994); Denison v. Swaco Geolograph Co., 941 F.2d 1416 (10th Cir. 1991); NLRB v. General Wood Preserving Co., 905 F.2d 803, 811 (4th Cir.), *cert. denied*, 498 U.S. 1016 (1990); United States v. Durham, 868 F.2d 1010 (8th Cir.), *cert. denied*, 493 U.S. 954 (1989); United States v. Drougas, 748 F.2d 8, 26 (1st Cir. 1984); United States v. Sliker, 751 F.2d 477, 488 (2d Cir. 1984), *cert. denied*, 470 U.S. 1058 (1985); United States v. Brown, 688 F.2d 1112, 1116 (7th Cir. 1982); Bury v. Marietta Dodge, 692 F.2d 1335, 1338 (11th Cir. 1982); United States v. Bruner, 657 F.2d 1278, 1284 (D.C. Cir. 1981); Bridger v. Union Ry., 355 F.2d 382, 391-92 (6th Cir. 1966).

When appropriate, proof of recording of the document is helpful. *See* 28 U.S.C. § 1739 (1994); Amoco Prod. Co. v. United States, 852 F.2d 1574, 1580 (10th Cir. 1988); Compton v. Davis Oil Co., 607 F. Supp. 1221 (D. Wyo. 1985).

In some cases it is possible to satisfy the Federal Rule of Evidence 901(a) requirement of sufficiency of evidence for authentication by drawing an inference from the lack of evidence. *See, e.g., In re* James E. Long Constr. Co., 557 F.2d 1039, 1041 (4th Cir. 1977). In *In re James E. Long Construction Co.*, the court held that there existed a permissible inference, from silence and other evidence, that a signature was genuine in light of Federal Rule of Evidence 901(a).

Under Federal Rule of Evidence 803(14), evidence of the recording of a document that purports to establish or effect an interest in property is sufficient proof of the content of the original recorded document, and of its execution and delivery by each person by whom it purports to have been executed. The rule provides, however, that the evidence of the recording must be a record from a public office authorized by statute to record documents of that kind in that office. The rule specifically exempts such records from the hearsay doctrine. *See* Connecticut Light & Power Co. v. Federal Power Comm'n, 557 F.2d 349 (2d Cir. 1977); Amoco Prod. Co. v. United States, 455 F. Supp. 46 (D. Utah 1977), *rev'd on other grounds*, 852 F.2d 1574 (10th Cir. 1988); Compton v. Davis Oil Co., 607 F. Supp. 1221 (D. Wyo. 1985). *See generally* Greycas, Inc. v. Proud, 826 F.2d 1560, 1567 (7th Cir. 1987), *cert. denied*, 484 U.S. 1043 (1988); United States v. Ruffin, 575 F.2d 346, 357 (2d Cir. 1978); United States v. Weinstock, 863 F. Supp. 1529, 1534 (D. Utah 1994).

Some of the other methods used to authenticate private writings include: (1) testimony of a non-expert witness as to the genuineness of handwriting, based upon the witness's familiarity with that handwriting. *See infra* chapter 5.D for an illustration of this technique; *see also* Fed. R. Evid. 901(b)(2); (2) the expert opinion of a document examiner. *See infra* chapter 6.H, for an illustration of this technique; *see also* Fed. R. Evid. 901(b)(3); (3) comparison by the trier of fact or expert with exemplars, which have been authenticated. *See* Fed. R. Evid. 901(c)(3); (4) the distinctive characteristic method, which allows a witness to authenticate a document by its contents when, for example, a letter is shown to contain information that persons other than the purported sender are unlikely to possess. *See* Fed. R. Evid. 901(b)(4); and (5) the so-called reply doctrine, which allows a private writing to be authenticated when it has been mailed and shown by its contents to be in reply.

Authentication requirements are similar in civil and criminal cases. Nevertheless, criminal cases place on the prosecution the additional burden of establishing chain of custody, the procedures of which are in many instances governed by statutes. *See* Fed. R. Evid. 901(b)(10).

B. BUSINESS RECORDS

John Smith, defendant in a criminal case, claims that at the time of the murder he was purchasing stereophonic equipment at Sears. Defense counsel wants to introduce the sales slip and then call the salesman as a witness. Counsel subpoenas the Area Credit Manager, requesting all credit records pertaining to John Smith during the summer of 1995.

Defense Counsel:

Q. Would you state your name, please?
A. Margaret Jefferson.
Q. Where do you live?
A. 214 Gough Street in Baltimore City.
Q. What is your present occupation?
A. Area Credit Manager for Sears.
Q. What are your responsibilities in that position?
A. I am responsible for maintaining all records pertaining to charge accounts with Sears stores in the Baltimore metropolitan area.
Q. Did you receive a subpoena to come to court today?
A. Yes.

Q. And what did that subpoena request you to bring with you?
A. All sales slips and records pertaining to John Smith for the summer of 1995.
Q. Did you bring those records with you?
A. Yes.
Q. May I please have those records? (Witness hands documents to counsel.)

Defense Counsel: Your Honor, may we have these records marked as Defendant's Exhibits Nos. 1(a) through (c) for identification?

Q. Were these documents that you handed to me, which have been marked as Defendant's Exhibits Nos. 1(a) through (c) for identification, maintained by you?
A. Yes.
Q. Please identify the documents.
A. They consist of three sales slips made out by our salesperson, all pertaining to the account of John Smith.
Q. Were these documents prepared in the regular course of business? (Alternatively: "Were these records kept in the regular course of a regularly conducted business activity?")
A. Yes.
Q. Was it the regular course of business for Sears to have records such as these prepared?
A. Yes.
Q. Do you know the circumstances of their being prepared?
A. Yes.
Q. Please explain.
A. On the day of sale, the salesperson would fill out these slips, the purchaser would sign in the presence of a salesperson, and the salesperson would hold the original sales slip to be forwarded to my office at the end of the day.
Q. How do you know this?
A. From years of working at Sears—it is standard operating procedure.

Defense Counsel: We offer Exhibits Nos. 1(a) through (c) for identification in evidence.

Comment

The business records exception to the hearsay rule applies in both civil and criminal cases when (1) the records were made and kept in the regular course of business activity; (2) it was a regular practice of the business to make and keep such written records; (3) the records were made at or near the time of the act, event, or diagnosis; and (4) they were made by a person with knowledge, or from information transmitted by a person with knowledge. *See* Shelton v. Consumer Prods. Safety Comm'n, 277 F.3d 998, 1010 n.9 (8th Cir. 2002); United States v. Salgado, 250 F.3d 438, 451 (6th Cir.), *cert. denied*, 122 S. Ct. 306 (2001); United States v. Williams, 205 F.3d 23, 32-33 (2d Cir.), *cert. denied*, 531 U.S. 885 (2000); United States v. Sutton, 2000 U.S. App. LEXIS 31929, at *4 (7th Cir. Dec. 6, 2000); United States v. Reyes, 157 F.3d 949, 951 (2d Cir. 1998); Phoenix Assocs. III v. Stone, 60 F.3d 95, 100 (2d Cir. 1995); Firemen's Fund Ins. Co. v. Thien, 63 F.3d 754, 757 (8th Cir. 1995); United States v. Warren, 42 F.3d 647, 656 (D.C. Cir. 1994); United States v. Console, 13 F.3d 641, 656 (3d Cir. 1993), *cert. denied*, 511 U.S. 1076, *cert. denied*, 513 U.S. 812 (1994); United States v. Emenogha, 1 F.3d 473, 483 (7th Cir. 1993), *cert. denied*, 510 U.S. 1080 (1994); United States v. Bland, 961 F.2d 123, 127 (9th Cir.), *cert. denied*, 506 U.S. 858 (1992); United States v. Arboleda, 929 F.2d 858, 869 (1st Cir. 1991); *In re* Custodian of Records of Variety Distrib., Inc., 927 F.2d 244, 246 (6th Cir. 1991); United States v. Saunders, 886 F.2d 56, 58 (4th Cir. 1989); United States v. Veytia-Bravo, 603 F.2d 1187, 1191-92 (5th Cir. 1979), *cert. denied*, 444 U.S. 1024 (1980); United States v. Snyder, 787 F.2d 1429, 1434 (10th Cir.), *cert. denied*, 479 U.S. 836 (1986); United States v. Dreer, 740 F.2d 18, 19 (11th Cir. 1984); United States v. Ortiz, 182 F. Supp. 2d 443, 451 (E.D. Pa. 2000). Hospital records, police reports, computer printouts, and even summaries or compilations made from business records can be included within this business record doctrine. Federal Rule of Evidence 803(6) defines "business" to include: "institution, association, profession, occupation and calling of every kind, whether or not conducted for profit." As discussed ahead, federal court practice does not require the custodian or person who has possession of the record to have been the maker of the record.

Although a proper foundation is required for introduction of evidence under the business record doctrine, it is not always necessary that the foundation consist of direct testimony that the document was prepared in the regular course of business. For example, one of the sales slips in this pattern examination could have been introduced by the defendant, claiming that it was the sales slip he received when he made the purchase. The court could conclude from the circumstances and the nature of the document that it was made in the regular course of business. *See* United States v. Salgado, 250 F.3d 438, 451 (6th Cir.), *cert. denied*, 122 S. Ct. 306 (2001); Arbuckle v. Dorsey, 1999 U.S. App. LEXIS 20687, at *12 (10th Cir. Aug. 30, 1999) (person supplying information must be under a legal duty of accuracy); City of Tuscaloosa v. Harcros Chems., 159 F.3d 548, 559 (11th Cir. 1998), *cert. denied*, 528 U.S. 812 (1999); United States v. Johnson, 971 F.2d 562, 570-72 (10th Cir. 1992); United States v. Linn, 880 F.2d 209, 216 (9th Cir. 1989); Itel Capital Corp. v. Cups Coal Co., 707 F.2d 1253, 1259 (11th Cir. 1983); Jones v. R.R. Donnelley & Sons Co., 1999 U.S. Dist. LEXIS 1592, at *6 (N.D. Ill. Feb. 12, 1999); United States v. Hing Shair Chan, 680 F. Supp. 521 (E.D.N.Y. 1988); Zenith Radio Corp. v. Matsushita Elec. Indus. Co., 505 F. Supp. 1190, 1236 (E.D. Pa. 1980), *aff'd in part, rev'd in part*, 723 F.2d 238 (3d Cir. 1983), *rev'd on other grounds*, 475 U.S. 574 (1986). However, the more prudent practice is to authenticate the document by formal foundation. Alternatively, the Federal Rules of Evidence do provide for self-authentication of business records. See Rule 902(11). Self-authentication involves providing a written declaration from the custodian of the records that sets out the elements of a business record under Rule 803(6) sufficiently in advance of trial to allow adverse parties to inspect and challenge the admissibility of the documents. Many local rules often establish a procedure for the introduction of all documents, including business records.

In this pattern counsel questioned: "Were these documents prepared in the regular course of business," and "Was it the regular course of business for Sears to have records such as these prepared?" An alternative form of question is, "Were these records kept in the regular course of a regularly conducted business activity?" *See* Fed. R. Evid. 803(6). This alternative is suggested by at least one commentator. *See* MICHAEL H. GRAHAM, HANDBOOK OF FEDERAL EVIDENCE, § 803.6 at 875 (3d ed. 1991); *see also* MICHAEL H. GRAHAM, EVIDENCE: TEXT, RULES, ILLUSTRATIONS & PROBLEMS 163-64 (2d ed. 1988), where the author reprints with approval this pattern for establishing a proper foundation for introducing business records.

Federal Rule of Evidence 803(6) requires testimony for establishing foundation by either the custodian of the records or other qualified witnesses. *See* Butler v. IMA Regiomontana S.A. de C.V., 2000 U.S. App.

LEXIS 1607, at *11 (9th Cir. Feb. 3, 2000); Hoselton v. Metz Baking Co., 48 F.3d 1056 (8th Cir. 1995); United States v. Chatman, 994 F.2d 1510 (10th Cir.), *cert. denied*, 510 U.S. 883 (1993); United States v. Patrick, 959 F.2d 991 (D.C. Cir. 1992); Elgabri v. Lekas, 964 F.2d 1255 (1st Cir. 1992); Raphaely Int'l, Inc. v. Waterman S.S. Corp., 972 F.2d 498 (2d Cir. 1992), *cert. denied*, 507 U.S. 916 (1993); United States v. Pelullo, 964 F.2d 193, 201 (3d Cir. 1992), *appeal after remand*, 14 F.3d 881 (3d Cir. 1994), *on remand to* 895 F. Supp. 718 (E.D. Pa. 1995); United States v. Jacoby, 955 F.2d 1527 (11th Cir. 1992), *cert. denied*, 507 U.S. 920 (1993); United States v. Muhammad, 928 F.2d 1461 (7th Cir. 1991); United States v. Ray, 930 F.2d 1368, 1370 (9th Cir. 1990), *cert. denied*, 498 U.S. 1124 (1991) ("[t]he phrase 'other qualified witness' is broadly interpreted to require only that the witness understand the record-keeping system"); Ledbetter v. Commissioner, 837 F.2d 708 (5th Cir.), *cert. denied*, 488 U.S. 856 (1988); United States v. Mahar, 801 F.2d 1477 (6th Cir. 1986); United States v. Ortiz, 182 F. Supp. 2d 442, 451 (E.D. Pa. 2000); *In re* Denslow, 104 B.R. 761, 765 (E.D. Va. 1989).

Federal procedures require all those transmitting and recording to do so in the "regular practice of that business." Fed. R. Evid. 803(6); *see* United States v. Kelly, 349 F.2d 720, 772 (2d Cir. 1965), *cert. denied*, 384 U.S. 947 (1966). For example, a letter recording a settlement demand in the regular course of an insurance company's business is a business record. *See* Twin City Fire Ins. Co. v. Country Mut. Ins. Co., 23 F.3d 1175, 1182 (7th Cir. 1994). However, the contents of the letter is double hearsay and must meet an exception to be admitted. In *Twin City Fire Ins. Co.*, the settlement demand referred to in the letter was a verbal act, and therefore non-hearsay. *Id.* at 1183. Therefore, both the letter and its contents were admissible. *See* Chadwell v. Koch Ref. Co., 251 F.3d 727, 731-32 (8th Cir. 2001); Schering Corp. v. Pfizer Inc., 189 F.3d 218, 239 (2d Cir. 1999), *amended in part*, 2000 U.S. Dist. LEXIS 9446 (S.D.N.Y. July 7, 2000). *See also* United States v. Nicholson, 924 F.2d 1053 (4th Cir.), *cert. denied*, 501 U.S. 1211 (1991), where the Court held that although a sales receipt constituted a business record, the hearsay exception could not be extended to the name of the purchaser.

Use of the business records exception at the second level of hearsay is analyzed in two interesting cases: *United States v. Bortnovsky*, 879 F.2d 30, 34 (2d Cir. 1989), and *United States v. Snyder*, 787 F.2d 1429, 1434 (10th Cir.), *cert. denied*, 479 U.S. 836 (1986). These cases held that in order for second- and third-level hearsay to be admissible under the business records exception to the hearsay rule, each level of hearsay must satisfy one of the exceptions to the hearsay rule. *See also* United States v. Walker, 272 F.3d 407, 417 (7th Cir. 2001), *cert. denied*, 122 S. Ct. 1456 (2002); United States v. Pena-Gutierrez, 222 F.3d 1080, 1087-88 (9th Cir.), *cert. denied*, 531 U.S. 1057 (2000); United States v. Vigneau, 187 F.3d 70, 76 (1st Cir. 1999), *cert. denied*, 528 U.S. 1172 (2000); Sana v. Hawaiian Cruises, Ltd., 181 F.3d 1041, 1046 (9th Cir. 1999); Twin City Fire Ins. Co. v. Country Mut. Ins. Co., 23 F.3d 1175 (7th Cir. 1994); United States v. Franks, 939 F.2d 600 (8th Cir. 1991); Baxter Healthcare Corp. v. Healthdyne, Inc., 944 F.2d 1573, 1577 (11th Cir. 1991), *opinion vacated and case dismissed*, 956 F.2d 226 (11th Cir. 1992) (based on parties' joint motion to withdraw); United States v. Cruz, 894 F.2d 41 (2d Cir.), *cert. denied*, 498 U.S. 837 (1990); United States v. Furst, 886 F.2d 558 (3d Cir. 1989), *cert. denied*, 493 U.S. 1062 (1990), *appeal after remand*, 918 F.2d 400 (3d Cir. 1990); Rassoulpour v. Washington Metro. Area Transit Auth., 826 F.2d 98, 100-01 (D.C. Cir. 1987); Ricciardi v. Children's Hosp. Med. Ctr., 811 F.2d 18, 22 (1st Cir. 1987); Clark v. City of Los Angeles, 650 F.2d 1033, 1037 (9th Cir. 1981), *cert. denied*, 456 U.S. 927 (1982); United States v. Yates, 553 F.2d 518, 521 (6th Cir. 1977); Florida Canal Indus., Inc., v. Rambo, 537 F.2d 200 (5th Cir. 1976); United States v. Burruss, 418 F.2d 677, 678 (4th Cir. 1969); Boca Investerings Pshp. v. United States, 128 F. Supp. 2d 16, 20-21 (D.D.C. 2000), *j. entered*, 167 F. Supp. 2d 298 (D.D.C. 2001); Santa Fe Natural Tobacco Co. v. Spitzer, 2001 U.S. Dist. LEXIS 7548, at *47 (S.D.N.Y. June 8, 2001), *motion granted*, 2002 U.S. Dist. LEXIS 5384 (S.D.N.Y. Mar. 29, 2002); 2 JOHN W. STRONG ET AL., MCCORMICK ON EVIDENCE 501 (4th ed. 1992).

Under the Federal Rules, the same hearsay, offered in a civil case or offered against the government in a criminal case, might be viewed differently, if the 803(6) business record is also admissible as a public record pursuant to Federal Rule of Evidence 803(8). Rule 803(8) exempts certain types of investigative reports from the hearsay rule, e.g., factual findings in investigative reports in civil cases. However, whether an inadmissible hearsay declaration in a business record will be admitted via the public record and report doctrine will depend on whether the trial judge deems the statement and full report reliable. *See generally* Wilson v. Zapata Off-Shore Co., 939 F.2d 260 (5th Cir. 1991); United States v. Gray, 852 F.2d 136 (4th Cir. 1988); United States v. Nixon, 779 F.2d 126 (2d Cir. 1985); Wilson v. Attaway, 757 F.2d 1227 (11th Cir. 1985); Washington Cent. R.R. Co. v. Nat'l Mediation Bd., 830 F. Supp. 1343 (E.D. Wash. 1993).

The term "factual findings" can be construed to include opinions. *See* Beech Aircraft Corp. v. Rainey, 488 U.S. 153 (1988); United States v. Midwest Fireworks Mfg. Co., 248 F.3d 563, 566 (6th Cir. 2001); Bank of Lexington & Trust Co. v. Vining-Sparks Sec., Inc., 959 F.2d 606 (6th Cir. 1992); Ellis v. Int'l Playtex, Inc., 745 F.2d 292 (4th Cir. 1984). The justification for allowing opinions and conclusions into evidence when they are contained within a public record is the assumption that a public official will perform his duty properly and not remember details independently of the record. Factors used to determine admissibility of such opinions and conclusions include: timeliness of the investigation; special skills of the official; and possible motivation problems. *See* 4 WEINSTEIN'S EVIDENCE 803-287 (Jack B. Weinstein et al., eds. 1995). *See also infra* chapter 2.F, relating to police accident reports; *infra* chapter 2.G.i, relating to certified public records; *infra* chapter 2.D, relating to computer printouts; and *supra* chapters 1.A and 1.B, for discussions of hearsay problems and first-hand knowledge problems with present recollection revived and past recollection recorded.

C. COPIES OF BUSINESS RECORDS

Defendant in a criminal case claims he was elsewhere at the time of the murder, purchasing stereophonic equipment at Sears. Defense counsel desires to introduce a microfilm copy of the sales slip consummating the sale. Defense counsel subpoenas the Area Credit Manager, requesting all credit records pertaining to the defendant, John Smith, during the summer of 1995.

Defense Counsel

Q. Would you state your name, please?

A. Margaret Jefferson.

Q. Where do you live?

A. 214 Gough Street in Baltimore City.

Q. Mrs. Jefferson, what is your present occupation?

A. Area Credit Manager for Sears.

Q. What are your responsibilities in that position?

A. I am responsible for maintaining all records pertaining to charge accounts with Sears stores in the Baltimore Metropolitan area.

Q. Did you receive a subpoena to come to court today?

A. Yes.

Q. And what did that subpoena request you to bring with you?

A. All sales slips and records pertaining to John Smith for the summer of 1995.

Q. Did you bring those records with you?

A. Yes, but they are microfilm copies.

Q. Where are the originals?

A. After my office receives the originals and they are placed on microfilm, we destroy the originals.

Q. Is that what occurred in this case?

A. Yes.

Q. May I please have those records? (Witness hands documents to counsel.)

Defense Counsel: Your Honor, may we have these records marked as Defendant's Exhibits Nos. 1(a) through (c) for identification?

Q. Were these documents that you handed to me, which have now been marked as Defendant's Exhibits Nos. 1(a) through (c) for identification, maintained by you?

A. Yes.

Q. Can you identify them?

A. Yes. They consist of three sales slips pertaining to the account of John Smith.

Q. Were these documents prepared in the regular course of business?

A. Yes.

Q. Was it the regular course of business for Sears to have records such as these prepared?

A. Yes.

Q. And was it in the regular course of business to place the original sales slips on microfilm?

A. Yes.

Q. Do you know the circumstances and procedure of the microfilm copies being prepared?

A. Yes.

Q. Please explain.

A. Well, on the day of sale, the salesperson would fill out sales slips, the purchaser would sign in the presence of a salesperson, and the salesperson would hold the original sales slip to be forwarded to my office at the end of the day. Then the slips are reproduced by a microfilm process on a weekly basis. The records are copied on an Eastman Kodak microfilm machine, under the direction of the custodian of records. The microfilm is saved and the original sales slip discarded.

Q. Does the microfilm copy machine accurately reproduce the original?

A. Yes, it does.

Q. How do you know this?

A. From years of working at Sears—it is standard operating procedure, and from personal observations.

Defense Counsel: Now, Your Honor, we offer Defendant's Exhibits Nos. 1(a) through (c) for identification in evidence.

Comment

Under the Uniform Photographic Copies of Business and Public Records as Evidence Act, photographic copies, microfilm, microcard or miniature photographic copies of documents that qualify as business records or records maintained in the regular course of business activity may be introduced in evidence regardless of whether the original documents are in existence and available. 28 U.S.C. § 1732 (1994). Duplicates or other evidence of the contents of documents that do not fall within the business record doctrine are not governed by the Uniform Photographic Copies of Business and Public Records as Evidence Act. However, Federal Rule 1003 provides for the admissibility of duplicates in federal proceedings and Federal Rule 1004 provides for admissibility of other evidence of contents upon the loss or destruction of the original.

D. COMPUTER PRINTOUTS

The Government, in a criminal case involving credit card fraud, seeks to introduce computer printouts of records maintained by Second National Bank of Maryland. These computer printouts reflect the occasions when a merchant called the bank's computer record center for authorization to process a charge on the credit card allegedly used by the defendant.

Prosecutor:

Q. Would you state your name, please?

A. Margaret Jefferson.

Q. Where do you live?

A. 214 Gough Street in Baltimore City.

Q. What is your present occupation?

A. I am the supervisor of the data processing services of the credit card authorization department of the Second National Bank of Maryland.

Q. What are your responsibilities in that position?

A. I prepare weekly printouts of calls received by the bank from merchants throughout the country who are presented with credit cards and then call us to verify the validity of the cards.

Q. Did you receive a subpoena to come to court today?

A. Yes.

Q. And what did that subpoena request you to bring with you?

A. All computer printouts reflecting calls for verification of Visa card number 0006167 received during the months of January, February, and March, 1996.

Q. Did you bring those records with you?

A. Yes.

Q. May I please have those records? (Witness hands documents to counsel.)

Prosecutor: May we have these records marked as Government's Exhibits No. 1(a), (b), and (c) for identification?

Q. Were these documents that you handed to me, which have now been marked as Government's Exhibits No. 1(a) through (c) for identification, maintained by you?

A. Yes.

Q. Can you identify these for us?

A. Yes. They are the computer printouts of the calls received by the bank from merchants throughout the country seeking to verify the validity of Visa cards presented to them in January, February, and March, 1996, particularly with respect to Visa card number 0006167.

Q. Were these documents prepared in the regular course of business?

A. Yes.

Q. Was it the regular course of business for the bank to have computer printouts such as these prepared?

A. Yes.

Q. Do you know the circumstances of their being prepared?

A. Yes.

Q. Please explain.

A. The printouts are prepared from data fed to the computer by an experienced key punch operator. The information fed to the computer comes from the records maintained by the personnel who receive calls from the merchants to ascertain the validity of the cards. After the data is fed into the computer, a supervisor cross-checks the data input stored in the computer. The computer stores the data and prints it out on command.

Q. Were the records of the merchants' telephone calls made at or near the time the calls were received?

A. Yes.

Q. Was the computer that was used to produce the printout standard equipment?

A. Yes.

Q. What type of equipment was it?

A. IBM.

Q. Is the equipment reliable?

A. Yes, very reliable.

Q. Please describe the program used to enter, store, and retrieve the information.

A. The entry program allows entry to disk, which means the data is being keyed directly onto the permanent storage area, as opposed to being keyed to card or tape and then transferred to disk storage. The entry screen verifies the card holder's name, to allow confirmation of accuracy as well as the ability to cross-check at a later point. Once the information is entered and verified, the data is immediately available for reports upon request. Only specified personnel have access to modify data once it is entered and verified.

Q. Is the process you just described standard and reliable?

A. Yes.

Q. Can you tell us whether the entry process is checked for accuracy?

A. The entry process is regularly checked for accuracy by staff personnel.

Q. Can you tell us whether the data stored in the computer is secure from loss or alteration?

A. Yes.

Q. Can you explain?

A. The system is equipped with user security to insure that only quali-fied users can have access to change data once it is entered and verified. The database is backed up daily, which means the data is copied to tape and stored in a safe place solely as a means of secu-rity.

Q. Is this printout an accurate representation of the data stored in the computer?

A. Yes, most definitely. It is a routine process and all our records are stored on the computer.

Prosecutor: We offer Exhibits No. 1(a) through (c) for identification in evidence.

Comment

There are basically two types of computer evidence: (1) evidence that de-rives from computer-stored declarations of individuals, such as computer-generated bills, accounting records, charges and summaries, e-mail; and (2) computer evidence that includes output generated automatically by a programmed process without input fed into the computer by individuals, such as automated telephone call records, computer-generated simulations or computer-enhanced photographic images. GREGORY P. JOSEPH, MODERN VISUAL EVIDENCE § 7.01 (Law Journal Seminars-Press, Inc. 1995).

Computer-generated hearsay evidence often derives from business records and may qualify for admission under the business records excep-tion to the hearsay rule. Fed. R. Evid. 803(6). See the last paragraph of the Advisory Committee Note to Fed. R. Evid. 803(6). *See* United States v. Salgado, 250 F.3d 438, 451 (6th Cir.), *cert. denied*, 122 S. Ct. 306 (2001); Hardison v. Balboa Ins. Co., 2001 U.S. App. LEXIS 2409, at *15 (10th Cir. Feb. 16, 2001); United States v. Jackson, 208 F.3d 633, 638 (7th Cir.), *cert. denied*, 531 U.S. 973 (2000); United States v. Goodchild, 25 F.3d 55 (1st Cir. 1994); United States v. Cestnik, 36 F.3d 904 (10th Cir. 1994), *cert. denied*, 513 U.S. 1175 (1995) (wire transfer records were ruled ad-missible); United States v. Loney, 959 F.2d 1332 (5th Cir. 1992); United States v. Bowers, 920 F.2d 220, 223 (4th Cir. 1990); United States v. Croft, 750 F.2d 1354 (7th Cir. 1984); United States v. Scholle, 553 F.2d 1109 (8th Cir.), *cert. denied*, 434 U.S. 940 (1977); United States v. Davey, 543 F.2d 996, 999 (2d Cir. 1976); United States v. Liebert, 519 F.2d 542, 547

(3d Cir.), *cert. denied*, 423 U.S. 985 (1975); United States v. Russo, 480 F.2d 1228 (6th Cir. 1973), *cert. denied*, 414 U.S. 1157 (1974); United States v. De Georgia, 420 F.2d 889 (9th Cir. 1969); United States v. Fusero, 106 F. Supp. 2d 921, 924-25 (E.D. Mich. 2000).

The authentication of computer-based evidence in federal courts is generally deemed sufficient when counsel adheres to Federal Rule of Evidence 901(b)(9). This rule provides that authentication requirements for introducing a process or system are satisfied when there is a showing that the process or system produces an accurate result. The proponent of computerized evidence must satisfy the burden of establishing the following: (1) the accuracy of the computer printout; (2) that the process was properly operated; (3) that the computer data were secure; and (4) that the information printed out was accurate. *See also* United States v. Linn, 880 F.2d 209 (9th Cir. 1989); United States v. Hutson, 821 F.2d 1015 (5th Cir. 1987); United States v. Glasser, 773 F.2d 1553 (11th Cir. 1985); United States v. Croft, 750 F.2d 1354 (7th Cir. 1984); *In re* Dow Corning Corp., 250 B.R. 298, 317-18 (E.D. Mich. 2000), *j. entered*, 2001 U.S. Dist. LEXIS 10660 (E.D. Mich. July 27, 2001), *dismissed without prejudice*, 2002 U.S. Dist. LEXIS 6484 (E.D. Mich. Mar. 29, 2002), for additional discussions on establishing foundations of computer evidence.

Authentication problems with computer evidence can be minimized by pretrial cooperation between counsel. The *Manual for Complex Litigation* recommends that discovery of computerized evidence should be undertaken to avoid unnecessary delay of trial. MANUAL FOR COMPLEX LITIGATION § 21.446 (3d ed. Federal Judicial Center 1995).

Other hearsay exceptions may be applicable to computer printouts, e.g., public records. *See* Fed. R. Evid. 902(4); United States v. Ryan, 969 F.2d 238 (7th Cir. 1992). Computer evidence that is not derived from business records requires proper authentication as well, for example, evidence derived from scientific experiments, or computer-generated visual animations. *See, e.g., infra* chapter 4.C.

This pattern was cited in LYNN MCLAIN, MARYLAND EVIDENCE: STATE AND FEDERAL § 803(6).1 n.13 (1987 & Supp. 1995).

E. LAW ENFORCEMENT REPORTS

Defendant is charged with felony murder on a federal reservation. The crucial evidence against defendant was the decedent's wife's identification of defendant as the assailant. Defense counsel wishes to introduce the police report to develop inconsistencies between the wife's description of the assailant moments after the incident and her testimony in court. The wife initially indicated to the police that the robbery occurred at 7:00 p.m., although she testified in court that the robbery occurred at 6:00 p.m. The wife also reported to the police that the assailant was approximately 5 feet 8 inches tall. The defendant is 5 feet 3 inches. She testified in court that she had observed the defendant in the neighborhood prior to the incident, although she reported the opposite to the police at the time of the incident.

Defense Counsel:

Q. Officer, would you state your name please?

A. James Stone.

Q. And where are you now employed?

A. Federal Bureau of Investigation.

Q. How long have you been employed by the FBI?

A. Twenty years.

Q. Directing your attention to August 5, 1995, did you have occasion to report to the scene of a homicide?

A. Yes, I did.

Q. Where?

A. 1413 Highlander Road.

Q. Can you explain to us the circumstances of your being called to that location?

A. I received a radio dispatch that a shooting and robbery had occurred. I immediately drove to that location from a point approximately two-and-a-half miles away.

Q. What, if anything, did you do upon arriving at the scene?

A. I conducted a routine investigation.

Q. What did that investigation consist of?

A. Interviewing witnesses, inspecting the crime scene to see if there was any physical evidence left by the assailant or assailants, and I called for the crime lab.

Q. When you arrived at the scene, who, if anyone, was present?

A. When I entered the bar I saw three people. One woman stated that she was the wife of the decedent, and two other individuals approached and indicated that they had been entering the bar when two people ran out.

Q. Did you obtain any statements from these individuals?

A. Yes.

Q. Did you record these statements as part of your report?

A. Yes.

Q. Do you have a copy of your report with you?

A. Yes.

Defense Counsel: We would like to have the agent's report marked as Defense Exhibit No. 1 for identification.

Q. Was this report prepared in the regular course of business?

A. Yes.

Q. Was it in the regular course of business for police officers to prepare records such as these?

A. Yes.

Q. When did you prepare this report?

A. Within minutes after I arrived at the scene.

Q. And when was that?

A. 7:30 p.m.

Q. And when did the incident occur?

A. At approximately 7:15 p.m.

Q. We offer Defense Exhibit No. 1 for identification in evidence.

Q. Referring to your report, did Mrs. Smith, the wife of the decedent, give you a description of the assailant?

A. Yes, she did.

Q. What description did she give?

A. The assailant was approximately 5 feet 8 inches or 5 feet 9 inches with long stringy hair and a mustache.

Q. Did Mrs. Smith indicate that the robbery occurred at a particular time?

A. Yes, she did.

Q. What did she tell you?

A. She said the robbery occurred at 6:00 p.m.

Q. Did Mrs. Smith indicate to you whether she had ever seen the assailant prior to the incident?

A. She indicated and I noted in the report that she had never seen the assailant before the incident.

Comment

Considered as business records, police offense reports, law enforcement agency reports, and similar records are admissible in a criminal case when offered by a defendant to support a defense. *See* United States v. Versaint, 849 F.2d 827, 830-32 (3d Cir. 1988); United States v. Smith, 521 F.2d 957 (D.C. Cir. 1975); Virgin Islands v. Peterson, 131 F. Supp. 2d 707, 712 (D.V.I.), *aff'd*, 281 F.3d 220 (3d Cir. 2001).

The prosecution is usually prohibited from introducing police offense reports in evidence, because of the right of the defendant under the confrontation clause to insist on having witnesses against him appear in court and testify. Palmer v. Hoffman, 318 U.S. 109 (1943). *See* United States v. Smith, 521 F.2d 957 (D.C. Cir. 1975); United States v. Burruss, 418 F.2d 677 (4th Cir. 1969). *See also* Fed. R. Evid. 803(8)(C), which recognizes that offense reports can also be treated as public records, but are not admissible against a defendant in a criminal case.

The issue that has sparked some disagreement among the circuits is whether the prosecution can introduce "matters observed by police officers and other law enforcement personnel," proscribed by Federal Rule 803(8)(B), into evidence through another hearsay exception. *See* United States v. Yakobov, 712 F.2d 20, 25 (2d Cir. 1983) (permitting the introduction of hearsay through rule 803(10)); United States v. Sawyer, 607 F.2d 1190, 1193 (7th Cir. 1979), *cert. denied*, 445 U.S. 943 (1980); United States v. Oates, 560 F.2d 45 (2d Cir. 1977), *remanded to* 445 F. Supp. 351 (E.D.N.Y.), *aff'd*, 591 F.2d 1332 (2d Cir. 1978). *See also* United States v. Ybarra, 2000 U.S. App. LEXIS 26000, at *2 (9th Cir. Aug. 7, 2000); United States v. Pena-Gutierrez, 222 F.3d 1080, 1087 (9th Cir.), *cert. denied*, 531 U.S. 1057 (2000); United States v. Brown, 9 F.3d 907 (11th Cir. 1993), *cert. denied*, 513 U.S. 852 (1994); United States v. Smith, 973 F.2d 603 (8th Cir. 1992); United States v. Dancy, 861 F.2d 77, 79 (5th Cir. 1988); United States v. Hayes, 861 F.2d 1225 (10th Cir. 1988); United States v. Coleman, 631 F.2d 908, 912 (D.C. Cir. 1980); United States v. Orozco, 590 F.2d 789 (9th Cir.), *cert. denied*, 442 U.S. 920 (1979). *See* discussion *infra* chapter 2.F on police accident reports.

As with all business records or evidentiary writings that are admissible, items recorded in offense reports based upon hearsay are inadmissible unless covered by an appropriate hearsay exception. However, in this particular pattern, even if a hearsay exception were not applicable to the witness's statements, hearsay is admissible to impeach a testifying witness by a prior inconsistent statement. In this pattern, since Mrs. Smith's in-court testimony was inconsistent with the report, the defense attorney could introduce the report regardless of its hearsay contents. Prior inconsistent statements are admissible in federal court proceedings to impeach a testifying witness. *See* Fed. R. Evid. 613. Under Federal Rule of Evidence 801(d)(1), the prior inconsistent statement could even be admissible as substantive evidence. The federal rule limits the admissibility as substantive evidence of the prior made "under oath" at a "proceeding," and views the prior inconsistent statement as non-hearsay.

F. POLICE ACCIDENT REPORTS

Plaintiff institutes suit for negligence against defendant, claiming damages for injuries sustained during an automobile collision. One of the issues at trial is whether the street where the collision occurred had three northbound lanes or two northbound lanes. Counsel for the plaintiff calls the police officer who reported to the accident scene to demonstrate that the defendant was incorrect when he testified that there were three northbound lanes.

Plaintiff's Counsel:

Q. Officer, what time did you arrive at the scene of the incident?

A. Around 10:30 a.m., ten minutes after the collision.

Q. How did you learn of the collision?

A. Radio report.

Q. What, if anything, did you do upon arriving at the scene?

A. I conducted a routine investigation.

Q. What did that investigation consist of?

A. I interviewed the drivers of both automobiles, inquired as to whether or not there were any witnesses and there were none, and prepared a report of the incident.

Q. Does your report contain a diagram of the location of the accident, as well as the positions of the automobiles after the impact?

A. Yes, it does.

Q. Who prepared that diagram?

A. I did, in my report.

Q. What was the diagram based upon?

A. Things that I personally observed.

Q. Do you have a copy of that report with you?

A. Yes.

Q. May I see it please? (Witness hands document to counsel.)

Plaintiff's Counsel: Please mark this police report as Plaintiff's Exhibit No. 1 for identification.

Q. With regard to this police report, Plaintiff's Exhibit No. 1 for identification, was this document prepared in the regular course of business?

A. Yes, it was.

Q. Was it in the regular course of business for police officers to prepare records such as these?

A. Yes.

Q. When did you prepare this report?

A. At the accident scene, approximately ten minutes after the accident had occurred.

Plaintiff's Counsel: We offer Plaintiff's Exhibit No. 1 for identification in evidence.

The officer may then be questioned on the basis of the police report as follows:

Q. Officer, where did this accident occur?

A. At the intersection of Old Court Road and Reisterstown Road in Pikesville, Maryland. The accident occurred in the northbound lane of Reisterstown Road near the parking lot of Foods Corp.

Q. How many northbound lanes were there on Reisterstown Road on the day of the accident?

A. Two.

Q. Does your diagram indicate the number of northbound lanes?

A. Yes.

Q. What does your diagram show?

A. Two northbound lanes.

Q. Is your diagram accurate?

A. I drew the diagram accurately reflecting the number of lanes on the road. There were only two lanes.

Q. Would you step down and come to the blackboard and please draw for us roughly how your diagram appears on the police report?

A. On my diagram, this is just roughly how it was. (Officer sketches diagram showing only two lanes.)

Comment

Police accident reports, and items appearing in them that are within the personal observation of the investigating officer, are admissible pursuant to Federal Rule of Evidence 803(6) (Records of Regularly Conducted Activity). *See, e.g.*, Ramrattan v. Burger King Corp., 656 F. Supp. 522 (D. Md. 1987); Juaire v. Nardin, 395 F.2d 373, 379 (2d Cir.), *cert. denied*, 393 U.S. 938 (1968). *See generally* United States v. Warren, 42 F.3d 647, 656 (D.C. Cir. 1994); United States v. Snyder, 787 F.2d 1429, 1434 (10th Cir. 1986), *cert. denied*, 479 U.S. 836 (1986); United States v. Pazsint, 703 F.2d 420 (9th Cir. 1983), *appeal after remand*, 728 F.2d 411 (9th Cir. 1984); United States v. Halperin, 441 F.2d 612 (5th Cir. 1971); United States v. Martin, 434 F.2d 275 (5th Cir. 1970); United States v. Graham, 391 F.2d 439 (6th Cir.), *cert. denied*, 390 U.S. 1035, *cert. denied*, 393 U.S. 941 (1968); Bowman v. Kaufman, 387 F.2d 582 (2d Cir. 1967); Coyle v. Kristjan Palusalu Maritime Co., 83 F. Supp. 2d 535, 544 (E.D. Pa. 2000), *aff'd without op.*, 254 F.3d 1077 (3d Cir. 2001). As is true of all business records, items based on hearsay and conclusions of the officer are not admissible through accident reports unless by way of some independent exception to the hearsay rule. An officer's notations of the length of skid marks and the dimensions of the road would be admissible within the police report. However, the officer's notation as to who is responsible would not be admissible, unless the officer saw the accident or unless a statement placing responsibility upon one driver or the other satisfied a hearsay exception. *See* Rassoulpour v. Washington Metro. Area Transit Auth., 826 F.2d 98 (D.C. Cir. 1987); United States v. Smith, 521 F.2d 957 (D.C. Cir. 1975). *See also* Fed. R. Evid. 805, which governs the admissibility of hearsay within hearsay.

Diagrams contained within police reports are also admissible if they reflect items within the personal observation of the investigating officer.

Federal Rule of Evidence 803(8) exempts from the hearsay rule factual findings in investigative reports, when offered in civil cases or against the government in criminal cases. However, to what extent an inadmissible hearsay declaration or conclusion presented without firsthand knowledge in a police accident report will be admitted under the public records and report doctrine will depend on the extent to which the trial judge deems the statement and full report reliable. *See* United States v. Versaint, 849 F.2d 827 (3d Cir. 1988); United States v. Hardin, 710 F.2d 1231, 1237 (7th Cir.), *cert. denied*, 464 U.S. 918 (1983); Ellis v. Int'l Playtex, Inc., 745 F.2d 292 (4th Cir. 1984); United States v. Stone, 604 F.2d 922, 925 (5th Cir. 1979); United States v. Orozco, 590 F.2d 789, 793-94 (9th Cir.), *cert. de-*

nied, 442 U.S. 920 (1979); Baker v. Elcona Homes Corp., 588 F.2d 551 (6th Cir. 1978), *cert. denied*, 441 U.S. 933 (1979). *See also* 4 JACK B. WEINSTEIN ET AL., WEINSTEIN'S EVIDENCE, 803-266 (1995).

Consider the following situation: In a police offense report, the officer recorded that, based upon his investigation determining skid marks measuring 100 feet, the operator of one motor vehicle was traveling at an excessive speed. This conclusion would be inadmissible under the business records exception of Federal Rule of Evidence 803(6). However, this report is arguably admissible pursuant to Federal Rule of Evidence 803(8).

This pattern was cited with approval in LYNN MCLAIN, MARYLAND EVIDENCE: STATE AND FEDERAL § 803(6).1 n.22 (1987 & Supp. 1995).

G. PUBLIC RECORDS

i. *Certified*

The government prosecutes a rape case. The victim testifies that after she was raped, her assailant asked her not to be angry and stated that he had been convicted of assault with intent to rape in 1990 and had been paroled in 1994. The defendant sought to establish that he was not the assailant, since he had not been paroled in 1994. The government, on rebuttal, desires to introduce in evidence a certified copy of the records of the Department of Parole and Probation of Baltimore City, which reflect that the defendant was on parole in 1994 from a conviction of assault with intent to rape. The records are to be offered for the limited purpose of establishing the identity of the accused by proving he had been paroled in 1994.

Prosecutor: Your Honor, before we call our next witness, the State would like to introduce in evidence a certified copy of the records of the Department of Parole and Probation of Baltimore City for the year 1994 insofar as they pertain to the defendant, Ron Smothers.
Defense Counsel: I would object to the introduction of this document unless a proper foundation is established. Certainly, an officer from the Department should be present to authenticate this record.
The Court: Is this document a copy of a public record certified as a true copy by the custodian of the records?
Prosecutor: Yes, Your Honor.

The Court: Federal Rule of Evidence 803(d). The objection is overruled.

Comment

Federal Rule of Evidence 803(8) provides the hearsay exception for public records in federal court. *See* Beech Aircraft Corp. v. Rainey, 488 U.S. 153 (1988); Ellis v. Int'l Playtex, Inc., 745 F.2d 292 (4th Cir. 1984). The rule does not distinguish between federal and nonfederal offices, and exempts three types of public records from the hearsay rule: (a) records of the performance of official duties; (b) reports of observations made pursuant to law as to which there was a duty to report; and (c) factual findings in investigative reports in civil cases, or if offered against the government, in criminal cases. If a public record meets the conditions of Rule 902(4) and the requirement for contemporaneousness imposed by Rule 803(6) (Records of Regularly Conducted Activity), Rule 803(8) eliminates foundation requirements. *See* 4 JACK B. WEINSTEIN ET AL., WEINSTEIN'S EVIDENCE 803-263 to 803-264 (1995). *See also supra* chapter 2.F (Police Accident Reports) and 2.B (Business Records). Another advantage of Rule 803(8) is that it might allow in evidence hearsay statements and statements based on other than the firsthand knowledge of the recorder. *See* 4 JACK B. WEINSTEIN ET AL., WEINSTEIN'S EVIDENCE 803-269 to 803-272 (1995).

The term "factual findings" is broadly construed. *See* Beech Aircraft Corp. v. Rainey, 488 U.S. 153 (1988). The rule established in *Beech* is that factual findings can include factually based conclusions or opinions. *See also* Clark v. Clabaugh, 20 F.3d 1290 (3d Cir. 1994); Bank of Lexington & Trust Co. v. Vining-Sparks Sec. Inc., 959 F.2d 606 (6th Cir. 1992); Lubanski v. Coleco Indus., 929 F.2d 42 (1st Cir. 1991); Hines v. Brandon Steel Decks, Inc., 886 F.2d 299 (11th Cir. 1989), *on remand to* 754 F. Supp. 199 (M.D. Ga. 1991), *aff'd*, 948 F.2d 1297 (11th Cir. 1991), *cert. denied*, 503 U.S. 971 (1992); Koonce v. Quaker Safety Prods. & Mfg. Co., 798 F.2d 700, 720 (5th Cir. 1986); Ellis v. Int'l Playtex, Inc., 745 F.2d 292 (4th Cir. 1984); Jenkins v. Whittaker Corp., 785 F.2d 720, 726 (9th Cir.), *cert. denied*, 479 U.S. 918 (1986); *In re* Air Crash Disaster at Stapleton Int'l Airport, 720 F. Supp. 1493 (D. Colo. 1989), *rev'd on other grounds*, 964 F.2d 1059 (10th Cir. 1992).

The justification for allowing opinions and conclusions into evidence when they are contained within a public record is the dual assumption that a public official will perform his or her duty properly and would not remember details independently of the record. Factors used to determine the admissibility of such opinions and conclusions include timeliness of the investigation, special skills of the official, and potential motivational problems. *See* supra chapter 2F, relating to police accident reports; chapter 2.D, relating to computer printouts; and chapters 1.A and 11.B, for discussions of hearsay problems and firsthand knowledge problems with present recollection revived and past recollection recorded.

Federal Rule of Evidence 902(4) provides that copies of public records, books, papers, or proceedings of any agency of the government or any of its political subdivisions shall be received in evidence in any court if certified as true copies by the custodian of the record, book, paper, or proceeding, and if otherwise admissible. Public records are self-authenticating when certified by the appropriate custodian. Federal Rule of Evidence 1005 provides that if a copy that complies with Rule 902(4) cannot be obtained by exercise of reasonable diligence, then other evidence of the contents may be given.

This pattern was cited with approval in LYNN MCLAIN, MARYLAND EVIDENCE: STATE AND FEDERAL § 803(8).1 n.2 (1987 & Supp. 1995).

ii. *Uncertified*

Same facts as stated in previous pattern, except the government calls the Custodian of Records of the Department of Parole and Probation of Baltimore City for purposes of demonstrating that the defendant's record corresponds to that of the assailant.

Prosecutor:

Q. Would you state your name?

A. Henry Jones.

Q. Where are you employed?

A. The Baltimore City Department of Parole and Probation.

Q. For how long have you been employed in that Department?

A. For 16 years.

Q. What position do you hold within the Department?

A. Custodian of Records.

Q. How long have you occupied that position?

A. For the past six months.

Q. Did you receive a subpoena to come to court today?

A. Yes.

Q. What, if anything, did the subpoena direct you to bring to court?

A. The records of Ron Smothers for the year 1994.

Q. Do you have those records, sir?

A. Yes, I do.

Q. May I please see them? (The witness hands the records to counsel.)

Prosecutor: May we have this document marked as Government's Exhibit No. 1 for identification?

Q. Are the records that you brought today recorded or filed in the office of the Department of Parole and Probation for Baltimore City?

A. Yes.

Q. Why does the Department of Parole and Probation of Baltimore City maintain such records?

A. Department policy requires that our office maintain complete and accurate records of each individual who has been paroled and whether or not he has complied with the conditions of parole.

Q. How do you know that these records were recorded or filed within the Department?

A. As the custodian of the records, I have access to all reports and documents, and when I received your subpoena, I went to our office files and located the particular document required.

Q. Do you know who prepared the record pertaining to the defendant?

A. Yes. It has the initials A.Q. at the bottom.

Q. And what do those initials stand for?

A. Adam Quarles; he was my predecessor.

Q. Was this document prepared within the course of law, regulation, or public duty?

A. Yes, it was.

Prosecutor: We offer State's Exhibit No. 1 in evidence.

Comment

Introduction of an uncertified public record is similar to the introduction of business records, except that in authenticating uncertified public records, counsel must establish that the record was authorized or required to be recorded or filed pursuant to law, regulation, or public duty and that the document was in fact recorded or filed in a public office and is from the public office where items of such nature are kept. Fed. R. Evid. 901(b)(7); United States v. Lock, 425 F.2d 313 (5th Cir. 1970). Rule 901(b)(7) extends the authentication principle to include data stored in computers and by similar methods. *See* United States v. Meienberg, 263 F.3d 1177, 1181 (10th Cir. 2001); United States v. Hernandez-Herrera, 952 F.2d 342, 343 (10th Cir. 1991). *See also* 7 JOHN HENRY WIGMORE, WIGMORE ON EVIDENCE § 2158 (Chadbourn rev. ed. 1978 & Supp. 1995).

However, in light of Federal Rule of Evidence 902 providing for self-authentication of certified public documents, counsel should think twice before requiring clerks of public offices to appear in court to authenticate public records.

This pattern has been cited with approval in the following texts: MICHAEL H. GRAHAM, EVIDENCE: TEXT, RULES, ILLUSTRATIONS & PROBLEMS 172-73 (2d ed. 1988); LYNN MCLAIN, MARYLAND EVIDENCE: STATE AND FEDERAL § 803(8).1 n.2 (1987 & Supp. 1995).

H. HOSPITAL RECORDS

Plaintiff sues Aetna Trucking Company for personal injuries suffered as a result of an automobile collision. Defendant wishes to introduce hospital records relating to a previous injury sustained by plaintiff in an automobile accident in which plaintiff injured her lower back. The hospital records contain a statement by an orthopedic surgeon describing plaintiff's back injury resulting from the previous automobile accident. Defense counsel subpoenas the custodian of records of the hospital.

Defense Counsel:

Q. Please state your occupation and tell us where you work?

A. I am the medical records custodian of Exeter Hospital in Philadelphia.

Q. What are your duties as custodian of records?

A. I am in charge of the keeping and filing of medical records made in the hospital.

Q. Were you served with a subpoena to produce the hospital records of Bernice Feldapple, plaintiff in this case, who was a patient at Exeter Hospital in November of 1995?

A. Yes.

Q. Did you bring those records with you today?

A. Yes.

Defense Counsel: Please mark these hospital records as Defendant's Exhibit No. 1 for identification.

Q. Where did you obtain these medical records of Bernice Feldapple?

A. In the medical records file in our hospital.

Q. How do you know that these are the medical records of the plaintiff, Bernice Feldapple?

A. The file reflects the full name of the patient, her home address, the date she was admitted to the hospital, and the date she was discharged, and I matched this information with that contained on your subpoena.

Q. Were these records prepared in the regular course of business?

A. Yes.

Q. Was it the regular course of business for Exeter Hospital to prepare and maintain records such as these?

A. Yes.

Q. Is it the regular course of business of the hospital for the entries in these records to be made at or near the time that the matters recorded are observed?

A. Yes.

Q. Was it the regular course of business for a history of the patient's complaint to be included in the medical records?

A. Yes.

Q. Who records this history?

A. The doctor on duty when the patient comes into the receiving room.

Q. From whom does the doctor obtain the history he or she records?

A. From the patient, or if the patient is unable to communicate, from anyone else who is able to give it.

Q. Is a statement of the patient's condition on discharge ordinarily included as a part of the medical records of the hospital?

A. Yes.

Q. How is this statement prepared?

A. The physician takes notes while giving the patient a final examination, reviews the chart to the extent necessary and, as promptly as possible, dictates a statement of the patient's condition, and this statement is typed by the secretary.

Q. When is this report made?

A. Either right after the examination or at the end of the day.

Defense Counsel: We offer Exhibit No. 1 for identification in evidence.

(Subsequently, during the course of direct examination of Plaintiff's doctor, the following questions are asked.)

Q. Doctor, please refer to the discharge report. Does the report describe Bernice Feldapple's condition at the time of her discharge?

A. There is a statement that she was in poor condition.

Q. What is the date of that discharge summary?

A. June 15, 1995.

Q. Does the discharge summary indicate why Mrs. Feldapple was admitted to the hospital?

A. No.

Q. Does the history contained in the hospital records indicate the reason Mrs. Feldapple was admitted to the hospital?

A. The history reflects that she was admitted to the hospital following a motor vehicle accident.

Q. What treatment, if any, is described in the records?

A. A disc operation, among other things.

Q. Who noted in the discharge summary that Mrs. Feldapple underwent surgery for her disc?

A. The operating surgeon made this statement in his operative report, and this was transferred to the discharge summary by Dr. Smock.

Comment

The introduction of hospital records follows basically the same form as the introduction of business records pursuant to Federal Rule of Evidence 803(6). *See* Petrocelli v. Gallison, 679 F.2d 286 (1st Cir. 1982); Rivers v. Union Carbide Corp., 426 F.2d 633 (3d Cir. 1970); Harris v. Smith, 372 F.2d 806 (8th Cir. 1967); Thomas v. Hogan, 308 F.2d 355 (4th Cir. 1962); Turner v. Inland Tugs Co., 689 F. Supp. 612 (E.D. La. 1988). Hospital records clearly fall within the business record doctrine.

See Wilson v. Zapata Off-Shore Co., 939 F.2d 260 (5th Cir. 1991); Bondie v. Bic Corp., 947 F.2d 1531 (6th Cir. 1991); Baxter Healthcare Corp. v. Healthdyne, Inc., 944 F.2d 1573 (11th Cir. 1991), *opinion vacated and case dismissed*, 956 F.2d 226 (11th Cir. 1992) (based on the parties' joint motion to withdraw); Stull v. Fuqua Indus. Inc., 906 F.2d 1271 (8th Cir. 1990); United States v. Hershenow, 680 F.2d 847 (1st Cir. 1982); United States v. Sackett, 598 F.2d 739 (2d Cir. 1979); Ascher v. Gutierrez, 533 F.2d 1235 (D.C. Cir. 1976); United States v. Bohle, 445 F.2d 54 (7th Cir. 1971), *appeal after remand*, 475 F.2d 872 (2d Cir. 1973); Rivers v. Union Carbide Corp., 426 F.2d 633 (3d Cir. 1970); Picker X-Ray Corp. v. Frerker, 405 F.2d 916 (8th Cir. 1969); Thomas v. Hogan, 308 F.2d 355 (4th Cir. 1962); United States v. Grant, 2002 CAAF LEXIS 370, at *9 (C.A.A.F. Apr. 18, 2002).

However, the complete hospital record is not always admissible. Federal Rule of Evidence 803(4) and case law require for admissibility that statements in hospital records be pathologically germane to the physical condition that caused the patient to be hospitalized. Stull v. Fuqua Indus., Inc., 906 F.2d 1271, 1273 (8th Cir. 1990) (holding that the explanation that the accident occurred when the plaintiff "jumped off the mower" was inadmissible). A statement is pathologically germane if it has a significant bearing upon or relation to the disease or injury that one suffers. Thus, in the pattern examination, the surgeon's statement appearing in the hospital record about plaintiff's previous disc operation would be admissible. *See* Cook v. Hoppin, 783 F.2d 684, 690 (7th Cir. 1986).

Counsel appearing in federal court are not required to adhere to the distinction made in some state courts between the treating and nontreating physician. Federal Rule of Evidence 803(4) eliminated the distinction made by case law between the treating physician and the so-called examining physician. *See* Michael H. Graham, Handbook of Federal Evidence § 803.4, at 856 (3d ed. 1991). *See also* O'Gee v. Dobbs Houses, Inc., 570 F.2d 1084 (2d Cir. 1978); Conte v. AGF Assocs., 1999 U.S. Dist. LEXIS 21482, at *6 (D. Conn. Sept. 3, 1999).

If statements as to how an accident occurred appear within the hospital records, they are inadmissible unless they are part of the history taken by hospital personnel and are necessary information to aid in treatment or diagnosis. History includes physical and mental background, as well as present condition. Thus, for example, that part of the hospital record is admissible which reveals that the patient was in an automobile accident, but the particulars of how the accident occurred are not admissible unless the details of the occurrence are themselves pathologically germane. *See* McCollum v. McDaniel, 2002 U.S. App. LEXIS 4825, at *12 (4th Cir. Mar. 25, 2002); Rock v. Huffco Gas & Oil Co., 922 F.2d 272 (5th Cir. 1991); United States v. Pollard, 790 F.2d 1309 (7th Cir. 1986); United

States v. Nick, 604 F.2d 1199 (9th Cir. 1979); Walker v. West Coast Fast Freight, Inc., 233 F.2d 939 (9th Cir. 1956); Lewis v. Velez, 149 F.R.D. 474 (S.D.N.Y. 1993); Virgin Islands v. Morris, 191 F.R.D. 82, 85-87 (D.V.I. 1999). Statements identifying the perpetrator of sexual abuse are admissible as statements made for diagnosis and treatment under Federal Rule of Evidence 803(4). *See, e.g.*, United States v. Yazzie, 2002 U.S. App. LEXIS 4504, at *9 (9th Cir. Mar. 12, 2002); United States v. Gabe, 237 F.3d 954, 957-58 (8th Cir. 2001); United States v. King, 2000 U.S. App. LEXIS 18108, at *21 (10th Cir. July 26, 2000), *cert. denied*, 531 U.S. 1028 (2000); United States v. Tome, 61 F.3d 1446 (10th Cir. 1995); United States v. Yazzie, 59 F.3d 807 (9th Cir. 1995); United States v. Yellow, 18 F.3d 1438 (8th Cir. 1994); United States v. Joe, 8 F.3d 1488 (10th Cir. 1993), *cert. denied*, 510 U.S. 1184 (1994); United States v. Cherry, 938 F.2d 748 (7th Cir. 1991).

The foundation for hospital records need not always consist of testimonial evidence. In some instances the court may properly conclude from the circumstances and the nature of the documents involved that they were made in the regular course of business. *See generally* United States v. Johnson, 971 F.2d 562, 570-72 (10th Cir. 1992); United States v. Linn, 880 F.2d 209, 216 (9th Cir. 1989); Itel Capital Corp. v. Cups Coal Co., 707 F.2d 1253, 1259 (11th Cir. 1983); United States v. Hing Shair Chan, 680 F. Supp. 521 (E.D.N.Y. 1988); Zenith Radio Corp. v. Matsushita Elec. Indus. Co., 505 F. Supp. 1190, 1236 (E.D. Pa. 1980), *aff'd in part, rev'd in part*, 723 F.2d 238, *rev'd on other grounds*, 475 U.S. 574 (1986).

I. MEDICAL AND REPAIR BILLS, PAID AND UNPAID

Plaintiff institutes suit against defendant for personal injuries sustained as a result of slipping on a banana peel in defendant's supermarket. Plaintiff's special damages included a $1,500 medical bill from Dr. Willard Applejack, an orthopedic surgeon. Plaintiff's attorney introduces the orthopedic surgeon's medical bill as an exhibit for identification during plaintiff's testimony and follows up with the orthopedic surgeon to establish the document's competency to be admitted in evidence.

Plaintiff's Counsel Examining Plaintiff:

Q. You testified that from September 1, 1992, to October 14, 1993, you visited Dr. Willard Applejack on sixteen occasions for purposes of medical examinations and treatment?

A. Yes, that's right.

Q. How many bills did you receive?

A. Sixteen bills.

Q. What were these bills for?

A. For the examinations, tests, and treatment that I received.

Q. Does this treatment rendered by Dr. Applejack include the physical therapy about which you testified?

A. No, that was separate. I received separate bills from the therapist for those.

Plaintiff's Counsel: Please mark these documents as Plaintiff's Exhibit No. 13(a) through (p) for identification.

Q. Mrs. Smith, I show you Plaintiff's Exhibit No. 13(a) through (p) for identification and ask you if you recognize these documents?

A. Yes, they are the medical bills I received from Dr. Applejack.

Q. What was the total amount of those medical bills?

A. $1,500.

Plaintiff's Counsel:

Q. Dr. Applejack, I show you Plaintiff's Exhibit No. 13(a) through (p) for identification and ask you if you recognize these documents, sir?

A. Yes, these documents represent medical bills that I sent to Mrs. Smith after each of her numerous visits to my office and after rendering various treatments to her.

Q. Can you tell us whether these bills are fair and reasonable?

A. Yes, they are, in my opinion, fair and reasonable.

Q. Were the services that you rendered to Mrs. Smith necessary?

A. Yes. Because of the serious injury that she sustained, the services that I rendered were necessary.

Plaintiff's Counsel: If the Court please, we offer Plaintiff's Exhibit No. 13(a) through (p) in evidence.

Comment

In federal court sufficient foundation exists for admissibility of medical bills and repair bills if there is testimony that the service was necessary, provided there is no evidence to show that the charges were unreasonable.

Galard v. Johnson, 504 F.2d 1198 (7th Cir. 1974). *See generally* DePonte v. Kamada, 42 F.3d 1399 (9th Cir. 1994); United States v. Lebovitz, 669 F.2d 894, 901 (3d Cir. 1982), *cert. denied*, 456 U.S. 929 (1982); 222 Liberty Assocs. v. Eesco Elec., Inc., 101 B.R. 856, 864 (E.D. Pa. 1989).

The practice for marking and introducing exhibits varies from court to court. Consult local rules. For example, Local Rule 106.2(h) of the Rules of the United States District Court for the District of Maryland requires the listing of all documents and records, other than impeachment documents, to be offered in evidence by each side. The rule also requires the parties to agree on which documents may be offered in evidence without the usual authentication. This requirement may be satisfied by attaching an exhibit list to the pretrial order. Though documents may be stipulated as authentic, they may be inadmissible on other grounds. The stipulation as to authenticity does not preclude objections for any other reason. Authentication stipulations avoid the time-consuming process of identification.

Local Rule 106.7(a) requires counsel, prior to trial, to attach tags to all exhibits. These tags may be obtained from the Clerk. At least one business day before trial, counsel are required to file and serve upon each other two copies of an exhibit list. Prior to trial, in accordance with Local Rule 106.7(b), counsel are required to meet, review each other's proposed exhibits, and make the same available for copying.

Local Rule 107.5(b) provides that, unless counsel requests that an exhibit be marked for identification only, whenever an exhibit number is first mentioned by counsel during examination of a witness at trial, the exhibit will be considered admitted into evidence, unless opposing counsel asserts an objection.

Federal Rule of Civil Procedure 26(a)(3) provides that the parties shall disclose, at least 30 days before trial, an identification of all trial exhibits. Within 14 days, a party may serve objections. Failure to object timely may result in a waiver.

Each judge uses his or her own format for prenumbering exhibits. Generally, prenumbering means that, prior to trial, counsel tags with a number each document intended to be used during the course of the litigation. Prenumbering does not mean that the exhibits have been marked for identification. This could require the Clerk to retain the documents, even if they were never used during the trial by counsel.

Best Evidence or Original Document Problems

3

A. DUPLICATES—PHOTOGRAPHIC COPIES

Henry Witherspoon instituted suit against Ti-Con Pool Company for breach of contract resulting from the alleged failure of the pool company to properly install a swimming pool. The contract price was $15,000, and after full payment was made and the pool installed, cracks appeared in the pool. The pool company denies receiving notice that the pool was cracked until 6 weeks prior to the institution of suit, 2½ years after the appearance of the cracks.

Witherspoon's attorney intends to introduce a copy of a letter Witherspoon received from the president of the pool company. The original letter was sent to a subcontractor, requesting the subcontractor to investigate the claim of plaintiff that cracks appeared in the lining of the pool. The copy received by Witherspoon was dated three months after the alleged cracking appeared, and would disprove the pool company's claim that it had no knowledge of the cracking.

Plaintiff's Counsel:

Q. When did you first observe cracks appearing in the pool?

A. Approximately 2 or 3 weeks after we filled the pool with water.

Q. When did you first advise the pool company of this problem?

A. The day after I saw the first cracks appear, I telephoned the main office and told the secretary to have Mr. Winston, the president of the company, call me immediately.

Q. Did you ever attempt to contact him through other means than telephone?

A. Yes, I wrote to him.

Q. Do you remember when you wrote?

A. No, I don't remember the exact date, but I do remember it was sometime during the month of June, 1994.

Q. What response, if any, did you receive?

A. I received a copy of a letter that the president of the pool company wrote to one of his subcontractors, requesting that he drop by my house to investigate the report of cracks.

Q. Do you have with you now the copy of the letter?

A. Yes, I do.

Q. May I see it, please? (Witness hands the documents to counsel.)

Plaintiff's Counsel: Please mark this document as Plaintiff's Exhibit No. 4 for identification.

Q. Can you identify what is marked as Plaintiff's Exhibit No. 4 for identification?

A. Yes, I can. It is the copy of the letter I received from the president of the pool company.

Q. Do you know where the original of that letter is?

A. I presume the original document is in the possession of the subcontractor.

Plaintiff's Counsel: We offer Plaintiff's Exhibit No. 4 for identification in evidence.

Comment

The "Best Evidence Rule" stands for the principle that requires the production of the original of a document to prove the contents of that document. However, in practice, because of all the exceptions accorded by the federal rules of evidence, the rule manifests itself as a mere "preference" for the original.

Certain types of "copies" such as printouts from computers, carbon copies of contracts, and prints from photographic negatives are considered to be originals in and of themselves. Fed. R. Evid. 1001(3). Other types of copies, which are produced by methods that virtually eliminate the possibility of error, are considered duplicates. A photocopy is an example. Federal Rule of Evidence 1001(4) provides:

> A "duplicate" is a counterpart produced by the same impression as the original, or from the same matrix, or by means of photography, including enlargements and miniatures, or by mechanical or electronic recording, or by chemical reproduction, or by other equivalent technique which accurately reproduces the original.

Federal Rule of Evidence 1003 permits the admissibility of duplicates, unless a genuine question is raised about the authenticity of the document or it would be unfair to admit the duplicate in place of the original. *See* United States v. Hicks, 2001 U.S. App. LEXIS 27085, at *14 (6th Cir. Dec. 18, 2001), *pet. for cert. filed* Feb. 12, 2002; United States v. Grimmer, 1999 U.S. App. LEXIS 26218, at *4 (2d Cir. Oct. 14, 1999); United

States v. Moore, 30 F.3d 135 (6th Cir. 1994); United States v. Harris, 898 F.2d 148 (4th Cir.), *cert. denied*, 497 U.S. 1030 (1990); United States v. Patten, 826 F.2d 198 (2d Cir.), *cert. denied*, 484 U.S. 968 (1987); United States v. Garmany, 762 F.2d 929 (11th Cir. 1985), *cert. denied*, 474 U.S. 1062 (1986); United States v. Balzano, 687 F.2d 6 (1st Cir. 1982); Amoco Prod. Co. v. United States, 619 F.2d 1383 (10th Cir. 1980); CTS Corp. v. Piher Int'l Corp., 527 F.2d 95 (7th Cir. 1975), *cert. denied*, 424 U.S. 978 (1976); United States v. Gerhart, 538 F.2d 807 (8th Cir. 1976); Myrick v. United States, 332 F.2d 279 (5th Cir.), *cert. denied sub nom.* Bergman v. United States, 377 U.S. 952 (1964); Sauget v. Johnston, 315 F.2d 816 (9th Cir. 1963); United States v. Bertoli, 854 F. Supp. 975 (D. N.J.), *aff'd in part, vacated in part*, 40 F.3d 1384 (3d Cir. 1994), *cert. denied*, 517 U.S. 1137 (1996).

Furthermore, Federal Rule of Evidence 1004 provides that other evidence of the contents of original documents is admissible: when the originals have been lost or destroyed through no bad faith of the proponent, when the originals are unobtainable, when the originals are under control of the opponent and not produced after notice, or when the documents pertain to collateral matters. Essentially, these rules restate the common law, but without recognizing "degrees" of secondary evidence. Thus, if the original document is unavailable, the proponent need not introduce the most reliable copy, and once the conditions of the rules are satisfied, the proponent may prove the contents of the writing by any secondary evidence properly admitted. *See, e.g.*, Nicholas v. Wal-Mart Stores, Inc., 2002 U.S. App. LEXIS 6206, at *13 (4th Cir. Apr. 4, 2002) (relying on transcript of missing recording); United States v. Jimenez, 256 F.3d 330, 348 (5th Cir. 2001) (relying on evidence of custom and regular business practice to establish existence and contents of missing business documents); Sicherman v. Diamoncut, 2000 U.S. App. LEXIS 3357, at *11 (6th Cir. Feb. 29, 2000) (relying on handwritten ledger sheet, computer printouts, and photocopies of adding machine tapes in place of missing inventory cards and computer records).

Consider also that photocopies of business records and public records are admissible under certain circumstances. *See supra* chapter 2.B, 2.G.

B. USE OF SECONDARY EVIDENCE

Same facts as stated in previous pattern, except Witherspoon's attorney intends to introduce a manually prepared duplicate of the original letter Witherspoon received from the president of the pool company disputing that cracks appeared. The letter negates the defense. The original letter was destroyed by fire.

Plaintiff's Counsel:

Q. When did you first observe cracks appearing in the pool?

A. Approximately 2 to 3 weeks after we filled the pool with water.

Q. When did you first advise the pool company of this problem?

A. The day after I saw the first cracks appear, I telephoned the main office and told the secretary to have Mr. Winston, the president of the company, call me immediately.

Q. Did you ever attempt to contact him through other means than telephone?

A. Yes, I wrote to him.

Q. Do you remember when you wrote?

A. No, I don't remember the exact date, but I do remember it was sometime during the month of June, 1994.

Q. Did you receive a reply?

A. Yes, I did. I received a letter from Mr. Winston.

Q. Do you have that letter with you in court today?

A. No, sir, I do not.

Q. Can you tell us where that letter is now?

A. It was destroyed in a fire.

Q. What kind of fire?

A. There was a fire in my office and some of my records were destroyed. This letter was among those documents destroyed.

Q. Did you ever have occasion to make any copies of the original letter?

A. Yes, I did.

Q. When and for what reason?

A. After I received the letter at the office, I requested that my secretary retype the document. I wanted to bring a duplicate home to my wife, keep the original in my office files, and our Xerox machine was broken.

Q. Do you have that duplicate with you in court now?

A. Yes, I do.

Plaintiff's Counsel: Please mark this typed copy as Plaintiff's Exhibit No. 4 for identification.

Q. Is this copy of the letter now marked as Plaintiff's Exhibit No. 4 for identification an exact copy of the letter that you initially received?

A. Yes, it is.

Plaintiff's Counsel: We offer this typed copy in evidence as Plaintiff's Exhibit No. 4.

Comment

Since the federal rules have abandoned the hierarchy of "degrees" of secondary evidence, if Mr. Witherspoon testified that the original letter he received from the pool company was destroyed by fire, he could establish the contents of the original letter by oral testimony rather than by introducing the duplicate, even if he had the copy available. *See infra* chapter 3.C. Also, if Witherspoon knew of the existence of the copy of the destroyed letter, which the defendant maintained in his files, the federal rules would not require him to attempt to obtain it by summons or notice to produce. *See* Fed. R. Evid. 1004; United States v. Dudley, 941 F.2d 260 (4th Cir. 1991), *cert. denied*, 502 U.S. 1046 (1992); United States v. Gerhart, 538 F.2d 807 (8th Cir. 1976); Davis v. Baron's Creditors Serv. Corp., 2001 U.S. Dist. LEXIS 19008, at *6 (N.D. Ill. Nov. 20, 2001); Takeall v. Pepsico, Inc., 809 F. Supp. 19 (D. Md. 1992), *aff'd*, 14 F.3d 596 (4th Cir. 1993), *cert. denied*, 512 U.S. 1236 (1994); Seiler v. Lucasfilm, Ltd., 613 F. Supp. 1253 (N.D. Cal. 1984), *aff'd*, 797 F.2d 1504 (9th Cir.), *opinion superseded by* 808 F.2d 1316 (9th Cir. 1986), *cert. denied*, 484 U.S. 826 (1987).

C. USE OF SECONDARY EVIDENCE ESTABLISHING THE CONTENTS OF A DOCUMENT BY ORAL EVIDENCE

Same facts as stated in previous pattern except counsel seeks to establish the content of the destroyed document by oral testimony.

Plaintiff's Counsel:

Q. When did you first observe cracks appearing in the pool?

A. Approximately 2 to 3 weeks after we filled the pool with water.

Q. When did you first advise the pool company of this problem?

A. The day after I saw the first cracks appear, I telephoned the main office and told the secretary to have Mr. Winston, the president of the company, call me immediately.

Q. Did you ever attempt to contact him through other means than telephone?

A. Yes, I wrote to him.

Q. Do you remember when you wrote?

A. No, I don't remember the exact date, but I do remember it was sometime during the month of June, 1994.

Q. Did you receive a reply?

A. Yes, I did. I received a letter from Mr. Winston.

Q. Do you have that letter with you in court today?

A. No, sir, I do not.

Q. Can you tell us where that letter is now?

A. It was destroyed in a fire.

Q. What kind of fire?

A. There was a fire in my home and some of my records were destroyed. This letter was among those documents.

Q. Do you recall the contents of that letter?

A. Yes, I do.

Q. What were the contents of the letter?

Defense Attorney: Objection.

The Court: What's the basis of the objection?

Defense Attorney: Before Mr. Witherspoon testifies as to the contents of the original letter, a proper foundation should be established to demonstrate that no copies of that letter are available.

The Court: Not under Rule 1004 of the Federal Rules of Evidence. Under this rule, there is no demarcation between degrees of secondary evidence. Even if a photographic copy does exist, the rules do not require that the copy be introduced in evidence as long as the original is lost or destroyed or not obtainable. Objection overruled.

Q. You may answer the question.

A. The letter was from Mr. Winston, president of the pool company. He wrote that he would send one of his subcontractors to my home to investigate my complaints that cracks had appeared in the swimming pool that he installed two months ago.

Comment

Under the federal rules, when the original is unavailable, any form of secondary evidence is admissible as long as it meets other evidentiary requirements. Fed. R. Evid. 1004. *See, e.g.*, Simas v. First Citizens' Fed. Credit Union, 170 F.3d 37, 51 (1st Cir. 1999) ("There is no general rule that proof of a fact will be excluded unless its proponent furnishes the best evidence in his power."); United States v. Beltre, 1999 U.S. App. LEXIS 20056, at *5 (4th Cir. Aug. 23, 1999); Burt Rigid Box Inc. v. Travelers Prop. Cas. Corp., 126 F. Supp. 2d 596, 609 (W.D.N.Y. 2001); Paul Revere Annuity Ins. Co. v. Zang, 81 F. Supp. 2d 227, 230 (D. Mass), *aff'd*, 226 F.3d 15 (1st Cir. 2000), *aff'd*, 248 F.3d 1 (1st Cir. 2001).

Demonstrative and Real Evidence

4

A. PHOTOGRAPHS

Plaintiffs instituted a wrongful death action against defendant swimming club, which owned and operated a quarry used by the general public, upon payment of an admission fee, for swimming and sunbathing. Plaintiffs' decedent allegedly dived from a pier into the water, which was extremely shallow, and suffered a fatal fracture of the skull. Defendant claims that plaintiffs' decedent dived off the side of the pier, which was blocked by a guardrail, instead of diving off the proper side, which had no guardrail. Defense counsel seeks to introduce a black and white photograph of the pier depicting the two sides and the end of the pier. On the side of the pier with the guardrail, the photograph shows a sign stating: "Caution, shallow water." A lifeguard has testified on the witness stand that she was on duty, in the lifeguard chair on Pier No. 4, at the time of the accident:

Defense Counsel:

Q. Can you describe Pier 4 for us, Miss Smith?

A. Pier 4 was the farthest pier away from the first pier that you would see when you came onto the beach after you would pay your admission fee.

Q. Were there any railings on Pier 4?

A. There were railings on only one side of the pier, the left side facing the beach.

Q. Why were there railings on that side but not on the other?

A. On the side where the railing was located, the water was approximately 3 to 4 feet in depth, but on the other side the water was very deep.

Q. Were there any notices or signs that indicated the depth of the water?

A. Yes, on the railing side there was a sign every 5 feet that said, "Caution, shallow water."

Defense Counsel: Please mark this photograph as Defendant's Exhibit No. 12 for identification.

Q. I show you Defendant's Exhibit No. 12 for identification and ask you whether or not you can identify what is portrayed in this picture?

A. Yes, sir, I can.

Q. Please tell us what it is?

A. This is the pier that I described as Pier 4, where I sat as a lifeguard last summer.

Q. Does the photograph fairly and accurately represent Pier 4 in June, when the accident occurred?

A. Yes, it does.

Defense Counsel: We offer Defendant's Exhibit No. 12 for identification in evidence.

The Court: It will be received.

Q. May I show the photograph to the jury at this time, Your Honor?

The Court: You may hand it to the foreman, Counsel, and he will pass the photograph to the other jury members. (Proceedings suspended while jury examines photograph.)

Comment

Photographs include still photographs, x-ray films, videotapes, and motion pictures. Fed. R. Evid. 1001(2). The foundation for introducing photographs is the same in state and federal court. Photographs are admissible in the discretion of the court when the picture is shown to be a correct representation of the site, person, or object depicted. *See* United States v. Hicks, 2001 U.S. App. LEXIS 27085, at *15 (6th Cir. Dec. 18, 2001), *pet. for cert. filed* Feb. 12, 2002; United States v. Joe, 8 F.3d 1488, 1499 (10th Cir. 1993), *cert. denied*, 510 U.S. 1184 (1994); Hurt v. Coyne Cylinder Co., 956 F.2d 1319 (6th Cir. 1992); Lubanski v. Coleco Indus., Inc., 929 F.2d 42, 47 (1st Cir. 1991); Radford v. Seaboard Sys. R.R., Inc., 828 F.2d 1552 (11th Cir. 1987); Shipp v. General Motors Corp., 750 F.2d 418, 427 (5th Cir. 1985); United States v. Akers, 702 F.2d 1145, 1149 (D.C. Cir. 1983); United States v. Oaxaca, 569 F.2d 518 (9th Cir.), *cert. denied*, 439 U.S. 926 (1978); Luther v. Maple, 250 F.2d 916 (8th Cir. 1958); Meurling v. County Transp. Co., 230 F.2d 167, 168 (2d Cir. 1956); McEachron v. Glans, 1999 U.S. Dist. LEXIS 21926, at *9 (N.D.N.Y. Aug. 23, 1999), *amended*, 1999 U.S. Dist. LEXIS 21928 (N.D.N.Y. Aug. 25, 1999). Shushereba v. R.B. Indus., Inc., 104 F.R.D. 524, 531 (W.D. Pa. 1985). *But see* Sprynczynatyk v. General Motors Corp., 771 F.2d 1112, 117-18 (8th Cir. 1985), *cert. denied*, 475 U.S. 1046 (1986) (abuse of discretion to introduce a videotape of a hypnosis session because of its prejudicial effect). Often the requisite foundation is stated in these terms: that the photograph is fair and accurate, or that the photograph depicts a correct likeness of the scene it purports to represent. Gilliam v. Foster, 75 F.3d 881, 897 (4th Cir.), *cert. denied*, 517 U.S. 1220 (1996); Bibbins v. Dalsheim, 21 F.3d 13, 15 (2d Cir.), *cert. denied*, 513 U.S. 901 (1994); United States v. Van Wyhe, 965 F.2d 528, 532 (7th Cir. 1992); Lubanski v. Coleco Indus., Inc., 929 F.2d 42 (1st Cir. 1991); United States v. Rembert, 863 F.2d 1023, 1027 (D.C. Cir. 1988); Bannister v. Town of Noble, 812 F.2d 1265, 1269-70 (10th Cir. 1987); Saturn Mfg., Inc. v. Williams Patent Crusher & Pulverizer Co., 713 F.2d 1347, 1356 (8th Cir. 1983); United States v. Stearns, 550 F.2d 1167, 1168-69 (9th Cir. 1977); United States v. Taylor, 530 F.2d 639, 641 (5th Cir.), *cert. denied*, 429 U.S. 845 (1976); McEachron v. Glans, 1999 U.S. Dist. LEXIS 21926, at *9 (N.D.N.Y. Aug. 23, 1999), *amended*, 1999 U.S. Dist. LEXIS 21928 (N.D.N.Y. Aug. 25, 1999). Gregory P. Joseph, Modern Visual Evidence § 4.02 (Law Journal Seminars-Press 1995).

A witness or party can verify photographs, and it is not necessary to verify the photograph through the person who took the picture. United States v. Rembert, 863 F.2d 1023, 1026 (D.C. Cir. 1988); United States v. Abayomi, 820 F.2d 902, 908 (7th Cir. 1987), *cert. denied*, 484 U.S. 866 (1987); United States v. Wilson, 719 F.2d 1491, 1495 (10th Cir. 1983); United States v. Rochan, 563 F.2d 1246, 1251 (5th Cir. 1977); McEachron v. Glans, 1999 U.S. Dist. LEXIS 21926, at *9 (N.D.N.Y. Aug. 23, 1999), *amended*, 1999 U.S. Dist. LEXIS 21928 (N.D.N.Y. Aug. 25, 1999). The witness must have familiarity with the subject of the photograph and so testify. United States v. Jackman, 48 F.3d 1, 4 (1st Cir. 1995); United States v. Henderson, 68 F.3d 323, 324 (9th Cir. 1995); United States v. Stormer, 938 F.2d 759, 762 (7th Cir. 1991); United States v. Wright, 904 F.2d 403, 404 (8th Cir. 1990); United States v. Rembert, 863 F.2d 1023, 1026 (D.C. Cir. 1988); United States v. Rochan, 563 F.2d 1246, 1251 (5th Cir. 1977); United States v. Calhoun, 544 F.2d 291, 295 (6th Cir. 1976); United States v. Wilson, 719 F.2d 1491, 1495 (10th Cir. 1983); United States v. McNair, 439 F. Supp. 103, 105 (E.D. Pa. 1977), *aff'd*, 571 F.2d 573 (3d Cir.), *cert. denied*, 435 U.S. 976 (1978).

Frequently, photographs are taken subsequent to an occurrence and will reflect changes that would cause the witness not to be able to testify that the object depicted is "correct" in its representation of the scene at the relevant time. Under these circumstances, counsel should qualify his or her question, e.g., "with the exception of the telephone pole in the left-hand corner of this photograph, is this photograph, Defendant's Exhibit

No. 12 for identification, a fair and accurate representation of the northwest corner of 42d Street and Taylor Avenue at the time of the accident?" If the changed condition depicted in the photograph substantially alters the identity of the original subject, the photograph might not be admissible. *See* United States v. Stearns, 550 F.2d 1167, 1170 (9th Cir. 1977); United States v. White, 454 F.2d 435, 438 (7th Cir. 1971), *cert. denied*, 406 U.S. 962 (1972); Sears, Roebuck & Co. v. Penn Cent. Co., 420 F.2d 560, 563 (1st Cir. 1970); Blum v. Cottrell, 276 F.2d 689, 694 (4th Cir. 1960). However, once the court determines that a photograph is a correct likeness of what it purports to represent, differences between the actual portrayal and the photograph relate to the weight rather than the admissibility of the evidence. Bridges v. Equitable Life Assur. Soc'y of the United States, 1999 U.S. App. LEXIS 16282, at *4 (6th Cir. July 14, 1999); Lubanski v. Coleco Indus., Inc., 929 F.2d 42, 47 (1st Cir. 1991); Reed v. Tiffin Motor Homes, Inc., 697 F.2d 1192 (4th Cir. 1982); Pritchard v. Downie, 326 F.2d 323 (8th Cir. 1964); McEachron v. Glans, 1999 U.S. Dist. LEXIS 21926, at *9 (N.D.N.Y. Aug. 23, 1999), *amended*, 1999 U.S. Dist. LEXIS 21928 (N.D.N.Y. Aug. 25, 1999); Int'l Union, United Auto., Aircraft, & Agric. Implement Workers v. Russell, 88 So. 2d 175, 186 (Ala. 1956), *aff'd*, 356 U.S. 634 (1958).

It is not always appropriate to request that the jury view the photograph during the course of the trial, but counsel should consider this approach at appropriate times.

B. MOTION PICTURES AND VIDEOTAPE EVIDENCE

Plaintiff instituted suit against defendant trucking company for damages allegedly sustained when Defendant's tractor-trailer collided with the plaintiff's vehicle. Plaintiff sustained lower back injuries and testified that as a result of these injuries he was unable to participate in any athletics or household chores. Defendant engaged a professional photographer to take motion pictures of plaintiff playing tennis six months after the accident. Counsel for defendant attempts to introduce the motion pictures in evidence. He calls the photographer to the witness stand.

Defense Counsel:

Q. What is your full name?

A. Harry Pentaquod.

Q. And with whom are you employed?

A. I am self-employed.

Q. What is your occupation?

A. I am a professional photographer.

Q. Do you take moving pictures?

A. I do.

Q. Did you have occasion to take moving pictures of the plaintiff, Bernard Howell?

A. Yes.

Q. Describe the circumstances.

A. You engaged me to take motion pictures of Mr. Howell participating in any types of sports activities or doing any type of work outside of his home.

Q. And did you take such motion pictures?

A. Yes, I did.

Q. Tell us when and the circumstances of your taking those pictures.

A. On August 18, 1995, I accompanied Mr. Dan Thoerosa, a private investigator, to the home of Mr. Howell. We arrived at 9:30 in the morning. Approximately 15 minutes after we arrived, Mr. Howell left the house, entered a 1984 Oldsmobile, and proceeded to drive one mile north to the Sweetwater Tennis Courts. We followed his automobile to those tennis courts. I took my camera and equipment and positioned myself in a place where I could view the tennis courts and proceeded to take moving pictures of Mr. Howell playing tennis.

Q. What type of camera did you use?

A. I used a Model 201X, 16mm, Kodak.

Q. Can you tell us what type of lens was used?

A. I used a F 1.2, s=8.5 to 30 mm.

Q. What film were you using?

A. Ansco Tri-X.

Q. Was your camera in good working order that day?

A. Yes, it was.

Q. What did you do with the camera as you started taking pictures?

A. I focused the camera for the position, taking into consideration the distance and the appropriate lighting conditions.

Q. What speed was used to take these pictures?

A. I used 16 frames per second.

Q. Is that the usual speed for taking motion pictures?

A. Yes, particularly when I am focusing on a sports event such as tennis.

Q. What pictures did you take that day?

A. I took pictures of Mr. Howell serving and playing tennis.

Q. How long did Mr. Howell play tennis?

A. Thirty minutes.

Q. Did you photograph all of his activity during the entire 30 minutes?

A. No, I photographed about 20 of the 30 minutes Mr. Howell was on the court.

Q. Was there anything that Mr. Howell did during the 30 minutes he was on the tennis court that you did not photograph?

A. Yes.

Q. What actions of Mr. Howell did you not photograph?

A. I stopped shooting when they changed sides of the court or had conversations with each other.

Q. After you took the film, what did you do?

A. I took the film to the Kodak laboratory for development and picked it up three days later and have had it in my possession since that time.

Q. And did you run it off on a projector after that?

A. Yes.

Q. And were the pictures a true and accurate representation of the actions of Mr. Howell that you have testified to and that you witnessed while you were taking the pictures?

A. Absolutely.

Q. Did you edit in any way or cut these pictures?

A. They have not been tampered with in any way.

Q. Do you have the films with you today?

A. Yes, I do.

Defendant's Attorney: I would like to have this film marked as Defendant's Exhibit A for identification.

Q. Sir, I show you Defendant's Exhibit A for identification and ask if this is the film that you took and have described in your testimony?

A. Yes.

Defendant's Attorney: I offer the film in evidence and ask that the movies be shown to the jury.

The Court: The ruling will be reserved subject to cross-examination by plaintiff's counsel.

Comment

The foundation required to introduce motion pictures is similar to the foundation for the introduction of still photographs. Photographs include still photographs, x-ray films, videotapes, and motion pictures. Fed. R. Evid. 1001(2). The foundation for introducing photographs is the same in state and federal courts. The basic testimony essential to authenticate motion pictures includes the identification of the person or place pictured, proof that the film is accurately representative of the person or place depicted, and testimony or evidence as to the circumstances of taking, developing, and projection. *See* Bannister v. Town of Noble, 812 F.2d 1265, 1269-70 (10th Cir. 1987); Louis Vuitton S.A. v. Spencer Handbags Corp., 765 F.2d 966, 973 (2d Cir. 1985); Saturn Mfg., Inc. v. Williams Patent Crusher & Pulverizer Co., 713 F.2d 1347, 1356 (8th Cir. 1983); United States v. Brannon, 616 F.2d 413, 416-17 (9th Cir. 1980), *cert. denied sub nom.* Cox v. United States, 447 U.S. 908 (1980); United States v. Bynum, 567 F.2d 1167, 1171 (1st Cir. 1978); United States v. Richardson, 562 F.2d 476, 478-79 (7th Cir. 1977), *cert. denied*, 434 U.S. 1072 (1978); Grimes v. Employers Mut. Liab. Ins. Co., 73 F.R.D. 607 (D. Alaska 1977). *See generally* United States v. Patterson, 277 F.3d 709, 713 (4th Cir. 2002); Gilliam v. Foster, 75 F.3d 881, 897 (4th Cir. 1996), *cert. denied*, 517 U.S. 1220 (1996); United States v. Rembert, 863 F.2d 1023, 1027 (D.C. Cir. 1988); United States v. Taylor, 530 F.2d 639, 641 (5th Cir.), *cert. denied*, 429 U.S. 845 (1976). It is desirable, but not required, to establish the photographer's experience and qualifications and to elicit testimony as to the speed of the exposed frames per second, the type of lens used, and the distances. If the photographer is unavailable, an eyewitness can testify that the motion pictures were taken and were representative of the scene or individual depicted. *See* Kortz v. Guardian Life Ins. Co., 144 F.2d 676 (10th Cir.), *cert. denied*, 323 U.S. 728 (1944). *See generally* United States v. Rembert, 863 F.2d 1023, 1026 (D.C. Cir 1988); United States v. Abayomi, 820 F.2d 902, 908 (7th Cir.), *cert. denied*, 484 U.S. 866 (1987); United States v. Wilson, 719 F.2d 1491, 1495 (10th Cir. 1983); United States v. Rochan, 563 F.2d 1246, 1251 (5th Cir. 1977).

Opposing counsel is furnished the opportunity to voir dire the photographer or qualifying witness and to oppose the showing of motion pictures. In this pattern, plaintiff's counsel could cross-examine the photographer to prove that, while the movies were taken, the plaintiff stopped frequently to rest and constantly rubbed the lower part of his back, as if suffering discomfort. Counsel could attempt to establish that the photographer was guilty of selective photography and that the film does not fairly portray all of the relevant activity.

Before the court determines that the pictures can be shown to the jury, the movies should be viewed out of the presence of the jury. In most instances, counsel is aware that his or her adversary will use movies, and the filing of a motion in limine (prior to trial) can often be a vehicle for determining whether a sufficient foundation has been established for the movies to be shown to the jury. After the movies are shown to the jury, opposing counsel has the further opportunity for re-cross-examination of the witness.

The introduction of videotape recordings is similar to the introduction of motion pictures and photographs. *See* Hendricks v. Swenson, 456 F.2d 503 (8th Cir. 1972); GREGORY P. JOSEPH, MODERN VISUAL EVIDENCE § 4.02.2 (Law Journal Seminars-Press 1995). There is little difference in authentication. Videotape recordings are motion pictures made by recording both sight and sound electronically on magnetic tapes, whereas motion pictures and photographs rely on light to convey invisible images, which are then exposed or revealed through chemical processes. *See* Kucharek v. Hanaway, 714 F. Supp. 1499, 1511-14 (E.D. Wis. 1989), *rev'd on other grounds*, 902 F.2d 513 (7th Cir. 1990), *cert. denied*, 498 U.S. 1041 (1991). Videotape evidence often contains sound. Objections to narration on the basis of hearsay will usually be granted. If the narrator is available to testify and adopts the narration, the hearsay objection should be overruled. *See* Fed. R. Evid. 801 (d) (1) advisory committee's note; United States v. McKneely, 69 F.3d 1067, 1074 (10th Cir. 1995); United States v. Weisz, 718 F.2d 413, 430 n.104 (D.C. Cir. 1983), *cert. denied*, 465 U.S. 1027, *cert. denied sub nom.* Ciuzio v. United States, 465 U.S. 1034 (1984); GREGORY P. JOSEPH, MODERN VISUAL EVIDENCE § 4.02(4) (Law Journal Seminars-Press 1995).

Videotape evidence can be offered to depict damages, demonstrations, or experiments. Consider the admissibility of a videotaped test, the results of which are offered as a predicate to the opinion of an expert, even though the test results are not offered as substantive evidence. *See* Eagle-Picher Indus., Inc. v. Balbos, 578 A.2d 228 (Md. App. 1990), *aff'd in part, rev'd in part*, 604 A.2d 445 (Md. 1992), where the court admitted a videotape of the decedent, who was comatose at the time; United States v. Norris, 217 F.3d 262, 270 (5th Cir. 2000), *cert. denied*, 122 S. Ct. 161 (2001); Green v. Ford Motor Co., 2001 U.S. Dist. LEXIS 19883, at *3 (W.D. Va. Nov. 26, 2001); Misener v. General Motors, 165 F.R.D. 105, 108 (D. Utah 1996); Datskow v. Teledyne Cont'l Motors Aircraft Prods., 826 F. Supp. 677, 685 (W.D.N.Y. 1993); Culpepper v. Volkswagen of Am., Inc., 109 Cal. Rptr. 110, 117-18 (1973). *But see* Finchum v. Ford Motor Co., 57 F.3d 526, 530 (7th Cir. 1995) (barring test as similarity of test to actual occurrence would lead to prejudice and confusion of the jury). *See also* GREGORY P. JOSEPH, MODERN VISUAL EVIDENCE § 4.02(4) (Law Journal Seminars-Press 1995). It is helpful for appellate review to include a transcript of the video. *See* Howe v. Varity Corp., 36 F.3d 746, 749 (8th Cir. 1994), *aff'd*, 516 U.S. 489 (1996); United States v. Betancur, 24 F.3d 73, 75 (10th Cir. 1994). *See generally* Cox v. Louisiana, 379 U.S. 536, 547 (1965); LYNN McLAIN, MARYLAND EVIDENCE: STATE AND FEDERAL § 403.5 (Supp. 1995).

C. COMPUTER ANIMATION

Plaintiff instituted suit against Health Forever, Inc. for negligent manufacturing of a heart valve. Counsel for the plaintiff seeks to introduce computer animation showing how defective heart valves can malfunction over time. The witness, Dr. Peter Hornride, is an expert in the field of cardiac transplants.

Plaintiff's Counsel:

Q. Doctor Hornride, are you familiar with the heart valve manufactured by Health Forever, Inc., model number 401?

A. Yes, I am.

Q. What is the basis of your familiarity?

A. I have used this product in the course of treating many of my patients in need of a heart valve replacement.

Q. How many patients have you treated with this particular product?

A. Probably a total of 500 patients a year for the last four years.

Q. How was the valve used in the treatment that you gave these patients?

A. During open-heart surgery, I removed the defective heart valve from the patient and inserted and attached the artificial valve.

Q. Did you ever notice a problem with the defendant's product?

A. Yes. Early last year, I had several complaints from patients of mine who had received the valve two to three years earlier. They complained of numbness in certain areas of their bodies, shortness of breath, tiring out easily, and occasional chest pains. Upon further diagnosis, I determined that in nearly all of these cases, the component of the artificial valve designed to allow blood to flow in one direction, but not back in the other direction, was wedged in one position instead of moving freely as originally designed. In some patients, this resulted in the impediment of blood flow to certain parts of the body. In other patients, the result was an undertow of blood being pumped away from the heart in the wrong direction.

Q. Do you have a computer animation along with you today depicting the wedged valve and the end results, to help explain them to the jury?

A. Yes.

Plaintiff's Attorney: I ask that the computer animation contained on this diskette be marked as Plaintiff's Exhibit 24 for identification.

Q. Dr. Hornride, are you familiar with the computer animation introduced as Exhibit 24?

A. Yes.

Q. What is the basis of your familiarity?

A. I created the animation.

Q. How did you design it?

A. I used a pre-existing medical program depicting a three-dimensional cross-section of the heart. The artificial valve image was scanned into the computer and scaled to the same size as the heart. I attached the valve image to the heart image, and programmed in the ability to control the flow of the blood through the artificial valve. Using the actual data gathered from my patients, the computer image can show how the blood flows through the artificial valve as originally designed and installed, versus how the blood flows through after the component inside the artificial valve becomes wedged in different positions.

Q. Is the computer image a true and accurate representation of a heart with an artificial valve?

A. Yes.

Q. Is the underlying data regarding the flow of blood through the artificial valve accurate, and was it accurately entered in the computer?

A. Yes.

Plaintiff's Attorney: Your Honor, I offer the computer animation into evidence and ask that the jury be allowed to see it.

The Court: The ruling will be reserved subject to cross-examination by defendant's counsel.

Comment

Computer animations are often used to help an expert witness explain his or her testimony. *See supra* 1.2.D. (20), for discussion of computer evidence. These animations are admissible with the proper foundation. In the case of those animations that seek to illustrate, counsel must show sufficient similarity. *See* Robinson v. Missouri P. R.R., 16 F.3d 1083, 1088-89 (10th Cir. 1994); Green v. Ford Motor Co., 2001 U.S. Dist. LEXIS 19883, at 3-4 (W.D. Va. Nov. 26, 2001); Datskow v. Teledyne Cont'l Motors Aircraft Prods., 826 F. Supp. 677, 685 (W.D.N.Y. 1993); Harris v. State, 2000 Okla. Crim. App. LEXIS 20, at *10 and n.4 (Okla. Crim. App. Oct. 23, 2000), *cert. denied*, 532 U.S. 1025 (2001); MICHAEL H. GRAHAM, HAND-BOOK OF FEDERAL EVIDENCE § 401.7 (3d ed. 1991 & Supp. 1995). In the case of animations that go beyond illustration and present experimental elements, the issue of reliability comes into play.

Under *Daubert v. Merrell Dow Pharms., Inc.*, 509 U.S. 579 (1993), trial courts serve as gatekeepers to evaluate the admissibility of expert opinions. Factors to be considered in determining admissibility of scientific evidence are whether the opinion or scientific technique has been tested; whether the technique has been subjected to peer review; the technique's rate of error; and whether the technique is generally accepted in the scientific community. *See* Kumho Tire Co. v. Carmichael, 526 U.S. 137, 141 (1999) ("gatekeeping" obligation applies not only to "scientific" testimony but to all expert testimony); Downs v. Perstorp Components, Inc., 2002 U.S. App. LEXIS 382, *475 (6th Cir. Jan. 4, 2002) (chemical exposure); Dhillon v. Crown Controls Corp., 269 F.3d 865, 869 (7th Cir.

2001) (vehicle design; court notes 2000 amendment to Rule 702); Lauzon v. Senco Prods., 270 F.3d 687 (8th Cir. 2001) (sets out a collection of *Daubert* decisions in the Eighth Circuit); Oddi v. Ford Motor Company, 234 F.3d 136, 145-46 (3d Cir. 2000); Compton v. Subaru of Am., Inc., 82 F.3d 1513, 1518 (10th Cir. 1996); United States v. Dorsey, 45 F.3d 809 (4th Cir. 1995), *cert. denied*, 515 U.S. 1168 (1995); United States v. Posado, 57 F.3d 428 (5th Cir. 1995); American & Foreign Ins. Co. v. General Elec. Co., 45 F.3d 135 (6th Cir. 1995); Pestel v. Vermeer Mfg. Co., 64 F.3d 382 (8th Cir. 1995); Daubert v. Merrell Dow Pharms., Inc., 43 F.3d 1311 (9th Cir.), *cert. denied*, 516 U.S. 869 (1995); Iacobelli Constr., Inc. v. County of Monroe, 32 F.3d 19 (2d Cir. 1994); *In re* Paoli R.R. Yard PCB Litig., 35 F.3d 717 (3d Cir. 1994), *cert. denied sub nom.* General Elec. v. Ingram, 513 U.S. 1190 (1995); Bradley v. Brown, 42 F.3d 434 (7th Cir. 1994); United States v. Lee, 25 F.3d 997 (11th Cir. 1994); Agri-Mark, Inc. v. Niro, Inc., 2002 U.S. Dist. LEXIS 1866, at 31-33 (D. Mass. Feb. 5, 2002); Maurizio v. Goldsmith, 2002 U.S. Dist. LEXIS 6032, at *9 (S.D.N.Y. Apr. 9, 2002; United States v. Salim, 189 F. Supp. 2d 93 (S.D.N.Y. 2002); United States v. Gricco, 2002 U.S. Dist. LEXIS 7564, at 3-5 (E.D. Pa. Apr. 26, 2002) (handwriting analysis); Bourne v. E.I. DuPont de Nemours & Co., 189 F. Supp. 2d 482 (S.D. W. Va. 2002) (epidemiology); Cayuga Indian Nation of New York v. Pataki, 188 F. Supp. 2d 223, 247 (N.D.N.Y. 2002) (in Second Circuit, "rejection of expert testimony is the exception rather than the rule"); United States v. Santiago, 156 F. Supp. 2d 145, 147-48 (D. P.R. 2001) (stating that these four factors are not exclusive); MICHAEL H. GRAHAM, HANDBOOK OF FEDERAL EVIDENCE § 401.7 (3d ed. 1991 & Supp. 1995); Hoult v. Hoult, 57 F.3d 1 (1st Cir. 1995).

Many animations generated by computers present analyses of data to predict future events. In *Strock v. Southern Farm Bureau Cas. Ins. Co.*, 998 F.2d 1010 (4th Cir. 1993), the court admitted an animation re-creating hurricane damage. *See* HOTCHKESS AND THOMAS, THE USE OF COMPUTERIZED INFORMATION AT TRIAL, ABA Section of Litigation (1995), where the authors point out that:

> When animations are generated by computer, counsel should consider establishing that the data is accurate and was accurately entered; [should] present opinion testimony about the validity of the method used to present the animation; [and should establish] that the expert is familiar with the demonstrative exhibit; and that the

exhibit will aid the judge or jury in understanding the expert's testimony.

D. DIAGRAM NOT TO SCALE

Plaintiff sues defendant for personal injuries received in an automobile accident. Counsel for plaintiff seeks to have a witness draw, in court, a sketch depicting the relative positions of the automobiles involved in the collision.

Plaintiff's Counsel:

Q. Mrs. Jones, where were you standing when you saw the collision?

A. I was standing in front of my husband's store on the northwest corner of South and Third Streets.

Q. Tell us what you saw?

A. I saw a red Ford pickup truck turn right, and almost at the same time I saw this blue Ford go through a yellow light, and the red pickup truck and the blue Ford collided.

Q. At this point, Your Honor, I would like permission to have Mrs. Jones step down from the witness stand and draw freehand on the easel a diagram of the intersection where this accident occurred.

The Court: Proceed.

Q. Can you first draw the intersection?

Plaintiff's Counsel: Let the record reflect the witness drew the intersection.

Q. Now, place by drawing an "X," if you will, the position of your husband's store with respect to the intersection.

Plaintiff's Counsel: Let the record reflect that the witness marked an "X" reflecting the position of the store with respect to the intersection.

Q. Show us where the automobiles collided by marking the spot with a "Z." (Witness complies.)

Plaintiff's Counsel: Let the record reflect that the witness marked with a "Z" the spot where the automobiles collided.

Comment

Drawings, plats, maps, and graphs are admissible in the discretion of the trial judge when shown to accurately represent what they purport to depict. *See* United States v. Emmons, 24 F.3d 1210, 1216 (10th Cir. 1994); United States v. Chavez, 979 F.2d 1350, 1355 (9th Cir. 1992); Bower v. O'Hara, 759 F.2d 1117 (3d Cir. 1985); Kenney v. Lewis Revels Rare Coins, Inc., 741 F.2d 378, 383 (11th Cir. 1984); United States v. Hardin, 710 F.2d 1231, 1237 (7th Cir.), *cert. denied*, 464 U.S. 918 (1983); United States v. Carter, 522 F.2d 666, 685 (D.C. Cir. 1975); United States v. Jordano, 521 F.2d 695, 698 (2d Cir. 1975); Rhoads v. Virginia-Florida Corp., 476 F.2d 82, 86 (5th Cir. 1973), *appeal after remand*, 549 F.2d 985 (5th Cir. 1977); Beaty Shopping Center, Inc. v. Monarch Ins. Co. of Ohio, 315 F.2d 467, 470 (4th Cir. 1963); Hart v. Grim, 179 F.2d 334, 336 (8th Cir. 1950). Sketches or diagrams need not be drawn to scale as a qualification for admissibility, if the scene presented reasonably depicts the site. *See* United States v Espinosa, 771 F.2d 1382 (10th Cir.), *cert. denied sub nom.* Foreman v. United States, 474 U.S. 1023 (1985); United States v. D'Antonio, 324 F.2d 667 (3d Cir. 1963), *cert. denied*, 376 U.S. 909 (1964); *In re* Complaint of Nautilus Motor Tanker Co., 862 F. Supp. 1251, 1259 (D. N.J. 1994); Cardullo v. General Motors Corp., 378 F. Supp. 890, 892 (E.D. Pa. 1974), *aff'd*, 511 F.2d 1392 (3d Cir. 1975). *See generally* GREGORY P. JOSEPH, MODERN VISUAL EVIDENCE ch. 9 (Law Journal Seminars-Press 1995), in which the author devotes considerable attention to the use of diagrams, charts, and graphs. Admissibility of this type of evidence is commonplace and depends on whether the evidence fairly and accurately depicts that which it purports to depict. *See* United States v. Williams, 657 F.2d 199 (8th Cir. 1981).

Moreover, such diagrams need not be introduced in evidence, if counsel desires the sketch simply to serve as an aid to the witness's testimony. *See* United States v. Ricks, 475 F.2d 1326, 1328 (D.C. Cir. 1973); Weller Mfg. Co. v. Wen Prods., Inc., 135 F. Supp. 121, 129 (N.D. Ill. 1955), *aff'd*, 231 F.2d 795 (7th Cir. 1956). Diagrams of accident scenes, particularly from police reports, are admissible when based upon the personal observation of the police officer or of the authenticating witness. *See supra* chapter 2.F pertaining to police reports and diagrams contained therein. Police composite sketches based on eyewitness accounts are also admissible pursuant to Federal Rule of Evidence 801(d) (1) (C), which renders as non-hearsay statements of identification made by a witness who testifies at trial and is subject to cross-examination.

Counsel can also use a traffic board, and the witness can place model cars on the traffic board to correspond with the positions of the vehicles involved in an accident. As the witness places the model on the traffic board, it would be appropriate for counsel to state for the record that the witness is placing the model on the board in a position in which the witness testified that he had observed the object or motor vehicle. Counsel can also place the model on the board as the witness testifies and state for the record where he is placing the model. It may be desirable to introduce in evidence the sketch or a photograph of the sketch, although resort to the sketch or diagram during trial does not require that it be admitted. Even if the sketch is not introduced, it may be prudent to obtain a stipulation as to a photograph of it, or mark the sketch for identification, so that the appellate court can see what the jury saw, even if what they saw was not introduced as an exhibit. Whatever the jury sees should be in the record on appeal.

E. DIAGRAM TO SCALE

Plaintiff institutes a negligence suit against defendant for damages resulting from an injury sustained when defendant's automobile struck plaintiff, a pedestrian, at the intersection of Charles and Baltimore Streets. Plaintiff's attorney seeks to introduce a scaled diagram of the intersection and then request subsequent witnesses to depict the position of the motor vehicles on either side of the street, and particularly defendant's vehicle in relationship to the plaintiff, at the time of the collision.

Plaintiff's Counsel:

Q. Would you state your name, please?

A. John Bastelle.

Q. What is your occupation?

A. Surveyor.

Q. Mr. Bastelle, at my request, did you go to Charles and Baltimore Streets for purposes of preparing a diagram?

A. Yes, I did.

Q. When did you visit that intersection?

A. January 1, 1995.

Q. What time of day did you go to that intersection?

A. 6:00 a.m.

Q. What, if anything, did you do when you arrived at the scene?

A. I measured the width of Charles Street, the width of Baltimore Street, and took measurements in all directions as well as sketched a diagram of the intersection.

Q. Did there come a time when you prepared a diagram based upon your observations and sketch?

A. Yes.

Q. Do you have that diagram with you?

A. Yes, I do. (Witness hands diagram to counsel.)

Q. Can you tell us how you prepared this diagram?

A. It was drawn to scale. I measured the distance involved and made a rough sketch while I was at the scene and subsequently I prepared the scaled diagram.

Q. What was the scale?

A. 1 inch to 15 feet.

Q. What is meant by a scale of 1 inch to 15 feet?

A. That means that the distance measured as 1 inch on this diagram or model is equal to 15 feet on the streets of Baltimore and Charles.

Q. Is this drawing a true and correct diagram of the intersection as you saw it on January 1, 1995, drawn to the scale of 1 inch to 15 feet?

A. Yes, it is.

Plaintiff's Counsel: We offer the diagram in evidence as Plaintiff's Exhibit No. 3.

Comment

See *supra* chapter 4.D for comment on drawings not to scale.

F. MODEL OF ACCIDENT SCENE

Same facts as stated in previous pattern, except plaintiff's attorney seeks to introduce a model of the intersection. Counsel first introduces a scaled diagram as in the previous pattern and proceeds as follows:

Plaintiff's Counsel:

Q. What did you do after you prepared the scaled diagram?

A. I constructed a model from it.

Q. I show you Plaintiff's Exhibit No. 4 for identification and ask whether or not this is the model to which you referred?

A. Yes.

Q. Does this model accurately reflect the highway and the measurements according to the scale of your diagram?

A. Yes.

Q. Does Plaintiff's Exhibit No. 4 for identification clearly and accurately portray the intersection of Baltimore and Charles Streets?

A. Yes.

Q. We offer Plaintiff's Exhibit No. 4 for identification in evidence.

Comment

It is not necessary to introduce in evidence the diagram from which the model was made (if a diagram exists, as one did in this case). Models, as well as drawings, plats, and other demonstrative evidence, can be excluded by the court in its discretion. *See In re* Air Crash Disaster, 86 F.3d 498, 531 (6th Cir. 1996); Finchum v. Ford Motor Co., 57 F.3d 526, 530 (7th Cir. 1995); Pestel v. Vermeer Mfg. Co., 64 F.3d 382, 384 (8th Cir. 1995); United States v. Chavez, 979 F.2d 1350, 1355 (9th Cir. 1992); United States v. Rockwell, 781 F.2d 985, 987 (3d Cir. 1986); Petty v. Ideco, 761 F.2d 1146, 1150 (5th Cir. 1985); Daskarolis v. Firestone Tire & Rubber Co., 651 F.2d 937, 939 (4th Cir. 1981); Shepard v. General Motors Corp., 423 F.2d 406 (1st Cir. 1970); Colon v. BIC USA, 2001 U.S. Dist. LEXIS 21037, at *39 (S.D.N.Y. Dec. 19, 2001); L.S. Tellier, Annotation, *Propriety, in Trial of Civil Action, of Use of Model or Instrumentality, or of Site or Premises, Involved in the Accident or Incident*, 69 A.L.R.2d 424 (1960 & Supps. 1984, 1995). *See* generally Milanowicz v. Raymond Corp., 148 F. Supp. 2d 525, 533-37 (D. N.J. 2001). *See also* United States v. Aldaco, 201 F.3d 979, 986 (7th Cir. 2000) (replica of destroyed shotgun allowed jury to see what officer saw when he observed defendant holding a shotgun); Roland v. Langlois, 945 F.2d 956 (7th Cir. 1991) (the court held that it was not an abuse of discretion to admit a life-size model of an amusement ride that injured the plaintiff); *In re* Beverly Hills Fire Litig., 695 F.2d 207 (6th Cir. 1982), *cert. denied*, 461 U.S. 929 (1983), *on remand* 583 F. Supp. 1163 (E.D. Ky. 1984) (illustrates the wide discretion of the court in admitting models and other demonstrative evidence). *See also* MARK A. DOMBROFF, DOMBROFF ON DEMONSTRATIVE EVIDENCE (Wiley Law Publications, Supp. 1990).

G. ANATOMICAL MODEL

In a personal injury case, plaintiff's expert doctor is to refer to an anatomical model.

Plaintiff's Counsel:

Q. Dr. Jones, in the study of medicine and in the practice of medicine, are visual aids used to help members of your profession teach and work with various structures of the human body?

A. Yes.

Q. What types of aids are used?

A. Charts, diagrams, films, and models.

Q. Have you brought with you today an anatomical model of the leg of a human being?

A. Yes, I have.

Q. Would the use of this model aid you in explaining to the jury the injuries received by Billy Jones?

A. Yes.

Q. Doctor, may I see the model that you have brought?

A. Yes. (Witness hands model to the plaintiff's counsel.)

Q. Doctor, what does this model show?

A. Well, it is the model of a leg reflecting the various bones, cartilage, and joints.

Q. Does this model accurately portray the human leg and how its various parts fit and operate together?

A. Yes.

Plaintiff's Counsel: I offer this model in evidence as Plaintiff's Exhibit No. 32.

Comment

Anatomical models are admissible in the discretion of the court. *See* Flanagan v. Redondo, 595 N.E.2d 1077 (Ill. App. 1992), where the trial court properly admitted into evidence a skeletal model after the doctor had testified that the model was a true and accurate representation of the skeletal anatomy it purported to represent; Smith v. Ohio Oil Co., 134 N.E.2d 526 (Ill. App. 1956); Padgett v. S. Ry. Co., 396 F.2d 303, 308 (6th Cir. 1968); Honeywell v. Rogers, 251 F. Supp. 841, 845 (W.D. Pa. 1966). *See* L.S. Tellier, Annotation, *Propriety, in Trial of Civil Action, of Use of*

Skeleton or Model of Human Body or Part, 58 A.L.R. 2d 689 (1958 & Supp. 1994); B. Finberg, Annotation, *Propriety, in Trial of Criminal Case, of Use of Skeleton or Model of Human Body or Part*, 83 A.L.R. 2d 1097 (1962 & Supp. 1986, 1991, 1995).

Models or replicas may be used as visual aids, in the same manner as drawings and charts. *See* United States v. Wanoskia, 800 F.2d 235, 237 (10th Cir. 1986). In *Wanoskia*, the court permitted a demonstration by an animate human model to determine the distance from her head to the gun held by her, as her arms were exactly the same length as that of the deceased victim. *Id. See also* United States v. Turner, 528 F.2d 143, 167 (9th Cir.), *cert. denied*, 423 U.S. 996 (1975).

H. CHARTS OR SUMMARIES

Plaintiff instituted an employment discrimination action, under 42 U.S.C. § 2000(e) et seq., against defendant school board, on the basis that she was denied promotion to a department chairmanship solely on the basis of race. Defendant's counsel seeks to introduce a tabulation of all instructors appointed as chairman of a home economics department in each of the board's schools since plaintiff's affiliation with the school. The tabulations showed, inter alia, the starting salary, raises in salary, and qualifications of each employee promoted to a department chairmanship. The tabulation summarized information obtained by Clara Jones, the supervisor of all departments of home economics, from personnel files and other board data contained in the personnel department.

Defense Counsel:

Q. Mrs. Jones, why did you not appoint Joan Brown to the position of home economics chairman in one of the schools of the White Marsh County school system?

A. She did not meet the qualifications for the position, and there were others who did, and they were appointed.

Defense Counsel: Please have this document marked as Defense Exhibit No. 13 for identification.

Q. I show you what purports to be Defendant's Exhibit No. 13 for identification and ask if you can identify it.

A. Yes I can.

Q. Can you explain to us what is represented by this document?

A. This is a summary from information that is in the files of the supervisor of all of the home economic departments within the school system, of those individuals who were appointed to home economics department chairman positions from 1973 to 1975. The information includes the name of the individual, the race of the individual, the sex of the individual, the starting salary when the individuals first began employment with the school system, each raise in salary the individual received, the date of appointment to the position of department chairman, and the qualifications of that person.

Q. Who prepared this summary?

A. I did.

Q. Where did you obtain the information appearing in the summary?

A. From the records and files of the Board of Education.

Q. Does the tabulation accurately summarize the information from which it was compiled?

A. Yes.

Q. Does it accurately state the substance of the Board's records as to the matters set out in the tabulation?

A. Yes.

Defense Counsel: We offer Defendant's Exhibit No. 13 for identification in evidence at this time.

Comment

Contents of writings, recordings, or photographs that cannot be conveniently examined in court may be presented in the form of a chart or summary, provided the chart or summary is properly authenticated. Fed. R. Evid. 1006. *See* 7-UP Bottling Co. v. Archer Daniels Midland Co., 191 F.3d 1090, 1102 (9th Cir. 1999), *cert. denied sub nom.* Gangi Bros. Packing Co. v. Cargill, Inc., 529 U.S. 1037 (2000); United States v. Harmas, 974 F.2d 1262, 1269 (11th Cir. 1992); United States v. Williams, 952 F.2d 1504, 1519 (6th Cir. 1991); Fagiola v. National Gypsum Co. A.C. & S., Inc., 906 F.2d 53 (2d Cir. 1990); United States v. Duncan, 919 F.2d 981 (5th Cir. 1990), *cert. denied*, 500 U.S. 926 (1991); United States v. Briscoe, 896 F.2d 1476 (7th Cir.), *cert. denied sub nom.* Usman v. United States, 498 U.S. 863 (1990); United States v. Nivica, 887 F.2d 1110, 1125 (1st Cir. 1989), *cert. denied*, 494 U.S. 1005 (1990); United States v. Possick, 849 F.2d 332 (8th Cir. 1988); United States v. Poschwatta, 829 F.2d 1477 (9th Cir. 1987), *cert. denied*, 484 U.S.

1064 (1988); United States v. Porter, 821 F.2d 968 (4th Cir. 1987), *cert. denied*, 485 U.S. 934 (1988); United States v. Lemire, 720 F.2d 1327, 1347 (D.C. Cir. 1983), *cert. denied*, 467 U.S. 1226 (1984); United States v. Behrens, 689 F.2d 154 (10th Cir.), *cert. denied sub nom.* Wilkett v. United States, 459 U.S. 1088 (1982); United States v. Weaver, 281 F.3d 228, 232 (D.D.C. 2002); BD v. DeBuono, 193 F.R.D. 117, 129-30 (S.D.N.Y. 2000) (inaccuracy of summary goes to weight, not admissibility, of evidence). *See also* GREGORY P. JOSEPH, MODERN VISUAL EVIDENCE ch. 9 (Law Journal Seminars-Press 1995); 4 JOHN HENRY WIGMORE, WIGMORE ON EVIDENCE § 1230 (Chadbourn Rev. 1972 & Supp. 1991).

In addition to providing notice and the summary to opposing counsel, the proponent should also provide the original data prior to trial at a reasonable time and place. When possible, questions pertaining to the accuracy of the chart should be resolved during pretrial conferences or by stipulation. The court has discretion to order the underlying data to be produced in court. Significantly, the rules governing the admissibility of summaries and charts do not require that it be impossible to examine the records, but only that it would be inconvenient to do so. *See* United States v. Meshack, 225 F.3d 556, 582 (5th Cir. 2000), *cert. denied*, 122 S. Ct. 142 (2001); United States v. Osum, 943 F.2d 1394, 1405 (5th Cir. 1991); United States v. Campbell, 845 F.2d 1374 (6th Cir.), *cert. denied*, 488 U.S. 908 (1988); United States v. Possick, 849 F.2d 332 (8th Cir. 1988); R & R Assocs., Inc. v. Visual Scene, Inc., 726 F.2d 36, 37-38 (1st Cir. 1984); Keith v. Volpe, 618 F. Supp. 1132 (C.D. Cal. 1985); Doninger Metal Prods. Corp. v. United States, 50 Fed. Cl. 110, 130 (Fed. Cl. 2001). Moreover, the data contained in the summary themselves must be admissible, unless they serve as the basis of an expert's opinion. *See* Fraser v. Major League Soccer, LLC, 284 F.3d 47, 67 (1st Cir. 2002); Certain Underwriters at Lloyd's v. Sinkovich, 232 F.3d 200, 205 n.4 (4th Cir. 2000); United States v. Filippi, 1999 U.S. App. LEXIS 2840, at*19-20 (4th Cir. Feb. 23, 1999), *cert. denied*, 528 U.S. 846 (1999); AMPAT/Midwest, Inc. v. Illinois Tool Works, Inc., 896 F.2d 1035, 1045 (7th Cir. 1990); United States v. Dorta, 783 F.2d 1179 (4th Cir.), *cert. denied*, 477 U.S. 905 (1986); Hackett v. Housing Auth., 750 F.2d 1308 (5th Cir.), *cert. denied*, 474 U.S. 850 (1985); Paddack v. Dave Christensen, Inc., 745 F.2d 1254 (9th Cir. 1984); Ford Motor Co. v. Auto Supply Co., 661 F.2d 1171 (8th Cir. 1981); United States v. Scales, 594 F.2d 558, 562 (6th Cir.), *cert. denied*, 441 U.S. 946 (1979); United States v. Conlin, 551 F.2d 534, 538 (2d Cir.), *cert. denied*, 434 U.S. 831 (1977); United States v. Demjanjuk, 2002 U.S. Dist. LEXIS 6999, at *61-

62 (N.D. Ohio Apr. 22, 2002); Fisher v. Sellas, 2002 Bankr. LEXIS 253, at *22-*23 (Bankr. N.D. Ill. Jan. 11, 2002); Tucker v. Ohtsu Tire & Rubber Co., 49 F. Supp. 2d 456, 462 (D. Md. 1999); Fujsawa Pharm. Co. v. Kapoor, 1999 U.S. Dist. LEXIS 11381, at *35-36 (N.D. Ill. July 21, 1999); LYNN MCLAIN, MARYLAND EVIDENCE: STATE AND FEDERAL § 1006.2 (1987 & Supp. 1995). Charts and diagrams highlighting specific facts in evidence may be used to illustrate testimony, as well as in closing argument.

When the foundation requirements are not met, the court may exclude the chart or summary. For examples of instances where the chart or summary was excluded, see *United States v. North American Reporting, Inc.*, 740 F.2d 50 (D.C. 1984) (a chart that collected a "jumble of the defendant's wishes, guesses and undocumented recollections" was not admissible) and *United States v. Pelullo*, 964 F.2d 193 (3d Cir 1992) (a government agent's summary of defendant's financial activity was not admissible because the underlying materials were out-of-court statements).

It is important to keep in mind the difference between charts or summaries presented under Rule 1006 on the one hand and those that are simply used to demonstrate or explain on the other. The former are admissible in evidence. The latter are not. White Indus. v. Cessna Aircraft Co., 611 F. Supp. 1049 (W.D. Mo. 1985) contains a good discussion of the differences—distinguishing between a Rule 1006 summary (which is admitted as substantive evidence) and a so-called "pedagogical" summary (which is a demonstrative aid shown to the fact-finder but not admitted into evidence.)

Counsel may also want to consider introducing summary evidence through the testimony of a witness. Cases discussing and permitting such evidence include United States v. Mortimer, 118 F.2d 266 (2d Cir. 1941) (stating general rule that statements compiled from voluminous records are admissible on the testimony of the supervising agent); Diamond Shamrock Corp. v. Lumbermens Mutual Casualty Co., 466 F.2d 722 (7th Cir. 1972) ("it is not necessary . . . that every person who assisted in the preparation of the original records or summaries be brought to the witness stand.)"; United States v. Soulard, 730 F.2d 1292 (9th Cir. 1984) (testimony of an agent to present a summary analysis is admissible); O'Dillon v. State, 265 S.E.2d 18 (Ga. 1980) (admitting a sheriff's testimony as "summarizing witness"); United States v. Johnson, 54 F.3d 1150 (4th Cir. 1995) (summary testimony admissible pursuant to Rule 611(a)); United States v. Baker, 10 F.3d 1374 (9th Cir. 1993) (summary chart and summary testimony are properly admissible).

I. TANGIBLE OBJECTS

The State institutes a criminal prosecution against John Jones, who is charged with stealing Sam Smith's wallet. The wallet was in Jones's possession when he was arrested, and eventually was placed in a property envelope at the police station where it remained until trial. The wallet was brought to trial by Officer Williams, who had not been involved in the arrest. The prosecutor attempts to introduce the wallet in evidence through Officer Williams.

Prosecuting Attorney:

Q. Officer Williams, you have with you a wallet that we have marked for identification as State's Exhibit 4. Please tell us how you came to possess this wallet.

A. I went to the evidence room at police headquarters and signed out a large envelope marked as containing items that were in the possession of Mr. Jones at the time of his arrest.

Q. Were you involved in the arrest of Mr. Jones?

A. No.

Q. Were you involved in placing items found in the possession of John Jones into the property envelope you just discussed?

A. No.

Q. Are you able to account for and describe to us, the custody of the wallet prior to the time you took it from the envelope?

A. No.

Q. Let me ask you to open the wallet and describe to us its contents?

A. The wallet contains an identification card stating it is the property of Sam Smith. It also contains several photographs of an individual I know to be Sam Smith.

Prosecuting Attorney: Your Honor, the State would at this time offer the Exhibit 4 wallet into evidence.

Defense Attorney: Objection, Your Honor, the State has failed to establish chain of custody with respect to the wallet.

The Court: The objection is overruled and the wallet will be admitted. While I agree that the State has not established a proper chain of custody, the wallet itself possesses characteristics which are fairly unique and which have been identified. In such a circumstance it is unnecessary to establish a chain of custody.

Comment

Assuming relevance, to gain admission of a tangible object into evidence the proponent of it must authenticate or identify it. Federal Rule of Evidence 901 states that the requirement is satisfied "by evidence sufficient to support a finding that the matter in question is what its proponent claims." The rule also provides several examples of authentication or identification that meet the requirement. The first is testimony by a witness with knowledge "that a matter is what it is claimed to be." Another is "appearance, contents, substance, internal patterns, or other distinctive characteristics, taken in conjunction with circumstances."

"Tangible objects . . . are admissible in evidence only when identified and shown to be in materially the same condition as at the time [at issue]." Lockhart v. Texas Dept. of Corrections, 782 F.2d 1275, 1280-81 (5th Cir. 1986) (citing McCormick's Handbook of the Law of Evidence, 527 (E. Cleary, 2d ed. 1972)). As McCormick notes, "If the offered item possesses characteristics which are fairly unique and readily identifiable, and if the substance of which the items is composed is relatively impervious to change, the trial court is viewed as having broad discretion to admit merely on the basis of testimony that the item is the one in question and is in a substantially unchanged condition." *Id.*

See also United States v. Kelly, 14 F.3d 1169 (7th Cir. 1994) (gap in chain of custody occurring after the testing is treated more permissively); and United States v. Thomas, 987 F.2d 1298 (7th Cir. 1993) (in cases where the evidence is unique and resistant to change—Korean-made sawed-off shotgun—the chain of custody is relatively unimportant); United States v. Miller, 994 F.2d 441 (8th Cir. 1993) (one-year gap in the chain of custody goes to the weight of the evidence and not the admissibility); United States v. Collado, 957 F.2d 38 (1st Cir. 1992) (the unique characteristic approach to authentication of real evidence is provided for by Fed. R. Evid. 901(b) (4) and the chain of custody analysis by rule 901(b) (1)); United States v. Clonts, 966 F.2d 1366 (10th Cir. 1992) ("the degree of proof needed to establish an uninterrupted chain of custody depends upon the nature of the evidence at issue"); United States v. Roberson, 897 F.2d 1092 (11th Cir. 1990) (gaps in the chain of custody go to the weight of the evidence and not the admissibility); United States v. Hon, 904 F.3d 803 (2d Cir. 1990) (deficiencies—such as incorrectly labeled evidence, evidence bags left open, and no written records—in the government's chain of custody go to the weight of the evidence and not the admissibility); United States v.

Browne, 891 F.2d 389 (1st Cir. 1989) (the trial court must be able to determine that it is reasonably probable that there was no material alteration of the evidence after it came into the custody of the proponent); United States v. Casamanto, 887 F.2d 1141 (2d Cir. 1989) (the chain of custody from the seizure of the substance to the analysis is subject to stricter scrutiny and deficiencies render the evidence inadmissible); United States v. Mahone, 537 F.2d 922 (7th Cir. 1976), *quoting* United States v. Blue, 440 F.2d 300, 303 (7th Cir. 1971) ("The chain of custody is not relevant when a witness identifies the object as the actual object about which he has testified."); United States v. Panczko, 353 F.2d 676 (7th Cir. 1965) (a chain of custody must be proved when the condition of the object at a prior time is in issue).

Opinions of the
Lay Witness **5**

A. LAY OPINION, GENERALLY

The United States indicts the local director of a federally funded program for willful misapplication of funds. The defendant places in issue the question of his willfulness, claiming he did not know and understand the particular requirements of the program that he is charged with violating. The Government calls the director's secretary, seeking to obtain her testimony on whether, in her opinion, the director fully understood the requirements of the program.

U.S. Attorney:

Q. State your name, please.

A. Gwendolyn Jackson.

Q. Where are you employed?

A. The office of Federal Support for Wild Animals.

Q. What is the office of Federal Support for Wild Animals?

A. It is a federally funded program to protect wild animals from cruelty.

Q. What is your position in that department?

A. I am secretary to the director, Mr. Smith.

Q. How long have you served as his secretary?

A. For the past three years.

Q. What are your responsibilities as his secretary?

A. General typing, administrative work, and serving as a liaison between other members in the office and the director.

Q. During the course of your employment as the director's secretary, do you have occasion to work with him on projects?

A. Yes, I do.

Q. Do you have occasion to attend meetings with him?

A. Yes, I do.

Q. Do you have occasion to observe him as he performs his responsibilities?

A. Yes, I do.

Q. Do you ever have occasion to attend meetings with him where the purposes and rules of operating the office are explained and discussed?

A. Yes, many times.

Q. Do you have an opinion as to whether Mr. Smith knew and under-

> stood the requirements of the program as to eligibility to receive federal funds?
>
> A. Yes, I do.
>
> Q. And what is that opinion?
>
> A. Mr. Smith fully appreciated and understood the rules and requirements of the program with regard to awarding and applying federal funds to those who were eligible.

Comment

Generally, lay witnesses may not state opinions in court. Nevertheless, the prevailing practice with regard to the admission of the opinions of lay witnesses manifests itself not as a rule of absolute prohibition, but rather as a preference for non-opinion testimony. *See* JOHN W. STRONG ET AL., MCCORMICK ON EVIDENCE § 11 (4th ed. 1992). Federal Rule of Evidence 701, in conjunction with Rule 602, provides that a lay witness may testify in the form of an opinion if the opinion is rationally based on the perception of the witness, is helpful to a clear understanding of the testimony or the determination of a fact in issue, and is not based on scientific, technical or specialized knowledge within the scope of Rule 702.

Lay witnesses have been permitted to express opinions on a wide variety of topics, including "[t]he appearance of person or things, identity, the manner of conduct, competency of a person, feelings, degrees of light or darkness, sound, size, weight, distance, and an endless number of things that cannot be described factually . . . ." Ladd, *Expert Testimony*, 5 VAND. L. REV. 414, 415-17 (1952). *See* United States v. Mendoza-Paz, 2002 U.S. App. LEXIS 6550, at *20-*21 (9th Cir. Apr. 10. 2002); United States v. Nelson, 2002 U.S. App. LEXIS 3628, at *13-*14 (9th Cir. Mar. 5, 2002) (no requirement that expert testimony be presented in child pornography cases to establish age of children in pictures); United States v. Caballero, 277 F.3d 1235, 1247 (10th Cir. 2002) (possible for same witness to provide both lay and expert testimony in same case); Research Sys. Corp. v. IPSOS Publicite, 276 F.3d 914, 924 (7th Cir. 2001) (lay testimony that product was not unique in the industry); Walton v. Nalco Chem. Co., 272 F.3d 13, 29-30 (1st Cir. 2001) (court upheld exclusion of lay opinion of district sales manager as to company's net profits lost); Meyers v. Wal-Mart Stores, Inc., 257 F.3d 625, 630 (6th Cir. 2001) (combination of both expert and lay testimony sufficient under Michigan law to present triable issue for jury; "before and after" lay testimony competent evidence on issue of damages); Mattison v. Dallas Carrier Corp., 947 F.2d 95 (4th Cir. 1991) (a lay witness was permitted to testify that emergency flashers on a vehicle did not provide sufficient warning); Asplundh Mfg. Div. v. Benton Harbor Eng'g, 57 F.3d 1190 (3d Cir. 1995); United States v. Newman, 49 F.3d 1 (1st Cir. 1995); Duluth Lighthouse for the Blind v. C.G. Bretting Mfg. Co., 199 F.R.D. 320, 325-26 (D. Minn. 2000) (discusses amended Rule 701 and advisory committee notes thereto).

Most often, lay witnesses are called upon to render opinions on speed, height and distance, sobriety, mental capacity, and the value of property. Lay witnesses can also testify that another person appeared nervous, United States v. Mastberg, 503 F.2d 465 (9th Cir. 1974); or excited, Asplundh Mfg. Div. v. Benton Harbor Eng'g, 57 F.3d 1190, 1196 (3d Cir. 1995); or about their own physical symptoms, Smolen v. Chater, 80 F.3d 1273 (9th Cir. 1996); or intoxicated, United States v. Horn, 185 F. Supp. 2d 530, 560 (D. Md. 2002); EEOC v. Oak-Rite Mfg. Corp., 2001 U.S. Dist. LEXIS 15621, at *8-*9 (S.D. Ind. Aug. 27, 2001). Counsel must be careful to elicit responses from the witness which demonstrate that the opinion is rationally based on the observation. *See, e.g.*, United States v. Cox, 633 F.2d 871 (9th Cir. 1980), *cert. denied*, 454 U.S. 844 (1981). When the opinion encompasses a legal conclusion or testimony that the court believes is not helpful, the court properly may exclude the opinion. *See* United States v. Roy, 881 F.2d 1070 (4th Cir. 1989); United States v. Ness, 665 F.2d 248 (8th Cir. 1981); United States v. Phillips, 600 F.2d 535 (5th Cir. 1979). *See also* Fed. R. Evid. 104(a) and 403. Certainly, superfluous opinions are rejected in favor of hearing testimony about underlying facts. Thus, for example, a witness's opinion about the believability of another witness's testimony is not admissible. *See* Lynn McLain, Maryland Rules of Evidence: State and Federal § 186-87 (1994). On the other hand, lay witnesses called as character witnesses may render opinions as to another witness's character traits for veracity.

While the federal rules express a preference for non-opinion testimony, there should be a natural inclination on the part of the trial attorney to avoid naked opinion testimony in the first place. The more concrete description, pushing a jury to infer the desired opinion, is more persuasive than an abstract, naked opinion. *See* John W. Strong et al., McCormick on Evidence § 11, at 45 (4th ed. 1992); Fed. R. Evid. 701 advisory committee's note.

In this example, the witness is asked to express an opinion concerning another individual's state of mind. *See* United States v. Fowler, 932 F.2d

306 (4th Cir. 1991), where the court permitted officials to render opinions that a person with defendant's experience would know the rules about classified documents not being available to contractors; United States v. Smith, 550 F.2d 277 (5th Cir.), *cert. denied sub nom.* Wallace v. United States, 434 U.S. 841 (1977); Gossett v. Oklahoma ex rel. Bd. of Regents for Langston Univ., 245 F.3d 1172, 1179 (10th Cir. 2001) (testimony as to pattern of discrimination against men); Xiangyuan Zhu v. Countrywide Realty Co., 165 F. Supp. 2d 1181, 1187, n.5 (D. Kan. 2001) (testimony about intent to deceive); United States v. Mirama Enters., 2002 U.S. Dist. LEXIS 1888, at *19-*20 (S.D. Cal. Jan. 24, 2002), *summ. j. granted (plaintiff)*, 185 F. Supp. 2d 1148 (S.D. Cal. 2002). Even if the lay opinion focuses on the ultimate issue of a case, Federal Rule of Evidence 704 would permit the opinion, subject to the discretion of the court. *See* Fed. R. Evid. 403.

Different judges could reach different determinations when confronted with the same facts. *See* 3 JACK B. WEINSTEIN ET AL., WEINSTEIN'S EVIDENCE § 701-31 to 701-32 (1995). The rules, however, relax the traditional view that lay opinions are not admissible, and relax the foundation requirements for the admissibility of those opinions.

B. VALUE OF PERSONAL PROPERTY

Plaintiff Margaret Sands institutes suit against John Smith, claiming that Smith was responsible for damages to plaintiff's automobile in a collision that allegedly occurred as a result of defendant's negligence. Counsel for plaintiff seeks to elicit plaintiff's opinion as to the value of her automobile at the time of the accident.

> Q. Mrs. Sands, when did you purchase the automobile that you were driving and that was involved in the collision?
> A. 1991.
> Q. And what was the purchase price of the car?
> A. $700.
> Q. Did you make any improvements to the automobile at the time or after you purchased it?
> A. Yes.
> Q. Tell us what type of improvements you made?
> A. I equipped the automobile with new tires and had other work done to it, such as installing a stereo sound system.

Q. Do you have an opinion as to the value of the automobile at the time of the accident?

A. Yes.

Q. Can you tell us what that opinion is?

A. The car was worth approximately $1,000 at the time of the accident.

Comment

Generally, lay witnesses may not state opinions in court. Nevertheless, the prevailing practice with regard to the admission of the opinions of lay witnesses manifests itself not as a rule of absolute prohibition, but rather as a preference for non-opinion testimony. *See* JOHN W. STRONG ET AL., MCCORMICK ON EVIDENCE § 11 (4th ed. 1992). Federal Rule of Evidence 701, in conjunction with Rule 602, provides that a lay witness may testify in the form of an opinion if the opinion is rationally based on the perception of the witness and helpful to a clear understanding of the testimony or the determination of a fact in issue and is not based on scientific, technical or specialized knowledge within the scope of Rule 702.

Lay witnesses have been permitted to express opinions on a wide variety of topics, including "[t]he appearance of person or things, identity, the manner of conduct, competency of a person, feelings, degrees of light or darkness, sound, size, weight, distance, and an endless number of things that cannot be described factually. . . ." Ladd, *Expert Testimony*, 5 VAND. L. REV. 414, 415-17 (1952). *See* United States v. Mendoza-Paz, 2002 U.S. App. LEXIS 6550, at *20-*21 (9th Cir. Apr. 10. 2002); United States v. Nelson, 2002 U.S. App. LEXIS 3628, at *13-*14 (9th Cir. Mar. 5, 2002) (no requirement that expert testimony be presented in child pornography cases to establish age of children in pictures); United States v. Caballero, 277 F.3d 1235, 1247 (10th Cir. 2002) (possible for same witness to provide both lay and expert testimony in same case); Research Sys. Corp. v. IPSOS Publicite, 276 F.3d 914, 924 (7th Cir. 2001) (lay testimony that product was not unique in the industry); Walton v. Nalco Chem. Co., 272 F.3d 13, 29-30 (1st Cir. 2001) (court upheld exclusion of lay opinion of district sales manager as to company's net profits lost); Meyers v. Wal-Mart Stores, Inc., 257 F.3d 625, 630 (6th Cir. 2001) (combination of both expert and lay testimony sufficient under Michigan law to present triable issue for jury; "before and after" lay testimony competent evidence on issue of damages); Asplundh Mfg. Div. v. Benton Harbor Eng'g, 57 F.3d

1190 (3d Cir. 1995); United States v. Newman, 49 F.3d 1 (1st Cir. 1995); Mattison v. Dallas Carrier Corp., 947 F.2d 95 (4th Cir. 1991) (a lay witness was permitted to testify that emergency flashers on a vehicle did not provide sufficient warning); Duluth Lighthouse for the Blind v. C.G. Bretting Mfg. Co., 199 F.R.D. 320, 325-26 (D. Minn. 2000) (discussing amended Rule 701 and advisory committee notes thereto).

As a general rule, an owner of personal property is permitted to express an opinion as to the value of that property. The rationale for the rule is somewhat disputed, sometimes leading to slightly different applications of the rule. *See* District of Columbia Redev. Land Agency v. Thirteen Parcels of Land, 534 F.2d 337 (D.C. Cir. 1976). One line of authority holds that the owner may give an opinion without qualification because of the close relationship he has to the property. *Id.* at 339. The owner is not draped in a cloak of expertise, but rather testifies from the unique position as the individual who stands to gain or lose the most from the tribunal's valuation of his property. *Id.* at 340. "The weight of such testimony is, of course, affected by the owner's knowledge of circumstances which affect value, and as an interested witness, it is for the jury to evaluate the credibility of his testimony." Berkshire Mut. Ins. Co. v. Moffett, 378 F.2d 1007, 1011 (5th Cir. 1967) (footnotes omitted). *See* Neff v. Kehoe, 708 F.2d 639, 643-44 (11th Cir. 1983); J & H Auto Trim Co., Inc. v. Bellefonte Ins. Co., 677 F.2d 1365, 1368 (11th Cir. 1982); District of Columbia Redev. Land Agency v. Thirteen Parcels of Land, 534 F.2d 337, 339 (D.C. Cir. 1976); *In re* Brown, 244 B.R. 603, 611-12 (Bankr. W.D. Va. 2000).

The other line of authority holds that the owner may give an opinion as to the value of his property based on his "quasi-expert" status. District of Columbia Redev. Land Agency v. Thirteen Parcels of Land, 534 F.2d 337 (D.C. Cir. 1976). That is, the owner is presumed to be qualified to give a valuation opinion based on his special knowledge arising out of ownership. This knowledge must rest on "some independent, competent, and relevant basis, such as experience in buying or selling [property], general knowledge of [property] values . . . , or some particular knowledge relating to the [property] in question." *Id* at 347. Where a lack of such knowledge is affirmatively shown, such as "where the opinion rest[s] on hypothesized facts or speculation on circumstances not in existence," the owner's opinion will be held inadmissible. *Id.* Robinson v. Watts Detective Agency, Inc., 685 F.2d 729, 739 (1st Cir. 1982), *cert. denied*, 459 U.S. 1204 (1983). While not clearly defined in the circuits, most federal courts align themselves within this second ideological camp. *See* Asplundh Mfg. Div. v. Benton Harbor Eng'g, 57 F.3d 1190, 1198 (3d Cir. 1995); Robinson v. Watts Detective Agency, Inc., 685 F.2d 729, 738 (1st Cir. 1982), *cert. denied,* 459 U.S. 1204 (1983); Dietz v. Consol. Oil & Gas, Inc., 643 F.2d 1088, 1093-94 (5th Cir.), *cert. denied,* 454 U.S. 968 (1981); Greenwood Ranches, Inc. v. Skie Constr. Co., 629 F.2d 518, 522 (8th Cir. 1980); Rich v. Eastman Kodak Co., 583 F.2d 435, 437 (8th Cir. 1978); Runge v. Lee, 441 F.2d 579, 582 (9th Cir.), *cert. denied,* 404 U.S. 887 (1971); Insurance Co. of Pa. v. Smith, 435 F.2d 1029, 1031 (10th Cir. 1971); Lee Shops, Inc. v. Schatten-Cypress Co., 350 F.2d 12, 17 (6th Cir. 1965), *cert. denied,* 382 U.S. 980 (1966); Knuppel v. American Ins. Co., 269 F.2d 163, 166 (7th Cir. 1959); *In re* Smith, 267 B.R. 568, 573 (Bankr. S.D. Ohio 2001); Lubecki v. Omega Logging, Inc., 674 F. Supp. 501, 509-10 (W.D. Pa. 1987); Granholm v. TFL Express, 576 F. Supp. 435, 452 (S.D.N.Y. 1983).

This pattern was cited with approval in LYNN MCLAIN, MARYLAND EVIDENCE: STATE AND FEDERAL § 701.4 n.2 (1987 & Supp. 1995).

C. VALUE OF REAL PROPERTY

Henry Armco, in a condemnation trial, desires to demonstrate that the fair market value of his home, which the city desires to acquire for a highway, is $200,000.

Plaintiff's Counsel:

Q. Mr. Armco, when did you acquire the premises known as 210 Madison Street?

A. 1989.

Q. What did you pay for the premises?

A. $120,000.

Q. Have you lived on the premises since the time you purchased it?

A. Yes, I have.

Q. Are you familiar with the real estate values in the vicinity of your home?

A. Yes, I am.

Q. What is the basis of your familiarity?

A. I have talked to neighbors living in similar type homes and they told me what their homes have sold for.

Q. When have you had these conversations?

A. Throughout the last five years.
Q. When did the sales that you discussed occur?
A. From 1989-1995.
Q. How many occurred during the past three years?
A. Five.
Q. Do you have an opinion as to the fair market value of your premises as of July 1, 1995?
A. Yes, I do.
Q. Please state your opinion of that value as of July 1, 1995?
A. $200,000.

Comment

Generally, lay witnesses may not state opinions in court. Nevertheless, the prevailing practice with regard to the admission of the opinions of lay witnesses manifests itself not as a rule of absolute prohibition, but rather as a preference for non-opinion testimony. *See* JOHN W. STRONG ET AL., MCCORMICK ON EVIDENCE § 11 (4th ed. 1992). Federal Rule of Evidence 701, in conjunction with Rule 602, provides that a lay witness may testify in the form of an opinion, if the opinion is rationally based on the perception of the witness and helpful to a clear understanding of the testimony or the determination of a fact in issue, and is not based on scientific, technical or specialized knowledge within the scope of Rule 702.

Lay witnesses have been permitted to express opinions on a wide variety of topics, including "[t]he appearance of person or things, identity, the manner of conduct, competency of a person, feelings, degrees of light or darkness, sound, size, weight, distance, and an endless number of things that cannot be described factually. . . ." Ladd, *Expert Testimony*, 5 VAND. L. REV. 414, 415-17 (1952). *See* United States v. Mendoza-Paz, 2002 U.S. App. LEXIS 6550, at *20-*21 (9th Cir. Apr. 10. 2002); United States v. Nelson, 2002 U.S. App. LEXIS 3628, at *13-*14 (9th Cir. Mar. 5, 2002) (no requirement that expert testimony be presented in child pornography cases to establish age of children in pictures); United States v. Caballero, 277 F.3d 1235, 1247 (10th Cir. 2002) (possible for same witness to provide both lay and expert testimony in same case); Research Sys. Corp. v. IPSOS Publicite, 276 F.3d 914, 924 (7th Cir. 2001) (lay testimony that product was not unique in the industry); Walton v. Nalco Chem. Co., 272 F.3d 13, 29-30 (1st Cir. 2001) (court upheld exclusion of lay opinion of district sales manager as to company's net profits lost); Meyers v. Wal-

Mart Stores, Inc., 257 F.3d 625, 630 (6th Cir. 2001) (combination of both expert and lay testimony sufficient under Michigan law to present triable issue for jury; "before and after" lay testimony competent evidence on issue of damages); Mattison v. Dallas Carrier Corp., 947 F.2d 95 (4th Cir. 1991) (a lay witness was permitted to testify that emergency flashers on a vehicle did not provide sufficient warning); Asplundh Mfg. Div. v. Benton Harbor Eng'g, 57 F.3d 1190 (3d Cir. 1995); United States v. Newman, 49 F.3d 1 (1st Cir. 1995); Duluth Lighthouse for the Blind v. C.G. Bretting Mfg. Co., 199 F.R.D. 320, 325-26 (D. Minn. 2000) (discussing amended Rule 701 and Advisory Committee Notes thereto).

As a general rule, an owner of real property is permitted to express an opinion as to the value of that property. The rationale for the rule is somewhat disputed, sometimes leading to slightly different applications of the rule. *See* District of Columbia Redev. Land Agency v. Thirteen Parcels of Land, 534 F.2d 337 (D.C. Cir. 1976). One line of authority holds that the owner may give an opinion without qualification because of the close relationship he has to the property. *Id.* at 339. The owner is not draped in a cloak of expertise, but rather testifies from the unique position as the individual who stands to gain or lose the most from the tribunal's valuation of his property. *Id.* at 340. "The weight of such testimony is, of course, affected by the owner's knowledge of circumstances which affect value, and as an interested witness, it is for the jury to evaluate the credibility of his testimony." Berkshire Mut. Ins. Co. v. Moffett, 378 F.2d 1007, 1011 (5th Cir. 1967). *See* LaCombe v. A-T-O, Inc., 679 F.2d 431 (5th Cir. 1982); District of Columbia Redev. Land Agency v. Thirteen Parcels of Land, 534 F.2d 337, 339 (D.C. Cir. 1976); *In re* Brown, 244 B.R. 603, 611-12 (Bankr. W.D. Va. 2000).

The other line of authority holds that the owner may give an opinion as to the value of his property based on his "quasi-expert" status. District of Columbia Redev. Land Agency v. Thirteen Parcels of Land, 534 F.2d 337 (D.C. Cir. 1976). That is, the owner is presumed to be qualified to give a valuation opinion based on his special knowledge arising out of ownership. This knowledge must rest on "some independent, competent, and relevant basis, such as experience in buying or selling land, general knowledge of land values . . . , or some particular knowledge relating to the land in question." *Id.* at 347. Where a lack of such knowledge is affirmatively shown, such as "where the opinion rest[s] on hypothesized facts or speculation on circumstances not in existence," the owner's opinion will be held inadmissible. *Id.* at 347; Robinson v. Watts Detective Agency, Inc., 685

F.2d 729, 739 (1st Cir. 1982), *cert. denied*, 459 U.S. 1204 (1983). While not clearly defined in the circuits, most federal courts align themselves within this second ideological camp. *See* White v. Atlantic Richfield Co., 945 F.2d 1130, 1132-33 (9th Cir. 1991); United States v. 7.92 Acres of Land, 769 F.2d 4, 12 (1st Cir. 1985), *cert. denied*, 484 U.S. 1011 (1988); LaCombe v. A-T-O, Inc., 679 F.2d 431, 434 (5th Cir. 1982); Justice v. Pennzoil Co., 598 F.2d 1339, 1344 (4th Cir.), *cert. denied sub nom.* McKinney v. Pennzoil Co., 444 U.S. 967 (1979); United States v. 534.28 Acres of Land, 442 F. Supp. 82, 84 (M.D. Pa. 1977); United States v. 3698.63 Acres of Land, 416 F.2d 65, 67 (8th Cir. 1969); United States v. Sowards, 370 F.2d 87, 92 (10th Cir. 1966); Kinter v. United States, 156 F.2d 5, 7 (3d Cir. 1946); *In re* Smith, 267 B.R. 568, 573 (Bankr. S.D. Ohio 2001); *In re* Jamison, 93 B.R. 595, 596 (Bankr. S.D. Ohio 1988).

This pattern was cited with approval in LYNN McLAIN, MARYLAND EVIDENCE: STATE AND FEDERAL § 701.4 n.2 (1987 & Supp. 1995).

D. HANDWRITING IDENTIFICATION

Patio, Inc. institutes suit against a general contractor, alleging cost delays caused by the contractor's failure to coordinate the operations of a subcontractor. The theory of Patio, Inc.'s case is that the general contractor warranted to Patio, Inc. that it would issue no change orders to the subcontractor without first obtaining the approval of Patio, Inc. and that the general contractor breached this aspect of its contract. Plaintiff's counsel seeks to introduce in evidence through the president of plaintiff corporation a change order issued by the general contractor's resident engineer, which was not shown to plaintiff and which resulted in delays causing damages to plaintiff. The president of plaintiff corporation, who is examined as to the source of the change order, is not a handwriting expert.

Plaintiff's Counsel:

Q. Mr. Johnson, are you familiar with the signature of the general contractor's resident engineer on the project that is the subject of this lawsuit.

A. Yes.

Q. Can you tell us the basis of your familiarity with his signature?

A. In my capacity as president of Patio, Inc., I have seen the resident engineer's signature on hundreds of change orders and other documents over the last five years.

Q. Would you recognize that signature if you saw it today?

A. Yes.

Plaintiff's Counsel: Please mark this document as Plaintiff's Exhibit No. 32 for identification.

Q. Mr. Johnson, I show you what has been marked as Plaintiff's Exhibit No. 32 for identification and ask you if you can identify the signature at the bottom of that document.

A. It is the signature of Tom Morrow, the general contractor's resident engineer.

Q. Can you identify the document?

A. It is a change order issued by the general contractor's resident engineer, requesting the sewer contractor to move a sewer line.

Plaintiff's Counsel: Your Honor, we offer Plaintiff's Exhibit No. 32 for identification in evidence.

Comment

Generally, lay witnesses may not state opinions in court. Nevertheless, the prevailing practice with regard to the admission of the opinions of lay witnesses manifests itself not as a rule of absolute prohibition, but rather as a preference for non-opinion testimony. *See* JOHN W. STRONG ET AL., MCCORMICK ON EVIDENCE § 11 (4th ed. 1992). Federal Rule of Evidence 701, in conjunction with Rule 602, provides that a lay witness may testify in the form of an opinion if the opinion is rationally based on the perception of the witness and helpful to a clear understanding of the testimony or the determination of a fact in issue, and is not based on scientific, technical or specialized knowledge within the scope of Rule 702.

Lay witnesses have been permitted to express opinions on a wide variety of topics, including "[t]he appearance of person or things, identity, the manner of conduct, competency of a person, feelings, degrees of light or darkness, sound, size, weight, distance, and an endless number of things that cannot be described factually. . . ." Ladd, *Expert Testimony*, 5 VAND. L. REV. 414, 415-17 (1952). *See* United States v. Mendoza-Paz, 2002 U.S. App. LEXIS 6550, at *20-*21 (9th Cir. Apr. 10. 2002); United States v. Nelson, 2002 U.S. App. LEXIS 3628, at *13-*14 (9th Cir. Mar. 5, 2002) (no requirement that expert testimony be presented in child pornography cases to establish age of children in pictures); United States v. Caballero,

277 F.3d 1235, 1247 (10th Cir. 2002) (possible for same witness to provide both lay and expert testimony in same case); Research Sys. Corp. v. IPSOS Publicite, 276 F.3d 914, 924 (7th Cir. 2001) (lay testimony that product was not unique in the industry); Walton v. Nalco Chem. Co., 272 F.3d 13, 29-30 (1st Cir. 2001) (court upheld exclusion of lay opinion of district sales manager as to company's net profits lost); Meyers v. Wal-Mart Stores, Inc., 257 F.3d 625, 630 (6th Cir. 2001) (combination of both expert and lay testimony sufficient under Michigan law to present triable issue for jury; "before and after" lay testimony competent evidence on issue of damages); Mattison v. Dallas Carrier Corp., 947 F.2d 95 (4th Cir. 1991) (a lay witness was permitted to testify that emergency flashers on a vehicle did not provide sufficient warning); Asplundh Mfg. Div. v. Benton Harbor Eng'g, 57 F.3d 1190 (3d Cir. 1995); United States v. Newman, 49 F.3d 1 (1st Cir. 1995); Duluth Lighthouse for the Blind v. C.G. Bretting Mfg. Co., 199 F.R.D. 320, 325-26 (D. Minn. 2000) (discussing amended Rule 701 and Advisory Committee Notes thereto).

A lay witness is permitted to testify as to the genuineness of handwriting based upon his or her familiarity with that handwriting, provided that the familiarity is not acquired for purposes of litigation. Fed. R. Evid. 901(b) (2). *See also* 5 JACK B. WEINSTEIN ET AL., WEINSTEIN'S EVIDENCE § 901-36 (1995). The minimum foundation requires the witness to testify that he or she is familiar with the handwriting in question and to describe the circumstances giving rise to that familiarity. Counsel should take care not to over-prepare a witness with regard to handwriting exemplars so as to create a familiarity based on trial preparation. In the case of *Murray v. United States*, 247 F. 874 (4th Cir. 1917), which predated the Federal Rules of Evidence, the court held that a lay opinion on handwriting was admissible based on the witness's observation of the questioned handwriting on only one other occasion. *Cf.* United States v. Pitts, 569 F.2d 343 (5th Cir.), *cert. denied*, 436 U.S. 959 (1978) (one-shot comparison does not meet standard of familiarity). In *United States v. Barron*, 707 F.2d 125 (5th Cir. 1983), the court permitted a lay witness to testify that the defendant forged another's signature. *See also* United States v. Chandler, 2001 U.S. App. LEXIS 3099, at *14-*15 (10th Cir. Mar. 1, 2001), *cert. denied*, 122 S. Ct. 120 (2001); United States v. Scott, 270 F.3d 30, 48-49 (1st Cir. 2001), *cert. denied*, 2002 U.S. LEXIS 2662 (U.S. Apr. 15, 2002); United States v. Dozie, 27 F.3d 95 (4th Cir. 1994); United States v. Tipton, 964 F.2d 650 (7th Cir. 1992); United States v. Binzel, 907 F.2d 746 (7th Cir. 1990) (witness may testify in non-absolute terms such as "I believe" or "the writing is similar to"); United States v. Barker, 735 F.2d 1280 (11th Cir.), *cert. denied*, 469 U.S. 933 (1984); United States v. Carriger, 592 F.2d 312 (6th Cir. 1979); United States v. Pitts, 569 F.2d 343 (5th Cir.), *cert. denied*, 436 U.S. 959 (1978); United States v. Kilgore, 518 F.2d 496 (5th Cir. 1975), *cert. denied*, 430 U.S. 905 (1977); United States v. Dreitzler, 577 F.2d 539 (9th Cir. 1978), *cert. denied*, 440 U.S. 921 (1979); United States v. Gallagher, 576 F.2d 1028 (3d Cir. 1978), *cert. denied sub nom.* McCarthy v. United States, 444 U.S. 1043 (1980); United States v. Standing Soldier, 538 F.2d 196 (8th Cir.), *cert. denied*, 429 U.S. 1025 (1976); Ryan v. United States, 384 F.2d 379 (1st Cir. 1967).

This pattern was cited with approval in LYNN MCLAIN, MARYLAND EVIDENCE: STATE AND FEDERAL § 701.5 n.1 (1987 & Supp. 1995).

E. VOICE IDENTIFICATION—LAY WITNESS

Newstime, Inc. sues Easy Wax Car Wash, claiming fees for advertisements placed in Newstime's publications. The defense is that the advertisements were never authorized. Plaintiff calls the vice president of Newstime, Inc. to prove that the president of Easy Wax Car Wash personally placed the advertisements by telephone.

Plaintiff's Counsel:

Q. Who placed these advertisements?

A. John Jones, president of Easy Wax Car Wash.

Q. How did he place these advertisements?

A. By telephone.

Q. Who called whom?

A. He called me.

Q. Did you recognize the voice of the person who telephoned you on each of these occasions?

A. Yes, I did.

Q. Do you remember the date of the first telephone call to place an ad?

A. Yes, January 1, 1995.

Q. Had you spoken to John Jones on the telephone prior to the date of January 1, 1995?

A. Yes, many times.

Q. On this occasion and the other occasions, did he identify himself as John Jones to you?

A. Yes.

Q. Did you ever telephone him?

A. Yes.

Q. Now, on each of the calls that he placed to you requesting that advertisements be published in Newstime publications, what did he say to you?

Comment

Generally, lay witnesses may not state opinions in court. Nevertheless, the prevailing practice with regard to the admission of the opinions of lay witnesses manifests itself not as a rule of absolute prohibition, but rather as a preference for non-opinion testimony. *See* JOHN W. STRONG ET AL., MCCORMICK ON EVIDENCE § 11 (4th ed. 1992). Federal Rule of Evidence 701, in conjunction with Rule 602, provides that a lay witness may testify in the form of an opinion if the opinion is rationally based on the perception of the witness and helpful to a clear understanding of the testimony or the determination of a fact in issue, and is not based on scientific, technical or specialized knowledge within the scope of Rule 702.

Lay witnesses have been permitted to express opinions on a wide variety of topics, including "[t]he appearance of person or things, identity, the manner of conduct, competency of a person, feelings, degrees of light or darkness, sound, size, weight, distance, and an endless number of things that cannot be described factually. . . ." Ladd, *Expert Testimony*, 5 VAND. L. REV. 414, 415-17 (1952). *See* United States v. Mendoza-Paz, 2002 U.S. App. LEXIS 6550, at *20-*21 (9th Cir. Apr. 10. 2002); United States v. Nelson, 2002 U.S. App. LEXIS 3628, at *13-*14 (9th Cir. Mar. 5, 2002) (no requirement that expert testimony be presented in child pornography cases to establish age of children in pictures); United States v. Caballero, 277 F.3d 1235, 1247 (10th Cir. 2002) (possible for same witness to provide both lay and expert testimony in same case); Research Sys. Corp. v. IPSOS Publicite, 276 F.3d 914, 924 (7th Cir. 2001) (lay testimony that product was not unique in the industry); Walton v. Nalco Chem. Co., 272 F.3d 13, 29-30 (1st Cir. 2001) (court upheld exclusion of lay opinion of district sales manager as to company's net profits lost); Meyers v. Wal-Mart Stores, Inc., 257 F.3d 625, 630 (6th Cir. 2001) (combination of both expert and lay testimony sufficient under Michigan law to present triable issue for jury; "before and after" lay testimony competent evidence on issue of damages); Mattison v. Dallas Carrier Corp., 947 F.2d 95 (4th Cir.

1991) (a lay witness was permitted to testify that emergency flashers on a vehicle did not provide sufficient warning); Asplundh Mfg. Div. v. Benton Harbor Eng'g, 57 F.3d 1190 (3d Cir. 1995); United States v. Newman, 49 F.3d 1 (1st Cir. 1995); Duluth Lighthouse for the Blind v. C.G. Bretting Mfg. Co., 199 F.R.D. 320, 325-26 (D. Minn. 2000) (discussing amended Rule 701 and advisory committee notes thereto).

Federal Rule of Evidence 901(b) (5) provides that voice identification may be made by opinion evidence based upon hearing the voice at any time under circumstances connecting it with the alleged speaker. *See* United States v. Bakal, 2001 U.S. App. LEXIS 21482, at *4 (2d Cir. Oct. 3, 2001); United States v. Tropeano, 252 F.3d 653, 661 (2d Cir. 2001); United States v. Jordan, 2000 U.S. App. LEXIS 15489, at *7-*8 (7th Cir. June 29, 2000); United States v. Duran, 4 F.3d 800 (9th Cir. 1993), *cert. denied*, 510 U.S. 1078 (1994), *appeal after remand*, 46 F.3d 1146 (9th Cir.), *cert. denied*, 514 U.S. 1135 (1995); United States v. Puentes, 50 F.3d 1567 (11th Cir.), *cert. denied*, 516 U.S. 933 341 (1995); United States v. Cooper, 868 F.2d 1505 (6th Cir.), *cert. denied*, 490 U.S. 1094 (1989); United States v. Vega, 860 F.2d 779 (7th Cir. 1988); United States v. Cambindo Valencia, 609 F.2d 603 (2d Cir. 1979), *cert. denied sub nom.* Prado v. United States, 446 U.S. 940 (1980); United States v. Vitale, 549 F.2d 71 (8th Cir.), *cert. denied*, 431 U.S. 907 (1977); United States v. Watson, 594 F.2d 1330 (10th Cir.), *cert. denied sub nom.* Brown v. United States, 444 U.S. 840 (1979); United States v. DiMuro, 540 F.2d 503 (1st Cir. 1976), *cert. denied*, 429 U.S. 1038 (1977); Millender v. Adams, 187 F. Supp. 2d 852, 869 (E.D. Mich. 2002); United States v. Robinson, 707 F.2d 811 (4th Cir. 1983); United States v. Verlin, 466 F. Supp. 155 (N.D. Tex. 1979); United States v. Whitaker, 372 F. Supp. 154 (M.D. Pa.), *aff'd sub nom.* Appeal of Nicola, 503 F.2d 1399 (3d Cir.), *aff'd*, 503 F.2d 1400 (3d Cir. 1974), *cert. denied*, 419 U.S. 1113 (1975).

McCormick on Evidence discusses the foundation for telephone voice identification, which requires preliminary testimony to establish the identity of the other person. JOHN W. STRONG ET AL., McCORMICK ON EVIDENCE § 226 (4th ed. 1992). McCormick also discusses the nature of the authentication requirements for identification of a voice. Authentication can arise from the witness's familiarity with and recognition of the voice. It can also arise from the circumstances. These circumstances can include: a situation where the call was a return call in response to a message left for the caller; or a conversation during which the caller displayed knowledge of facts that only the caller would have or the caller demonstrated a familiarity with facts that the person in question would likely know. The requisite familiarity may be acquired either before or after hearing the voice to be identified, and it may be acquired for the purpose of litigation. *See* MICHAEL H. GRAHAM, FEDERAL PRACTICE AND PROCEDURE: FEDERAL RULES OF EVIDENCE § 6826 (Interim Edition); 6 LYNN MCCLAIN, MARYLAND EVIDENCE § 901.17 (1987).

Sound recordings are also admissible in evidence. Proper foundation requires the following testimony: that the recording device was capable of taking the conversation offered in evidence; that the operator of the device was competent to operate the device; that the recording is authentic and correct; that changes, additions or deletions have not been made in the recording; that the recording has been preserved in a manner that is shown to the court; an identification of the speakers; and that the conversation elicited was made voluntarily and in good faith, without any kind of inducement. *See* United States v. McKeever, 169 F. Supp. 426, 430 (S.D.N.Y. 1958), *rev'd on other grounds*, 271 F.2d 669 (2d Cir. 1959). *See also* United States v. Green, 175 F.3d 822, 830 (10th Cir. 1999), *reprinted in full*, United States v. Browne, 2000 U.S. App. LEXIS 6773 (10th Cir. Apr. 13, 2000); United States v. Rengifo, 789 F.2d 975 (1st Cir. 1986); United States v. Rochan, 563 F.2d 1246 (5th Cir. 1977); 5 JACK B. WEINSTEIN ET AL., WEINSTEIN'S EVIDENCE §§ 901-89 to 901-90 (1995).

F. INTOXICATION—LAY WITNESS

Sam Sailor, employed aboard the vessel *Vagabond*, fell off the boat's ladder while attempting to climb it and broke his arm. He sued Olaf Yachter, the owner of the boat, for his injuries, claiming that the ladder was negligently maintained and that boat was unseaworthy. Yachter defended on the ground that Sailor's injuries were due solely to Sailor's own intoxication. John Jones happened upon Sam Sailor shortly after his fall.

Defendant's Attorney:

Q. Where were you, Mr. Jones?

A. I was patrolling the dock at the Wilson Marina. It was part of my job as a night watchman there.

Q. What, if anything, unusual happened that evening?

A. Well, I saw this fellow, who I later learned was Sam Sailor, staggering down the dock toward the *Vagabond*.

Q. Did he make it to the *Vagabond*?

A. He did. I watched him the whole way down the dock.

Q. Then what happened?

A. I watched him climb aboard the *Vagabond*. The next thing I heard was a big thud and then some frightful yelling and cursing.

Q. What did you do?

A. I ran to the *Vagabond* and found Sam Sailor stumbling around on the deck of the boat, holding his arm and cursing.

Q. How close did you get to him?

A. A foot or two. I wanted to see if he was okay.

Q. What kind of lighting was in the area?

A. There were plenty of lights. I could see well.

Q. What did you observe?

A. He smelled of alcohol. There was a look in his eye—on his face— the best way I can describe it is the relaxed muscles that an intoxicated person's face has and red, watery eyes.

Q. Do you have an opinion as to whether Sam Sailor was intoxicated?

A. Yes. In my opinion he was very intoxicated. He was dead drunk.

Comment

Lay opinions on intoxication are governed by Federal Rules of Evidence 701 and 704 and comparable state evidentiary rules. Such opinions generally are permitted, as long as the proponent of the evidence establishes that the witness had sufficient opportunity to observe the person in question. *See* Trousdale v. State, 500 So. 2d 1329 (Ala. Crim. App. 1986) (a police officer may "give his opinion as to sobriety vel non of the appellant"); Jolly v. State, 395 So. 2d 1135 (Ala. Crim. App. 1981) (lay opinion of intoxication is allowed to go to jury as evidence of intoxication); Loof v. Sanders, 686 P.2d 1205 (Alaska 1984) (lay witness can give opinion testimony on the issue of intoxication); Esquivel v. Nancarrow, 104 P.2d 399 (Ariz. 1969) ("the rule is well-settled, and nearly universal, that lay witnesses who have had a sufficient opportunity to observe a person may testify as to whether that person appears to be intoxicated . . ."); State v. Lummus, 190 P.2d 1190 (Ariz. 1997) (urges to apply caution in allowing testimony on the ultimate issue of intoxication; however, testimony on the degree of intoxication is admissible); State v. Russell, 575 S.W.2d 761 (Mo. App. 1978) (lay witnesses may give an opinion on the intoxication of another if preceded by evidence of conduct and appearance observed by them to support that opinion); State v. Locklear, 136 S.E.2d 813 (N.C. App. 2000) (lay witness may give opinion as of the intoxication or sobriety of another); State v. Wargo (Oct. 31, 1997), 1997 Ohio App. LEXIS 4846 (a police officer may provide lay testimony as to his or her opinion concerning a defendant's state of intoxication); Commonwealth v. Giehl, 32 Pa. D. & C.3d 282 (Pa. 1983) (opinion as to defendant's intoxication is admissible, as intoxication is a matter of common observation); People v. Williams, 751 P.2d 395 (Cal. 1988) (lay opinion as to drug-induced intoxication is admissible); State v. Lamme, 563 A.2d 1372 (Conn. App. 1989) (lay opinion on the issue of intoxication is admissible); State v. Bebb, 53 P.3d 1198 (Haw. App. 2001) ("lay point of view" of police officer as to intoxication is admissible); State v. Carlton, 785 P.2d 184 (Kan. App. 1989) (lay opinions on the issue of intoxication are admissible); State v. Turkowski (Jan. 15, 2002), 2002 Minn. App. LEXIS 62 ("A lay witness may give an opinion as to another person's state of intoxication based on an observation of that person's breath, walk, and speech."); State v. Slayton, 367 A.2d 575 (N.H. 1976) ("lay opinion testimony as to state of intoxication has always been admissible").

Opinions of the Expert 6

111

A. QUALIFYING THE EXPERT

Counsel for the plaintiff qualifies an expert to render an opinion in the following manner:

Plaintiff's Counsel:

Q. Doctor Sill, are you licensed to practice medicine in the State of Maryland?

A. Yes, I am.

Q. When were you so licensed, Doctor?

A. In 1972.

Q. And from what medical school did you graduate?

A. From St. Andrews University in Scotland.

Q. In what year?

A. In 1967.

Q. Doctor, when did you come to this country to practice medicine?

A. In 1968.

Q. What were the reasons that you came to this country?

A. I had an opportunity to do an internship at Johns Hopkins University here in Baltimore.

Q. Doctor, did you in fact complete that internship?

A. Yes, I did.

Q. For how long did that internship last, Doctor Sill?

A. Two years.

Q. What other post-graduate education did you undertake?

A. My post-graduate education spanned approximately four years. The first year I was an intern, which is the title given to recent graduates of medical school who remain in the hospital to continue their training. My internship lasted for two years. The third year I became a first-year resident, and in the fourth year I became the Chief Resident.

Q. In what field, if any, did you do your internship and residency?

A. General surgery.

Q. Doctor Sill, have you followed any particular specialty within your profession?

A. Yes. During the years following my internship and residency and thereafter, I have done almost exclusively traumatic surgery.

Q. What does that specialty involve?

A. Soft tissue surgery for injuries due to trauma, or violent bodily damage from any external cause.

Q. In addition to attending medical school and serving as an intern and resident, were there any other aspects of your training that further prepared you for your specialty?

A. I spent ten years doing emergency surgery and several years doing research in the field of trauma and shock.

Q. Doctor Sill, are you now in the private practice of medicine?

A. Yes, I am.

Q. For how long have you been in private practice?

A. For seven years.

Q. Approximately how many patients have you treated for traumatic injury?

A. Thousands.

Q. Did that treatment include surgery?

A. Yes.

Q. Are you affiliated with any hospitals?

A. Yes, I am affiliated with Fallston General Hospital, Johns Hopkins Hospital, and the Children's Hospital.

Q. Can you tell us what it means to be affiliated with a hospital as you are?

A. It means that I have the privilege of examining and treating patients at the hospital and performing necessary surgical operations.

Q. How does one become affiliated with a particular hospital?

A. He applies for the affiliation.

Q. What other hospitals have you been affiliated with in the course of your career in this country?

A. Only two other hospitals, Sinai Hospital and Greater Baltimore Medical Center.

Q. Doctor Sill, do you hold any teaching positions in your specialty?

A. I was an associate professor of surgery at Johns Hopkins Hospital for five years, from 1990 to 1995, and I am still an adjunct professor and on the surgical staff at that hospital.

Q. Have you had occasion to deliver lectures to professional groups or organizations concerning your specialty?

A. Yes.

Q. How often and to whom?

A. I have given about 100 lectures over the last four years, in almost every state, to medical students and doctors at seminars and medical association meetings.

Q. Of what professional organizations and honorary societies are you a member?

A. I am a member of several medical societies.

Q. Can you name just a few for us?

A. I am a member of the International Trauma Society, of which I was a cofounder, a member of the Medical and Chirurgical Faculty, which is the official name of the Maryland State Medical Society, the Surgical Research Society, and the Atlantic Society for Experimental Medicine, and others.

Q. Have you written any articles or books in your specialty?

A. I have written about 200 articles and I have completed a book on general traumatic surgery.

Q. Thank you, Doctor Sill. Mr. Jones, defendant's counsel, now has a right to ask you any questions he may have about your qualifications.

Does Mr. Jones have any questions about the doctor's qualifications as an expert in general traumatic surgery before I ask the doctor his opinion on this case?

Comment

The admissibility of expert testimony is governed in the federal courts by Federal Rule of Evidence 702. Such testimony is admitted when the expert testimony could assist the trier of fact in understanding the evidence or determining a fact in issue, and when the witness is properly qualified to give the testimony as an expert. Fed. R. Evid. 702; United States v. Barile, 2002 U.S. App. LEXIS 7149, at *25 (4th Cir. Apr. 18, 2002); United States v. Mathis, 264 F.3d 321, 340 (3d Cir. 2001), *cert. denied*, 122 S. Ct. 1211 (2002) (use of expert witness with respect to eyewitness identification); Hardyman v. Norfolk & W. Ry., 243 F.3d 255, 260 (6th Cir. 2001) (validity of expert's theory must be shown; discusses differential etiology); United States v. Langan, 263 F.3d 613, 621 (6th Cir. 2001) (use of expert witness with respect to eyewitness identification); Ralston v. Smith & Nephew Richards, Inc., 275 F.3d 965, 970 (10th Cir. 2001) (qualified expert witness not strictly confined to area of practice but may testify regarding related applications); United States v. Smithers, 212 F.3d 306, 314 (6th Cir. 2000) (use of expert witness with respect to eyewitness identification); United States v. Hall, 165 F.3d 1095, 1102 (7th Cir.), *cert. denied*, 527 U.S. 1029 (1999); Kopf v. Skyrm, 993 F.2d 374 (4th Cir. 1993); Sparks v. Gilley Trucking Co., 992 F.2d 50 (4th Cir. 1993); Hines v. Consol. Rail Corp., 926 F.2d 262 (3d Cir. 1991); United States v. Fowler, 932 F.2d 306 (4th Cir. 1991); Wheeler v. John Deere Co., 935 F.2d 1090 (10th Cir. 1991); Persinger v. Norfolk & Western Ry., 920 F.2d 1185, 1188 (4th Cir. 1990); Coleman v. Parkline Corp., 844 F.2d 863 (D.C. Cir. 1988); United States v. Christophe, 833 F.2d 1296 (9th Cir. 1987); United States v. Carson, 702 F.2d 351 (2d Cir.), *cert. denied*, 462 U.S. 1108 (1983); United States v. Burchfield, 719 F.2d 356 (11th Cir. 1983); Mannino v. Int'l Mfg. Co., 650 F.2d 846 (6th Cir. 1981); United States v. Webb, 625 F.2d 709 (5th Cir. 1980); United States v. Fosher, 590 F.2d 381 (1st Cir. 1979); United States v. Watson, 587 F.2d 365 (7th Cir. 1978), *cert. denied*, 439 U.S. 1132 (1979); Holmgren v. Massey-Ferguson, Inc., 516 F.2d 856 (8th Cir. 1975); Stewart v. Rowan Cos., 2002 U.S. Dist. LEXIS 4135, at *7 (E.D. La. Mar. 7, 2002) (qualified expert witness not strictly confined to area of practice but may testify regarding related applications); Sullivan v. Ford Motor Co., 2000 U.S. Dist. LEXIS 4114, at *13 (S.D.N.Y. Mar. 31, 2000); MICHAEL H. GRAHAM, HANDBOOK OF FEDERAL EVIDENCE § 702.1 (3d ed. 1991).

Although in this particular pattern the witness was qualified as an expert for purposes of eliciting an opinion, experts can also render explanations of technical principles relevant to the case, allowing the trier of fact to apply those principles. Hence, Federal Rule of Evidence 702 provides that the expert may testify in the form of an opinion or otherwise.

Many trial lawyers, particularly in non-jury cases, will introduce in evidence the expert's curriculum vitae instead of taking elaborate testimony establishing qualifications. Depending on the circumstances, counsel may employ this practice or may prefer to draw out the expert's qualifications. Consideration should also be given to how detailed voir dire should be after an expert's qualifications are presented. Sometimes it is more practical to stipulate to the expert's qualifications or simply not conduct a voir dire on his or her qualifications. *See* FEDERAL EVIDENCE PRACTICE GUIDE § 11.11[2][a] (Joseph M. McLaughlin ed., Matthew Bender 1990).

In the 1990s, a trilogy of decisions by the United States Supreme Court resulted in significant amendments to the Federal Rules of Evidence governing the admissibility of the opinions of experts. *See* Kumho Tire Co. v. Carmichael, 526 U.S. 137 (1999); Joiner v. General Electric Co., 522 U.S. 136 (1997); Daubert v. Merrell Dow Pharms., Inc., 509 U.S. 579 (1993).

Rule 702 now provides that proponents of expert opinion testimony must show: (1) the expert's testimony is based upon sufficient facts or data; (2) the testimony is the product of reliable principles and methods; and (3)"the witness has applied the principles and methods reliably to the facts of the case."

Until the United States Supreme Court decided *Daubert v. Merrell Dow Pharms., Inc.*, 509 U.S. 579 (1993), the federal courts followed the so-called *Frye* test in determining the admissibility of scientific evidence. The test established by *Frye v. United States*, 293 F. 1013 (D.C. Cir. 1923), provided that, before a scientific opinion could be received as evidence, the basis of the opinion had to be shown to be generally accepted as reliable within the expert's particular scientific field. However, in *Daubert*, the Supreme Court held that the *Frye* test was no longer valid, because the general acceptance test of *Frye* was incompatible with the liberal approach of the Federal Rules of Evidence in admitting opinion evidence of experts. In establishing the so-called *Daubert* test for the admissibility of scientific evidence, the Supreme Court listed the following factors to be considered for the presentation of an opinion relating to scientific evidence: first, whether the theory or technique has been tested; second, whether the theory or technique had been subject to peer review publication; third, the known or potential error rate, and whether standards and controls exist for the operation of the theory or technique; and fourth, whether the theory or technique is generally accepted in the scientific community. *See* Kumho Tire Co. v. Carmichael, 526 U.S. 137, 141 (1999) ("gatekeeping" obligation applies not only to "scientific" testimony but to all expert testimony); Downs v. Perstorp Components, Inc., 2002 U.S. App. LEXIS 382, *475 (6th Cir. Jan. 4, 2002) (chemical exposure); Dhillon v. Crown Controls Corp., 269 F.3d 865, 869 (7th Cir. 2001) (vehicle design; court notes 2000 amendment to Rule 702); Lauzon v. Senco Prods., 270 F.3d 687 (8th Cir. 2001) (sets out a collection of *Daubert* decisions in the Eighth Circuit); Oddi v. Ford Motor Company, 234 F.3d 136, 145-46 (3d Cir. 2000); Joiner v. General Elec. Co., 78 F.3d 524 (11th Cir. 1996), *cert. granted*, 520 U.S. 1114 (1997), *rev'd, remanded*, 522 U.S. 136 (1997), *on remand*, 134 F.3d 1457 (11th Cir. 1998); United States v. Dorsey, 45 F.3d 809 (4th Cir.), *cert. denied*, 515 U.S. 1168 (1995); United States v. Posado, 57 F.3d 428 (5th Cir. 1995); Gruca v. Alpha Therapeutic Corp., 51 F.3d 638 (7th Cir. 1995); United States v. Davis, 40 F.3d 1069 (10th Cir. 1994), *cert. denied*, 514 U.S. 1088 (1995); Iacobelli Constr., Inc. v. County of Monroe, 32 F.3d 19 (2d Cir. 1994); *In re* Paoli R.R. Yard P&B Litig., 35 F.3d 717 (3d

Cir. 1994), *cert. denied*, 115 S. Ct. 1253 (1995); United States v. Bonds, 12 F.3d 540 (6th Cir. 1993); United States v. Martinez, 3 F.3d 1191 (8th Cir. 1993), *cert. denied*, 114 S. Ct. 734 (1994); United States v. Amador-Galvan, 9 F.3d 1414 (9th Cir. 1993); Agri-Mark, Inc. v. Niro, Inc., 2002 U.S. Dist. LEXIS 1866, at 31-33 (D. Mass. Feb. 5, 2002); Maurizio v. Goldsmith, 2002 U.S. Dist. LEXIS 6032, at *9 (S.D.N.Y. Apr. 9, 2002); United States v. Salim, 189 F. Supp. 2d 93 (S.D.N.Y. 2002); Bourne v. E.I. DuPont de Nemours & Co., 189 F. Supp. 2d 482 (S.D. W. Va. 2002) (epidemiology); Cayuga Indian Nation of New York v. Pataki, 188 F. Supp. 2d 223, 247 (N.D.N.Y. 2002) (in Second Circuit, "rejection of expert testimony is the exception rather than the rule"); United States v. Gricco, 2002 U.S. Dist. LEXIS 7564, at 3-5 (E.D. Pa. Apr. 26, 2002) (handwriting analysis); United States v. Santiago, 156 F. Supp. 2d 145, 147-48 (D. P.R. 2001) (stating that these four factors are not exclusive); Am. Family Ins. Group v. JVC Ams. Corp., 2001 U.S. Dist. LEXIS 8001, at *6 (D. Minn. Apr. 30, 2001); Sanner v. Bd. of Trade, 2001 U.S. Dist. LEXIS 15458, at *7 (N.D. Ill. Sept. 28, 2001) (district court has wide discretion in determining the competency of a witness as an expert and the relevancy of the testimony with respect to a particular subject); Pride v. BIC Corp., 218 F.3d 566, 577-78 (6th Cir. 2000); Hollander v. Sandoz Pharms. Corp., 95 F. Supp. 2d 1230, 1233 (W.D. Okla. 2000). Although the United States Supreme Court's decision in *Kumho Tire Co. v. Carmichael*, 526 U.S. 137 (1999) broadened the applicability of *Daubert* to all expert testimony, even beyond that relating to scientific testimony, Rule 702 does not codify all of the criteria enunciated in *Daubert* for evaluating the admissibility of expert testimony. Nevertheless, the rule clearly denotes that all expert testimony must be the product of reliable principles based on sufficient facts. A question arises whether Rule 702 requires a proponent of expert testimony to elicit on direct examination testimony from the expert that specifically addresses the criteria promulgated in the rule. In most instances this approach will not be necessary. Usually the expert's testimony will encompass the criteria, if not specifically, at least sufficiently to satisfy the court that the criteria of the rule have been satisfied. For example, when during the examination of the expert at trial the proponent asks, "What is the basis of that opinion?," the answer will include a recitation of facts sufficient to justify an opinion. The testimony will also encompass explanations relating to the reliability of the methods used to form the opinion and to the applicability of the opinion to the facts of the case. If there is any doubt, then the proponent should pose specific questions to satisfy the rule, e.g., "What methods or principles did you use to form your opinion? Are these methods or principles accepted or recognized within the industry? Did you apply the methodology you adopted in a proper manner?" While arguably these questions go to the ultimate issue of admissibility, the answers they seek go to the heart of the criteria established by the rule to evaluate the admissibility of the testimony. In many instances, if doubt exists about the admissibility of the expert testimony, opposing counsel will most likely seek a so-called "*Daubert* hearing" prior to trial for purposes of obtaining a pretrial ruling to exclude the expert from giving testimony. Even if a *Daubert* hearing is not conducted, the court acting as "gatekeeper" to assess reliability can exclude the expert's testimony at trial. A cautious advocate will want to pay close attention to Rule 702 in conducting the direct examination of the expert.

In *Samuel v. Ford*, 96 F. Supp. 2d 491 (D. Md. 2000), Judge Paul Grimm, writing for the court, fashioned a *Daubert/Kumho Tire* "checklist," attached to the opinion as an appendix, that counsel should follow if seeking to challenge the admissibility of an expert's testimony at trial under *Daubert/Kumho Tire* standards. The checklist requires the following information: (1) the name of the expert whose opinion(s) is (are) challenged; (2) a brief summary of the opinion(s) challenged, including a reference to the source of the opinion (such as the FRCP 26(a) (2) (B) disclosure, deposition transcript, etc.); (3) a brief description of the methodology/reasoning used by the expert to reach the challenged opinion(s), including a reference to the source materials; (4) a brief explanation of the basis for the challenge to the reasoning/methodology used by the expert, including a reference to the source material for the challenge; (5) a discussion of the known or potential error rate associated with the methodology employed by the expert, if known; (6) a summary of the relevant peer review material, if available, with citation to the source; and (7) a discussion of whether the methods/principles used have been generally accepted within the relevant scientific or technical community, with citation to references. *Samuel*, 96 F. Supp. 2d at 504.

While all courts may not expect counsel to follow such a detailed checklist to present an evidentiary challenge to proffered expert testimony, it is a good reference tool, as it highlights the various components that must be considered in making a *Daubert/Kumho Tire* challenge. Further, it underscores that the facts related to the *Daubert/Kumho Tire* factors should be obtained during discovery. *See also* PAUL GRIMM, CHARLES FAX AND PAUL MARK SANDLER, DISCOVERY PROBLEMS AND SOLUTIONS (ABA Litigation Section).

The knowledge of the expert can be obtained from observation, experience, standard texts, or any other reliable source. The courts do have discretion in allowing expert testimony. *See* United States v. Jordan, 236 F.3d 953, 955 (8th Cir.), *cert. denied*, 122 S. Ct. 220 (2001) (trial court has broad discretion to admit or exclude expert testimony); Brown v. Wal-Mart Stores, Inc., 1999 U.S. App. LEXIS 32031, at *5-*6 (6th Cir. Nov. 24, 1999) (expert is permitted wide latitude to offer opinions, including those not based on firsthand knowledge or observation); United States v. Fosher, 590 F.2d 381 (1st Cir. 1979); Reno-West Coast Distrib. Co., Inc. v. Mead Corp., 613 F.2d 722 (9th Cir.), *cert. denied*, 444 U.S. 927 (1979); Soo Line R.R. Co. v. Fruehauf Corp., 547 F.2d 1365 (8th Cir. 1977). However, this discretion is not unbridled. In *Garrett v. Desa Indus., Inc.*, 705 F.2d 721 (4th Cir. 1983), the court reversed the trial court's ruling, which prohibited a mechanical engineer from opining on the unsafe design of a product. *Consider* Kopf v. Skyrm, 993 F.2d 374 (4th Cir. 1993). *See also* Allison v. McGhan Med. Corp., 184 F.3d 1300, 1306 (11th Cir. 1999); *In re* Japanese Elec. Prod. Antitrust Litig., 723 F.2d 238 (3d Cir. 1983), *rev'd on other grounds*, 475 U.S. 574 (1986) (reversing the trial court's refusal to admit expert testimony as error, where the trial court had substituted its own opinion as to what constitutes reasonable reliance for that of experts in the field); N.V. Maatschappij Voor Industriele Waarden v. A.O. Smith Corp., 590 F.2d 415 (2d Cir. 1978) (holding that the trial court had improperly concluded that a patent agent, because he lacked formal training and was not qualified to testify in a Canadian court, was not an expert qualified to testify on infringement).

Criminal cases pose unique issues when medical testimony is sought relating to the defendant's psychological condition. Since the defendant has a motivation to falsify, an expert is not permitted to base an opinion only on what the defendant has communicated. Rather, the expert must base the opinion, at least in part, on other admissible evidence. *See* Strickland v. Francis, 738 F.2d 1542 (11th Cir. 1984). *See also* Mims v. United States, 375 F.2d 135 (5th Cir. 1967).

B. DIRECT OBSERVATION—TREATING PHYSICIAN

Plaintiff, suing for personal injuries, wishes to elicit testimony from a surgeon as to the cause of the injuries.

Plaintiff's Counsel:

Q. Doctor, do you know the plaintiff in this case, Joan Smith?

A. Yes.

Q. Have you seen her professionally?

A. Yes.

Q. When?

A. On May 1, 1994.

Q. Where did you see her?

A. At the emergency room of University Hospital.

Q. What was the occasion?

A. She was admitted to the emergency room having been brought to the hospital in an ambulance.

Q. How long after her arrival did you first see her?

A. Almost immediately.

Q. What were the circumstances?

A. Joan Smith was met immediately upon her arrival at the hospital emergency room by a team of doctors from the Shock Trauma Unit, nurses and anesthesiologists of which I was in charge. These individuals, including myself, immediately performed specific tests and administered procedures according to a pre-set protocol.

Q. Can you tell us what that protocol involved with regard to Joan Smith?

A. Automatically she received intravenous fluid, a blood pressure monitor, pulse rate monitor, respiratory rate monitor, and various tubes placed into her throat and bladder.

Q. Doctor, at the time Joan Smith was admitted to the emergency room was a history taken by a responsible member of the hospital staff?

A. Yes.

Q. Who?

A. The nurse in charge.

Q. What do you mean by history?

A. The facts leading up to the injury, as well as the medical chronology of the patient.

Q. Who provided the history in this instance, if you know?

A. The child's mother.

Q. What was the pertinent history?

A. Joan Smith was a three-year-old child who had fallen from a fire escape.

Q. Doctor, did you personally examine Joan Smith in the emergency room after she was administered the tests to which you referred?

A. Yes.

Q. What did that examination consist of?

A. (Witness explains in detail.)

Q. Did you make a diagnosis?

A. Yes.

Q. What was that diagnosis?

A. The patient exhibited internal bleeding, multiple fractures of limbs, including the forefinger of the left hand, the lower limb of the right arm, and the lower left leg, a basilar skull fracture, and lacerations on the forehead.

Q. Doctor, did there come a time when you performed surgery on Joan Smith?

A. Yes. Approximately three hours after she was admitted to the hospital, I performed an operation to stop the internal bleeding.

Q. Why did you wait three hours before performing surgery?

A. Other tests had to be administered to the patient.

Q. Do you have an opinion, Doctor Sill, based upon reasonable medical certainty, as to what caused the injuries that you diagnosed?

A. Yes. It is my opinion that the injuries I described were caused by the child's fall from the fire escape.

Q. What was the basis of that opinion?

A. My examination of the patient in the Shock Trauma Unit and the history as reported in the medical records taken by the nurse in charge for purposes of my review as an aid for diagnosing the child's condition.

Q. Why did you reach that conclusion on that basis?

A. These were precisely the kind of injuries that such a fall would normally cause, and there was no other possible reason that could have produced these injuries.

Q. Are you satisfied that you had sufficient opportunity to observe Ms. Smith in the shock trauma unit and to review her history?

A. Yes, of course.

Comment

Expert witnesses may render opinions at trial using the following methods: firsthand knowledge, as in this case; hearsay, or a combination of firsthand knowledge and hearsay; facts related in the testimony of others; facts related to the expert in a hypothetical question (*see infra* 1.6.F-G (80, 82)); and even hearsay that the expert learned before trial, provided that the hearsay is of a type reasonably relied on by experts in the field (*see* section I, *infra* Fed. R. Evid. 703); *see* 1 JOHN W. STRONG ET AL., MCCORMICK ON EVIDENCE §§ 13-15 (4th ed. 1992); MICHAEL H. GRAHAM, FEDERAL PRACTICE & PROCEDURE: FEDERAL RULE OF EVIDENCE § 6651 (Interim Edition 1992 & Supp. 1996). *See* pp. 115-20, *supra,* for discussion of FRE 702 and the criteria for evaluation of the admissibility of expert testimony. Rule 702 codifies the United States Supreme Court decisions in *Daubert v. Merrell Dow Pharmaceuticals, Inc.,* 509 U.S. 579 (1993); *Joiner v. General Electric Co.,* 522 U.S.136 (1997); and *Kumho Tire Co. v. Carmichael,* 526 U.S. 137 (1999). The rule requires that expert testimony be based upon sufficient facts or data, that the testimony be derived from reliable principles and methods, and the principles and methods used be reliably applied to the facts of the case in which the expert will testify. Whether the proponent of expert testimony will ask the witness specific questions embracing the language of Rule 702 will be determined on a case-by-case basis. In this pattern counsel did pose a last question to the expert relating to whether he had a sufficient basis to form his opinion.

Federal Rule of Evidence 704 provides that the opinion of an expert that embraces the ultimate issue is not inadmissible merely on that basis. *See* United States v. Barile, 2002 U.S. App. LEXIS 7149, at *24 (4th Cir. Apr. 18, 2002); Crawford v. Bundick, 2002 U.S. App. LEXIS 5923, at *4 (8th Cir. Apr. 2, 2002); United States v. Caballero, 277 F.3d 1235, 1249 (10th Cir. 2002); Bonner v. ISP Techs, Inc., 259 F.3d 924, 929 (8th Cir. 2001) (neither Rule 702 nor *Daubert* requires that an expert's opinion resolve an ultimate issue of fact to a scientific absolute in order to be admissible); United States v. Glover, 265 F.3d 337, 345 (6th Cir. 2001), *cert. denied,* 122 S. Ct. 1103 (2002) ("expert was only drawing on common sense when he gave his opinion as to the ultimate issue, and the jury was informed that it could accept or reject the expert's test, as it could with any other witness"); NutraSweet Co. v. X-L Eng'g Co., 227 F.3d 776, 789 (7th Cir. 2000); United States v. McSwain, 197 F.3d 472, 483 (10th Cir. 1999), *cert. denied,* 529 U.S. 1138 (2000); *In re* Air Disaster at Lockerbie, Scot., 37 F.3d 804 (2d Cir. 1994), *cert. denied,* 513 U.S. 1126 (1995); United States v. Simpson, 7 F.3d 186 (10th Cir. 1993); United States v. Dunn, 846 F.2d 761 (D.C. Cir. 1988); Salas v. Wang, 846 F.2d 897 (3d Cir. 1988);

Adalman v. Baker, Watts & Co., 807 F.2d 359 (4th Cir. 1986); Torres v. County of Oakland, 758 F.2d 147 (6th Cir. 1985); Haney v. Mizell Mem'l Hosp., 744 F.2d 1467 (11th Cir. 1984); United States v. Fleishman, 684 F.2d 1329 (9th Cir.), *cert. denied*, 459 U.S. 1044 (1982); United States v. Fosher, 590 F.2d 381 (1st Cir. 1979); United States v. Scavo, 593 F.2d 837 (8th Cir. 1979); United States v. Masson, 582 F.2d 961 (5th Cir. 1978); Case & Co., Inc. v. Board of Trade, 523 F.2d 355 (7th Cir. 1975). *But see* Cottom v. Town of Seven Devils, 2002 U.S. App. LEXIS 3711, at *14 (4th Cir. Mar. 8, 2002) (expert simply assumed the truth of plaintiffs' allegations and concluded that police conduct was improper); C P Interests, Inc. v. Cal. Pools, Inc., 238 F.3d 690 (5th Cir. 2001) (neither Rule 702 nor Rule 704 permits experts to offer conclusions of law). Federal Rule of Evidence 704(b), on the issue of expert testimony with respect to the mental state of a defendant in a criminal case, differs from the practice in many state rules, which permit opinion testimony on the ultimate issue of criminal responsibility. Federal Rule of Evidence 704 does not. *See* United States v. Watson, 260 F.3d 301, 308 (3d Cir. 2001); United States v. Boyd, 55 F.3d 667 (D.C. Cir. 1995); United States v. Gastiaburo, 16 F.3d 582 (4th Cir.), *cert. denied*, 513 U.S. 829 (1994); United States v. Simmons, 923 F.2d 934 (2d Cir.), *cert. denied*, 500 U.S. 919 (1991); United States v. Kessi, 868 F.2d 1097 (9th Cir. 1989); United States v. Angiulo, 847 F.2d 956 (1st Cir.), *cert. denied*, 488 U.S. 928 (1988); United States v. Newman, 849 F.2d 156 (5th Cir. 1988); United States v. Cox, 826 F.2d 1518 (6th Cir. 1987), *cert. denied*, 484 U.S. 1028 (1988); United States v. Pohlot, 827 F.2d 889 (3d Cir. 1987), *cert. denied*, 484 U.S. 1011 (1988); United States v. Felak, 831 F.2d 794 (8th Cir. 1987); United States v. Esch, 832 F.2d 531 (10th Cir. 1987), *cert. denied*, 485 U.S. 991 (1988); United States v. Windfelder, 790 F.2d 576 (7th Cir. 1986); United States v. Alexander, 805 F.2d 1458 (11th Cir. 1986); *see also* 1 JOHN W. STRONG ET AL., MCCORMICK ON EVIDENCE § 12 (4th ed. 1992). *But see* United States v. Dixon, 185 F.3d 393, 401-02 (5th Cir. 1999); United States v. Alvarez, 837 F.2d 1024, 1030-31 (11th Cir.) (holding that an expert, while precluded under Federal Rule of Evidence 704(b) from expressing an opinion or inference as to the defendant's state of mind, can testify with respect to the defendant's mental state if the expert leaves the inference of the mental state to be drawn by the trier of fact), *cert. denied*, 486 U.S. 1026 (1988); *accord* United States v. Brown, 32 F.3d 236 (7th Cir. 1994).

In this pattern, the treating physician expressed his opinion concerning the cause of injuries based on his personal observations and firsthand knowledge. Fed. R. Evid. 703; *see* McGuire v. Davis, 437 F.2d 570 (5th Cir. 1971); *see also* Power v. Arlington Hosp. Ass'n, 42 F.3d 851 (4th Cir. 1994); Graham v. Wyeth Lab., Div. of Am. Home Prods. Corp., 906 F.2d 1399 (10th Cir.), *cert. denied*, 498 U.S. 981 (1990); Coleman v. De Minco, 730 F.2d 42 (1st Cir. 1984); United States v. McCoy, 539 F.2d 1050 (5th Cir. 1976), *cert. denied*, 431 U.S. 919 (1977); Sulesky v. United States, 545 F. Supp. 426 (S.D. W.Va. 1982). Federal Rule of Evidence 705 permits the expert to give his or her opinion without disclosure of the underlying data or basis of that opinion. Nevertheless, strategically, counsel frequently will prefer to elicit the underlying data or basis of an expert's opinion before asking the expert to express the opinion. In other instances, the furnishing of the basis of the opinion is deferred until after the expert renders the opinion.

In this pattern, the expert related his familiarity with the patient and the circumstances of his personal knowledge of her condition. Following the request by counsel for the expert to express his opinion, wrap-up questions were asked requesting the witness to specify not only the basis of his opinion, but also the reasons for his conclusion. Simply eliciting from the witness the basis of his opinion is not enough. Reasons are what persuade the trier of fact.

In this pattern, counsel asked the witness to express his opinion in terms of "certainty." However, all that is required is "probability." *See* United States v. Rahm, 993 F.2d 1405 (9th Cir. 1993); United States v. Baller, 519 F.2d 463 (4th Cir.), *cert. denied*, 423 U.S. 1019 (1975); *see also* DaSilva v. American Brands, Inc., 845 F.2d 356 (1st Cir. 1988); United States v. Fleishman, 684 F.2d 1329 (9th Cir.), *cert. denied*, 459 U.S. 1044 (1982). Counsel should appreciate that if an expert cannot express an opinion in terms of reasonable "medical certainty," the term "medical probability" should be used. However, if the expert can state an opinion in terms of reasonable "medical certainty," the question should be phrased in those terms, because the more strongly expressed the opinion, the more impact it is likely to have on the trier of fact. Federal cases, like state court cases, are unclear as to what degree of certainty is required from the expert in the expression of an opinion—particularly when the witness is a medical expert. *See, e.g.*, Mayhew v. Bell S.S. Co., 917 F.2d 961 (6th Cir. 1990) (expert testimony was excluded on the basis of speculation, because the doctor did not testify to any degree of certainty); Snodgrass v. Ford Motor Co., 2001 U.S. Dist. LEXIS 18555, at *14 (D. N.J. Sept. 4, 2001) (while absolute certainty is not required, expert opinion typically is excluded when testimony is speculative, using language such as "possibility"); Hollander

v. Sandoz Pharms. Corp., 95 F. Supp. 2d 1230, 1235 (W.D. Okla. 2000) (plaintiffs' expert's testimony insufficient when expert listed only "possible" ways drug could cause hypertension and study cited "presented only some suggestive evidence"). *But see* Omar v. Sea-Land Service Inc., 813 F.2d 986 (9th Cir. 1987) (allowing admission of physician's speculative testimony as to causation because jury was aware of the hypothetical nature of the testimony, and other medical evidence was offered). Nevertheless, opinions expressed in terms of "could" and "most probably" are admitted. Williams v. Wal-Mart Stores, Inc., 922 F.2d 1357 (8th Cir. 1990) (what could have caused back pain was proper subject for expert testimony); DaSilva v. American Brands, Inc., 845 F.2d 356 (1st Cir. 1988) (holding that medical expert's testimony as to causation, expressed in terms of "my belief" and "could have," was sufficient to reflect a reasonable degree of medical certainty); United States v. Longfellow, 406 F.2d 415 (4th Cir.), *cert. denied*, 394 U.S. 998 (1969); *see* City of Greenville v. W.R. Grace & Co., 827 F.2d 975, 980 n.2 (4th Cir. 1987). *But see* Renaud v. Martin Marietta Corp., 972 F.2d 304 (10th Cir. 1992); MICHAEL H. GRAHAM, HANDBOOK OF FEDERAL EVIDENCE § 702.1 (3d ed. 1991 & Supp. 1995). Professor Graham points out that courts may be more demanding in requiring a degree of certainty in the prediction of future consequences. MICHAEL H. GRAHAM, HANDBOOK OF FEDERAL EVIDENCE § 702.1 n.16 (Supp. 1995).

In the Fourth Circuit, for example, there is no distinction between events that may occur in the future and those that may have occurred in the past. Expert opinion must be expressed in terms of "probably," rather than "possibly," regardless of whether the expert is testifying to future events, *see* Standard Oil Co. v. Sewell, 37 F.2d 230 (4th Cir. 1930), or to past events, Sakaria v. Trans World Airlines, 8 F.3d 164 (4th Cir. 1993), *cert. denied*, 511 U.S. 1083, *reh'g denied*, 512 U.S. 1247 (1994); Rohrbough v. Wyeth Labs., Inc., 916 F.2d 970 (4th Cir. 1990); Crinkley v. Holiday Inns, Inc., 844 F.2d 156 (4th Cir. 1988); Fitzgerald v. Manning, 679 F.2d 341 (4th Cir. 1982); City of Richmond v. Atlantic Co., 273 F.2d 902 (4th Cir. 1960); Ralston Purina Co. v. Edmunds, 241 F.2d 164 (4th Cir.), *cert. denied*, 353 U.S. 974 (1957); Leakas v. Columbia Country Club, 831 F. Supp. 1231 (D. Md. 1993). *See also* Phillip E. Hassman, Annotation, *Admissibility of Expert Medical Testimony as to Future Consequences of Injury as Affected by Expression in Terms of Probability or Possibility*, 75 A.L.R. 3d 9 (1977 & Supp. 1995).

C. DIRECT OBSERVATION—NONTREATING PHYSICIAN

Plaintiff, suing for personal injuries, wishes to elicit testimony from a nontreating orthopedic surgeon as to the cause of the injuries.

Plaintiff's Counsel:

Q. Doctor, do you know the plaintiff in this case, Joan Smith?

A. Yes.

Q. Have you seen her professionally?

A. Yes.

Q. When?

A. On May 23, 1994.

Q. What were the circumstances of your seeing her?

A. At your request, she made an appointment to see me for an orthopedic examination.

Q. Did you in fact examine Miss Smith on May 23, 1994, Doctor?

A. Yes.

Q. Did you take a history before you examined her, Doctor?

A. Yes.

Q. What did that history consist of?

Defense Counsel: Objection; may we approach the bench?

[At bench conference.]

Defense Counsel: If the court please, this doctor is a nontreating physician who examined Miss Smith in order to qualify as an expert witness, and he cannot present the history and subjective symptoms of the plaintiff as distinguished from symptoms he uncovered as a result of his examination of the plaintiff.

The Court: Overruled. Rule 803(4) of the Federal Rules of Evidence has abolished the distinction between treating and nontreating physicians. The history and subjective symptoms as related to the nontreating doctor may be introduced as substantive evidence.

[bench conference concluded]

Plaintiff's Counsel:

Q. What did the history consist of, Doctor?

A. Miss Smith was involved in an automobile accident at the intersection of Calvert and Redwood Streets on May 3, 1992, when she was a passenger in the back seat of a car that was struck from behind. Since the accident she has experienced severe lower back pain, which she never experienced prior to the accident. She has difficulty walking, running, and participating in any sports activities. She feels more severe pain when she lifts objects, regardless of their weight, and her pain in her lower back frequently "shoots into her legs."

Q. What did your examination consist of, Doctor?

A. I did a gross orthopedic and neurological examination of the patient's body, upper and lower extremities.

Q. What does that mean?

A. I examined the musculoskeletal system, which includes the neck and back areas of the patient.

Q. As a result of the examination did you make a diagnosis?

A. Yes.

Q. What was that diagnosis?

A. (Witness responds with details of the diagnosis.)

Q. Do you have an opinion based upon reasonable medical certainty as to what caused the injuries that you diagnosed?

A. Yes.

Q. What is that opinion?

A. It is my opinion that the injuries that I described were caused by the automobile accident in which the plaintiff was involved on May 3, 1992.

Q. What is the basis of that opinion?

A. My examination of the patient, the history that she gave to me, as well as the subjective symptoms she reported to me.

Q. Why did you reach that conclusion on that basis?

A. These were precisely the kind of injuries that such an automobile accident would normally produce, when the patient was in a rear-end type collision in which she was sitting in the back seat of the automobile, and there is no other possible cause in this case to produce these injuries.

Comment

See pp. 115-20 *supra* for discussion of FRE 702 and the criteria for evaluation of the admissibility of expert testimony. Rule 702 codifies the United States Supreme Court decisions in *Daubert v. Merrell Dow Pharmaceuti-*

cals, Inc., 509 U.S. 579 (1993); *Joiner v. General Electric Co.,* 522 U.S.136 (1997); and *Kumho Tire Co. v. Carmichael*, 526 U.S. 137 (1999). The rule requires that expert testimony be based upon sufficient facts or data, that the testimony be derived from reliable principles and methods, and the principles and methods used be reliably applied to the facts of the case in which the expert will testify. Whether the proponent of expert testimony will ask the witness specific questions embracing the language of Rule 702 will be determined on a case-by-case basis.

Frequently, in cases requiring testimony of medical experts, a nontreating physician is engaged to examine a patient, not for the purpose of treatment, but in order to qualify as an expert witness. This nontreating physician is often asked to testify as to his or her medical conclusions and the information, including the history and subjective symptoms, received from the patient that provide the basis of the conclusions. Federal Rule of Evidence 803(4) provides that statements made for purposes of medical diagnosis are not excluded on the basis of the hearsay rule, and effectively abolishes the traditional view excluding from evidence the nontreating physician's testimony relating a patient's history and subjective symptoms as reported by the patient. *See* O'Gee v. Dobbs Houses, Inc., 570 F.2d 1084 (2d Cir. 1978) (nontreating physician may present history of patient as related to treating physician, if basis of opinion and history can be considered as substantive evidence); *see generally* McCollum v. McDaniel, 2002 U.S. App. LEXIS 4825, at *12 (4th Cir. Mar. 25, 2002); Swinton v. Potomac Corp., 270 F.3d 794, 808 (9th Cir. 2001), *cert. denied*, 2002 U.S. LEXIS 2870 (2002); United States v. Gabe, 237 F.3d 954, 957 (8th Cir. 2001); United States v. Edward J., 224 F.3d 1216, 1219 (10th Cir. 2000); United States v. Console, 13 F.3d 641 (3d Cir. 1993), *cert. denied sub nom.* Curcio v. United States, 511 U.S. 1076, *cert. denied sub nom.* Markoff v. United States, 513 U.S. 812 (1994); United States v. Farley, 992 F.2d 1122 (10th Cir. 1993); Navarro de Cosme v. Hospital Pavia, 922 F.2d 926 (1st Cir. 1991); Rock v. Huffco Gas & Oil Co., 922 F.2d 272 (5th Cir. 1991); Morgan v. Foretich, 846 F.2d 941 (4th Cir. 1988); Cook v. Hoppin, 783 F.2d 684 (7th Cir. 1986); United States v. Castaneda-Reyes, 703 F.2d 522 (11th Cir.), *cert. denied*, 464 U.S. 856 (1983); United States v. Iron Shell, 633 F.2d 77 (8th Cir. 1980), *cert. denied*, 450 U.S. 1001 (1981); United States v. Nick, 604 F.2d 1199 (9th Cir. 1979); Drayton v. Jiffee Chem. Corp., 591 F.2d 352 (6th Cir. 1978); United States v. Lechoco, 542 F.2d 84 (D.C. Cir. 1976); *see also* White v. Illinois, 502 U.S. 346 (1992).

D. EXPERT OPINION—BASED UPON INADMISSIBLE FACTS AND DATA

Plaintiff, a gasoline dealer, instituted an antitrust suit against defendant oil company, claiming damages resulting from the oil company's refusal to sell gasoline to plaintiff. Plaintiff calls an economist to express an opinion on the market value of the plaintiff's business. After qualifying the witness, counsel proceeds as follows:

Plaintiff's Counsel:

Q. Do you have an opinion as to the market value of plaintiff's gasoline station as of January 1, 1996?

A. Yes.

Q. What is that opinion?

A. $220,000.

Q. Can you tell us the basis of that opinion?

A. The history of the gasoline station from 1985 to 1996, consisting of information that was supplied to me by the proprietor; a survey of traffic flow on Baltimore Street by the Department of Transportation; and various service station problems that I was advised of when I interviewed representatives from the oil company.

Q. Can you tell us whether it is customary and reasonable for economists to rely on this type of information in formulating opinions on market values of gasoline stations?

A. Absolutely, it is the custom and practice in the field.

Q. What are the reasons upon which you base your conclusions?

A. (The witness gives his reasons.)

Comment

Federal Rule of Evidence 703 provides that the facts and data relied upon by the expert in reaching his or her opinion need not themselves be admissible in evidence, if the facts and data are of a type reasonably relied upon by experts in the particular field in forming opinions on the subject. *See* Burek v. Valley Camp Coal Co., 2001 U.S. App. LEXIS 13695, at *10 (4th Cir. June 18, 2001), *cert. denied*, 122 S. Ct. 927 (2002); United States v. Feliciano, 223 F.3d 102, 121 (2d Cir. 2000), *cert. denied*, 532 U.S. 943 (2001); Brennan v. Reinhart Institutional Foods, 211 F.3d 449, 450-51 (8th Cir. 2000); Tyger Constr. Co. v. Pensacola Constr. Co., 29 F.3d 137 (4th Cir. 1994), *cert. denied*, 1513 U.S. 1080 (1995); Engebretsen v. Fairchild

Aircraft Corp., 21 F.3d 721 (6th Cir. 1994); University of Rhode Island v. A.W. Chesterton Co., 2 F.3d 1200 (1st Cir. 1993); United States v. Locascio, 6 F.3d 924 (2d Cir. 1993), *cert. denied*, 511 U.S. 1070 (1994); South Cent. Petroleum, Inc. v. Long Bros. Oil Co., 974 F.2d 1015 (8th Cir. 1992); United States v. Elkins, 885 F.2d 775 (11th Cir. 1989), *cert. denied*, 494 U.S. 1005 (1990); United States v. Wright, 783 F.2d 1091 (D.C. Cir. 1986); United States v. Affleck, 776 F.2d 1451 (10th Cir. 1985); Paddack v. Dave Christensen, Inc., 745 F.2d 1254 (9th Cir. 1984); United States v. Lawson, 653 F.2d 299 (7th Cir. 1981), *cert. denied*, 454 U.S. 1150 (1982); United States v. Genser, 582 F.2d 292 (3d Cir. 1978), *cert. denied*, 444 U.S. 928 (1979); United States v. Williams, 447 F.2d 1285 (5th Cir. 1971), *cert. denied*, 405 U.S. 954, *reh'g denied*, 405 U.S. 1048 (1972); *In re* Lake States Commodities, Inc., 272 B.R. 233, 242-43 (Bankr. N.D. Ill. 2002); *see also* Dura Auto. Sys. of Ind., Inc. v. CTS Corp., 285 F.3d 609 (7th Cir. 2002) (expert witness is permitted to use assistants in formulating expert opinion, and usually the assistants need not testify). Thus, for example, expert testimony based on public opinion polls is admissible even though the poll itself may not be admissible. *See* Baumholser v. Amax Coal Co., 630 F.2d 550 (7th Cir. 1980).

Under the rules, counsel need not, as a matter of evidentiary requirement, prove the opinions and diagnoses of other doctors by calling them to the stand. *See In re* "Agent Orange" Prod. Liab. Litig., 611 F. Supp. 1223 (E.D.N.Y. 1985); *see also* United States v. Mann, 712 F.2d 941 (4th Cir. 1983). In this pattern, counsel need not prove the "traffic flow" on Baltimore Street to enable the expert to state that he relied upon that information as a basis for his or her opinion.

Query: Can the economist in this pattern or any expert actually relate or disclose the otherwise inadmissible data he reasonably relied upon and received from others to form an opinion? Under Federal Rule of Evidence 703, courts may not permit the expert to express or relate this information. The information can only be used as a basis for the opinion without specifically being presented to the jury. If, however, a request is presented to the court to allow such inadmissible data to be presented, such evidence at the discretion of the court may be admissible if the court determines that the probative value of the evidence substantially outweighs its prejudicial effect. *See* Brennan v. Reinhart Institutional Foods, 211 F.3d 449, 451 (8th Cir. 2000); Boone v. Moore, 980 F.2d 539 (8th Cir. 1992); United States v. Sims, 514 F.2d 147 (9th Cir.), *cert. denied*, 423 U.S. 845 (1975); however, Federal Rule of Evidence 705 provides that on cross-examination the expert may be required to disclose the underlying facts of an opinion. *See* O'Gee v. Dobbs Houses, Inc., 570 F.2d 1084 (2d Cir. 1978); *see also* University of Rhode Island, *supra*, 2 F.3d at 1217; *Wright, supra*, 783 F.2d at 1101.

The question asked of the economist in this pattern, "Can you tell us whether it is customary and reasonable for economists to rely on this type of information in formulating opinions on market values of filling stations?," is not a question required to establish a foundation for the opinion of the expert based upon the inadmissible data. In fact, it is a self-serving type question, because the standard of reasonableness that the court applies in determining whether to permit the expert to rely upon the otherwise inadmissible facts is a judicial one. *See* Fed. R. Evid. 104(a); Fed. R. Evid. 703 advisory committee's note. However, if the court wants guidance from the expert on what is reasonably relied upon by an expert in that particular field in forming opinions, the question may be of some benefit. *See also* MICHAEL H. GRAHAM, HANDBOOK OF FEDERAL EVIDENCE § 703.1 (3d ed. 1991). As Professor Graham points out, the advisory committee's note to Federal Rule of Evidence 703 stresses that reasonable reliance is a vital standard. Therefore, in accordance with the note, the opinion of an "accidentologist" as to the point of impact would not be admissible if that opinion were based on the statements of bystanders. *Id.* at 640.

A question arises as to whether reasonably reliable "facts or data" include opinions. The answer is in the affirmative. *See* James W. McElhaney, *Expert Witnesses and the Federal Rules of Evidence*, 28 MERCER L. REV. (1977), for an enlightening discussion of the Federal Rules as they pertain to experts. *See also* Fed. R. Evid. 703 advisory committee's note; American Universal Ins. Co. v. Falzone, 644 F.2d 65 (1st Cir. 1981); Nanda v. Ford Motor Co., 509 F.2d 213 (7th Cir. 1974); Ries v. CSX Transp., Inc., 2000 U.S. Dist. LEXIS 4763, at *6 (E.D. Pa. Mar. 29, 2000); MICHAEL H. GRAHAM, HANDBOOK OF FEDERAL EVIDENCE § 703.1 (3d ed. 1991).

In *Wilson v. Merrell Dow Pharms., Inc.*, 893 F.2d 1149 (10th Cir. 1990), the Tenth Circuit Court of Appeals clearly ruled that expert testimony may be based on inadmissible hearsay when such information is the type customarily relied upon by experts in the field. The court recognized that such information may be admissible to show the basis of the expert's opinion, but not as substantive evidence. Counsel should appreciate that such evidence could still be excluded on the basis of its prejudicial effect. *See* Emigh v. Consol. Rail Corp., 710 F. Supp. 608 (W.D. Pa. 1989) (holding that although Federal Rule of Evidence 703 allows an expert to base an opinion on otherwise inadmissible evidence, Federal Rule 403 precludes the use of Rule 703 as a device to put such evidence before the jury when the evidence would be more prejudicial than probative).

E. EXPERT OPINION WITHOUT DISCLOSURE OF DATA UNDERLYING OPINION

Don Smith institutes suit against Harry Stone. Smith claims Stone's deed from Smith's father should be set aside, because Smith's father lacked mental capacity to transfer the property. Plaintiff has retained a world-renowned psychiatrist as an expert witness. The witness will be asked to express an opinion on whether plaintiff's father possessed sufficient mental capacity to execute a valid deed. Plaintiff's counsel is unsure as to whether there exists a factual basis for the expert's opinion that would be deemed sufficient for the expert to render an opinion, because the expert never examined the grantor. Therefore, counsel does not examine the witness with regard to underlying facts or data in support of the opinion. Immediately after qualifying the expert and eliciting testimony that the expert discussed the grantor's condition with the plaintiff for the first time on the eve of trial, the following questions are asked.

Plaintiff's Counsel:

Q. Doctor, do you have an opinion based upon reasonable medical certainty as to whether Mr. Smith was of sound and disposing mind, capable of signing a deed, with an understanding of the nature of his act, its effect, and the natural objects of his bounty?

A. Yes.

Q. What is your opinion?

A. He was totally lacking in such mental capacity.

Q. What are your reasons for that opinion?

A. (Witness furnishes reasons.)

Q. Thank you, Doctor. That is all.

Comment

Federal Rule of Evidence 705 permits the expert to testify in terms of an opinion and give reasons, without first testifying to the underlying facts unless the court otherwise requires. *See* Guidroz-Brault v. Mo. Pac. R.R., 254 F.3d 825, 831-32 (9th Cir. 2001); United States v. Havvard, 260 F.3d 597, 601 (7th Cir. 2001); Ambrosini v. Labarraque, 966 F.2d 1464 (D.C.

Cir. 1992); Symbol Techs. Inc. v. Opticon, Inc., 935 F.2d 1569 (Fed. Cir. 1991); Monks v. General Elec. Co., 919 F.2d 1189 (6th Cir. 1990); Lewis v. Rego Co., 757 F.2d 66 (3d Cir. 1985); Bulthuis v. Rexall Corp., 789 F.2d 1315 (9th Cir. 1985); Evers v. General Motors Corp., 770 F.2d 984 (11th Cir. 1985); Deitchman v. E.R. Squibb & Sons, Inc., 740 F.2d 556 (7th Cir. 1984); Rock Island Improv. Co. v. Helmerich & Payne, Inc., 698 F.2d 1075 (10th Cir.), *cert. denied*, 461 U.S. 944 (1983); United Roasters, Inc. v. Colgate-Palmolive Co., 649 F.2d 985 (4th Cir.), *cert. denied*, 454 U.S. 1054 (1981); N.V. Maatschappij Voor Industriele Waarden v. A.O. Smith Corp., 590 F.2d 415 (2d Cir. 1978); United States v. Santarpio, 560 F.2d 448 (1st Cir.), *cert. denied*, 434 U.S. 984 (1977); Bryan v. John Bean Div. of FMC Corp., 566 F.2d 541 (5th Cir. 1978); Polk v. Ford Motor Co., 529 F.2d 259 (8th Cir.), *cert. denied*, 426 U.S. 907 (1976).

The rule in effect abolishes the requirement for the hypothetical question, because experts may render opinions pursuant to the rule without discussing the basis of the opinion. The expert may have no firsthand knowledge, but nevertheless be permitted to render an opinion without a hypothetical question. However, the rule can be a trap for the unwary litigator. Assume the expert renders an opinion pursuant to Federal Rule of Evidence 705 relying on otherwise inadmissible information received from third parties. Although the expert relies on this information, he does not disclose this on direct examination. On cross-examination, however, the basis of the opinion is elicited pursuant to the rules, and the court subsequently concludes that the expert's "reliance" was not reasonable. *See supra*, chapter 6.D discussing Fed. R. Evid. 703; *see also* James W. McElhaney, *Expert Witnesses and the Federal Rules of Evidence*, 28 Mercer L. Rev. 463 (1977). *Consider* Smith v. Ford Motor Co., 626 F.2d 784 (10th Cir. 1980), *cert. denied*, 450 U.S. 918 (1981), where the court commented that Federal Rule of Evidence 705 places upon opposing counsel the burden of exploring, through cross-examination, the facts and assumptions that serve as the basis of an expert's opinion. *Accord* Bryan v. John Bean Div. of FMC Corp., 566 F.2d 541 (5th Cir. 1978); *see also* Polk v. Ford Motor Co., 529 F.2d 259 (8th Cir.), *cert. denied*, 426 U.S. 907 (1976). *Consider* Studiengesellschaft Kohle v. Dart Inds., Inc., 862 F.2d 1564 (Fed. Cir. 1988) (holding that Federal Rule of Evidence 705 does not require a court or trier of fact to automatically credit an expert's testimony which is not cross-examined). Hence, careful pretrial discovery is important so that counsel can prepare for cross-examination of the expert witness at trial.

This pattern was cited with approval in Lᴙɴɴ McLᴀɪɴ, Mᴀʀʏʟᴀɴᴅ Eᴠɪ-
ᴅᴇɴᴄᴇ: Sᴛᴀᴛᴇ ᴀɴᴅ Fᴇᴅᴇʀᴀʟ § 705.2 n.2 (1987 & Supp. 1995).

F. THE LONG FORM—HYPOTHETICAL

Don Smith institutes suit against Henry Stone. Smith claims a deed to
Stone, signed by Smith's father on June 6, 1995, should be set aside, because Smith's father lacked mental capacity to transfer the property. Plaintiff
has retained as an expert witness a psychiatrist who did not examine Smith's
father or hear any of the evidence. After qualifying the expert, the following examination occurs:

Plaintiff's Counsel:

Q. Doctor, I will ask you what is known as a hypothetical question.
This question will request that you give an opinion based on facts
as submitted in this case. Please follow closely the statement of
facts that I present to you, assume them to be true, and then I will
ask you to express an opinion upon those facts. Are you ready, sir?

A. Yes, sir.

Q. Assume a man 89 years of age cannot stand up straight and needs
a cane. He suffered a stroke at the age of 87, and since that time he
constantly babbles and talks to himself. He professes frequently
that he is Abraham Lincoln reincarnated.

Now, Doctor, assuming all these facts and conditions as being
true, do you have an opinion based on reasonable medical certainty as to whether this man, on June 6, 1995, was of sound and
disposing mind, capable of signing a deed with an understanding
of the nature of his act, its effect, and the natural objects of his
bounty?

A. Yes, I do.

Q. What is your opinion, Doctor?

A. My opinion is that the gentleman did not have a sound and disposing mind, and was incapable of signing a deed with an understanding of the nature of his act, its effect, and the natural objects
of his bounty.

Q. What is the basis of that opinion?

A. The details suggested about the patient's state of mind, that is, his
constant babbling, his belief that he is Abraham Lincoln reincarnated, the fact that he had a stroke several years before, and his age.

Q. Why did you reach that conclusion on that basis?

A. The facts related by you indicate that the man has lost touch with reality and is incapable of the rational thinking necessary for one to understand the nature and extent of his property and the consequences of his transferring the property.

Comment

Experts are permitted to express opinions based not only on direct observation, but also on hypothetical questions. *See* United States v. Mancillas, 183 F.3d 682 (7th Cir. 1999), *cert. denied*, 529 U.S. 1005 (2000); United States v. Harley, 990 F.2d 1340 (D.C. Cir. 1993), *cert. denied*, 510 U.S. 885 (1993); Toucet v. Maritime Overseas Corp., 991 F.2d 5 (1st Cir. 1993); Williams v. Jader Fuel Co., Inc., 944 F.2d 1388 (7th Cir. 1991), *cert. denied*, 504 U.S. 957 (1992); Samples v. City of Atlanta, 916 F.2d 1548 (11th Cir. 1990); Taylor v. Burlington N. R.R., 787 F.2d 1309 (9th Cir. 1986); Ramsey v. Culpepper, 738 F.2d 1092 (10th Cir. 1984); United States v. Mann, 712 F.2d 941 (4th Cir. 1983); Teen-Ed, Inc. v. Kimball Int'l, Inc., 620 F.2d 399 (3d Cir. 1980); United States v. Kreimer, 609 F.2d 126 (5th Cir. 1980); Iconco v. Jensen Constr. Co., 622 F.2d 1291 (8th Cir. 1980); Cunningham v. Gans, 507 F.2d 496 (2d Cir. 1974); Garza v. Indiana & Michigan Elec. Co., 338 F.2d 623 (6th Cir. 1964); Holland v. Horn, 150 F. Supp. 2d 706, 745 (E.D. Pa. 2001); *see also* Barefoot v. Estelle, 463 U.S. 880, *reh'g denied*, 464 U.S. 874 (1983); *but see* Duluth Lighthouse for the Blind v. C.G. Bretting Mfg. Co., 199 F.R.D. 320, 324 (D. Minn. 2000) (if a person is a lay witness and not an expert witness, he cannot respond to hypothetical questions, even if he relies on specialized knowledge to form his opinions). Under Federal Rule of Evidence 705, counsel is no longer required to use hypothetical questions to obtain an opinion from an expert who does not have firsthand knowledge of facts upon which the expert bases an opinion. One of the primary reasons for the adoption of these rules was to free counsel from the burden of asking complex and lengthy hypothetical questions. *See* 1 JOHN W. STRONG ET AL., McCORMICK ON EVIDENCE § 16 (4th ed. 1992). Nevertheless, these questions can be very effective and are admissible in the court's discretion. *See* Newman v. Hy-Way Heat Sys., Inc., 789 F.2d 269 (4th Cir. 1986); *Taylor, supra*, 787 F.2d 1309; United States v. Kreimer, 609 F.2d 126 (5th Cir. 1980).

One technique for avoiding objections during trial to a complex hypothetical is to review the hypothetical with opposing counsel prior to presenting it in trial. For this reason, and also so that counsel's presentation in court can be smooth and complete, it is helpful to write out the hypothetical question prior to trial. Either of two forms of hypothetical questions can be utilized: the long form, as illustrated by this pattern, and the short form, as illustrated in chapter 6.G *infra*.

The long form of hypothetical question requires counsel to state for the witness such facts as are essential to the foundation of an opinion, and ask the witness to assume the truth of the facts so stated, and then to render an opinion based upon them. The question must contain a fair summary of the material facts in evidence that are essential to the formulation of a rational opinion concerning the subject matter. *See* Iconco v. Jensen Constr. Co., 622 F.2d 1291 (8th Cir. 1980); *see also* Theriot v. Bay Drilling Co., 783 F.2d 527, 537 n.8 (5th Cir. 1986) (noting that a hypothetical question must utilize a fair, undistorted collection of facts); Logsdon v. Baker, 517 F.2d 174 (D.C. Cir. 1975). However, the long-form hypothetical question need not contain all the facts in evidence, if it contains a fair summary of the facts. *See* Iconco v. Jensen Constr. Co., 622 F.2d 1291 (8th Cir. 1980); Twin City Plaza, Inc. v. Central Sur. & Ins. Corp., 409 F.2d 1195 (8th Cir. 1969); United States v. Aspinwall, 96 F.2d 867 (9th Cir. 1938); Napier v. Greenzweig, 256 F. 196 (2d Cir. 1919). If the question is framed inadequately, the court can require counsel to include additional facts. Minneapolis, St. Paul & Sault Ste. Marie R.R. v. Metal-Matic, Inc., 323 F.2d 903 (8th Cir. 1963).

On occasion it becomes necessary to ask a hypothetical question based on facts assumed to be true but not in evidence when the question is asked. This procedure can be adopted, when necessary, if counsel sufficiently satisfies the court by a proffer and assurances of definite intent to "connect up." *See* 1 John W. Strong et al., McCormick on Evidence § 14 (4th ed. 1992). This concept of "connecting up" is particularly important when the facts not in evidence are not within the reasonable reliance provision of Federal Rule of Evidence 703. *See* Vermont Food Indus., Inc. v. Ralston Purina Co., 514 F.2d 456 (2d Cir. 1975); Michael H. Graham, Handbook of Federal Evidence § 705.2 (3d ed. 1991). It may be argued that connecting up is not necessary, since federal rules do not require the expert to state the factual basis for his or her opinion on direct examination. However, it is suggested that if counsel resorts to the hypothetical question as a technique to prove the case, then the traditional rules applying to the hypothetical question should govern. *See generally* 1 John W. Strong et al., McCormick on Evidence § 14, at 61 (4th ed. 1994); Federal Rule of Evidence 705 allows the court, at its discretion, to require the expert to testify to the factual basis on direct examination. MICHAEL H. GRAHAM, HANDBOOK OF FEDERAL EVIDENCE § 705.2 (3d ed. 1991); *see* Fed. R. Evid. 705 advisory committee's note.

Concerning the use of the phrase "reasonable medical certainty" as opposed to "reasonable probability," *see supra* chapter 6.B.

This pattern has been cited with approval in the following texts: MICHAEL H. GRAHAM, EVIDENCE: TEXT, RULES, ILLUSTRATIONS & PROBLEMS 272 (2d ed. 1988); LYNN MCLAIN, MARYLAND EVIDENCE: STATE AND FEDERAL § 705.1 n.10 (1987 & Supp. 1995).

G. THE SHORT FORM—HYPOTHETICAL

Mr. Silver, son of the late Wilson Bonds, instituted suit against his cousin to set aside a deed transferring Bonds's Eastern Shore Estate, on the grounds that Bonds was incompetent to execute a deed at the time the land was conveyed.

Plaintiff's attorney called a psychiatrist as an expert witness. The psychiatrist attended the trial and listened to portions of the testimony. After he was qualified as an expert, counsel presented the psychiatrist with a hypothetical question in the following manner:

Q. Doctor, have you heard certain testimony in this case?

A. Yes, sir.

Q. Assuming the truth of all that testimony and excluding from that testimony any inferences, expressions of opinion, and conclusions of others, do you have any opinion based upon reasonable medical certainty whether or not Mr. Bonds was of sound and disposing mind, capable of signing a deed, with an understanding of the nature of his act, its effect, and the natural objects of his bounty?

A. Yes, sir.

Q. What is that opinion, Doctor?

A. My opinion is that the gentleman did not have a sound and disposing mind, and was incapable of signing a deed with an understanding of the significance of his act, its effect, and the natural objects of his bounty.

Q. What is the basis of that opinion?

A. The details suggested about the patient's state of mind, that is, his constant babbling, his belief that he is Abraham Lincoln reincarnated, the fact that he had a stroke several years before, and his age.

Q. Why did you reach that conclusion on that basis?

A. The testimony of Messrs. James and Collins, which I heard, indicate that the man has lost touch with reality and is incapable of the rational thinking necessary for one to understand the nature and extent of his property and the consequences of transferring the property.

Comment

The hypothetical question may be asked in either of two ways: the long-form method, *see supra* chapter 6.F, and the short-form method, reflected in this pattern, sometimes referred to as the "bare bones" method. A few jurisdictions are hesitant to allow the short-form method, and several others provide the trial court with a great degree of discretion to restrict and limit the practice. *See* 32 C.J.S. *Evidence* § 554 (1964 & Supp. 1996). The short-form method requires that the expert predicate his opinion upon uncontradicted evidence heard or read and assumed to be true. *See id.*; 1 JOHN W. STRONG ET AL., MCCORMICK ON EVIDENCE § 14 (4th ed. 1992); *see also* Bosse v. Ideco Div. of Dresser Indus., Inc., 412 F.2d 567 (10th Cir. 1969); Frankel v. Lull Eng'g Co., Inc., 334 F. Supp. 913 (E.D. Pa. 1971), *affirmed*, 470 F.2d 995 (3d Cir. 1973) (allowing an expert witness to answer a short-form hypothetical question that assumed as factual the testimony of a previous witness, after the court had determined that the question was intelligible to the jury). Counsel should take care to request the expert to exclude from consideration any inferences, expressions of opinion, or conclusions of others, unless reliance upon the aforesaid information is customary in the expert's particular specialty. Fed. R. Evid. 703; *infra* 1.6.I. (85); *see also* Concerned Area Residents for the Env't v. Southview Farm, 834 F. Supp. 1422 (W.D.N.Y. 1993), *rev'd on other grounds*, 34 F.3d 114 (2d Cir. 1994), *cert. denied*, 514 U.S. 1082 (1995).

The witness need not have heard all the evidence before giving an opinion in response to the short form; the witness must, however, have heard the evidence on which an opinion is sought. *See* 1 JOHN W. STRONG ET AL., MCCORMICK ON EVIDENCE § 14 (4th ed. 1992). Concerning the use of the phrase "reasonable medical certainty," *see supra* chapter 6.B.

H. EXPERT WITNESS—HANDWRITING COMPARISON

In a criminal matter, the Government's case hinges upon the fact that the defendant, Kirby Hempel, endorsed a check in the name of John Pelhem, which Hempel allegedly received for distributing contraband. The Government desires to prove through expert testimony the genuineness of the defendant's signature on the check. He proceeds as follows:

Government:

Q. Agent Hubbel, at the time the defendant was arrested, did you advise him of his rights?

A. Yes, I did.

Q. What, if anything, resulted after you advised the defendant of his rights?

A. He waived those rights.

Q. Did he sign a written waiver?

A. Yes.

Government: I wish to have this document marked as the State's Exhibit No. 1 for identification.

Q. Now, Agent, do you recognize this document?

A. Yes, this is the waiver of rights form that the defendant signed.

Q. Do you recognize the signature on the right-hand side of this card at the bottom?

A. Yes, it is the defendant's signature.

Q. How do you know it is the defendant's signature?

A. I was present when he signed the statement and saw him do it.

Government: We offer this waiver as Government's Exhibit No. 1.

* * *

We now call to the witness stand Johnson Heightford Teton.

(The witness is thereupon qualified as a handwriting expert. *See supra* 1.6.A. (66).

Government: We would like to have this check, which purports to bear the signature of the defendant as an endorsement, marked as Government's Exhibit No. 2 for identification.

Q. Mr. Teton, I show you State's Exhibit No. 1, which is a statement signed by the defendant in this case, and I also show you

Government's Exhibit No. 2 for identification, which is a check which purports to bear the signature of John Pelhem endorsed upon it, and I ask you if you have seen these documents before?

A. Yes, I have.

Q. What were the circumstances of your seeing these documents before today?

A. You requested that I examine these documents to determine if I could express an opinion on whether the check, Exhibit No. 2 for identification, was signed by the same person who signed Exhibit No. 1.

Q. What did your examination consist of?

A. I examined them microscopically as to line quality and slant and letter forms.

* * *

(Counsel requests that the expert explain each procedure and requests the expert to make use of enlarged photographs to illustrate his point.)

* * *

Q. Now, Mr. Teton, do you have an opinion based on reasonable certainty as to whether the same person who signed "Kirby Hempel" to Government's Exhibit No. 1 also signed "John Pelhem" to State's Exhibit No. 2 for identification?

A. Yes, I do.

Q. What is that opinion?

A. It is my opinion that the person who signed Exhibit No. 2 was the same person who signed Exhibit No. 1.

Q. What, sir, is the basis of that opinion?

A. My examination of the documents and comparisons that I made.

Q. What are the reasons upon which you base your conclusion?

A. (The witness explains his reasons in detail.)

Comment

Genuineness of a disputed signature may be established by the use of any writing proved to be genuine, and comparison of the writing on the genuine document with the signature on the contested document. *See, e.g.,* United States v. Henry, 164 F.3d 1304, 1309 (10th Cir.), *cert. denied,* 527 U.S. 1029 (1999); NLRB v. General Wood Preserving Co., 905 F.2d 803 (4th Cir.), *cert. denied,* 498 U.S. 1016 (1990); Ona Corp. v. NLRB, 729

F.2d 713 (11th Cir. 1984); United States v. Clifford, 704 F.2d 86 (3d Cir. 1983); United States v. Mauchlin, 670 F.2d 746 (7th Cir. 1982); United States v. Brink, 648 F.2d 1140 (8th Cir.), *cert. denied*, 454 U.S. 1031 (1981); United States v. Mangan, 575 F.2d 32 (2d Cir.), *cert. denied*, 439 U.S. 931 (1978); United States v. Turquitt, 557 F.2d 464 (5th Cir. 1977); Scharfenberger v. Wingo, 542 F.2d 328 (6th Cir. 1976); United States v. Greiser, 502 F.2d 1295 (9th Cir. 1974); United States v. Wagner, 475 F.2d 121 (10th Cir. 1973); Easterday v. United States, 292 F. 664 (D.C. Cir.), *cert. denied*, 263 U.S. 719 (1923); Overnight Transp. Co., 334 N.L.R.B. 134 (2001); Cogburn Healthcare Ctr., 335 N.L.R.B. 105 (2001).

In this pattern the prosecutor introduced a document with the genuine signature of the defendant and then requested the expert to compare the authenticated genuine specimen with the signature on the contested document. The initial document that bears the genuine signature of the party need not be a document relevant to the case, but it may be any document that is a genuine example of the writing of the person alleged to have written the contested document. Fed. R. Evid. 901(3). *See* United States v. Mauchlin, 670 F.2d 746 (7th Cir. 1982); Reece v. Reece, 212 A.2d 468 (Md. 1965); DiPietro v. State, 356 A.2d 599 (Md. App. 1976); Green v. State, 329 A.2d 731 (Md. App. 1974), *cert. denied*, 274 Md. 728 (1975). *See also* United States v. Wagner, 475 F.2d 121 (10th Cir. 1973).

I. EXAMINATION OF PSYCHIATRIST TO ESTABLISH INSANITY DEFENSE

Tom Jones is arrested for the murder of Mr. Apple. The homicide occurred on March 3, 1995. A plea of "not guilty by reason of insanity" is entered. At trial, testimony is sought from a psychiatrist as to the defendant's responsibility under the Insanity Defense Reform Act, 18 U.S.C. § 17 (1973, Supp. 1996). Defense counsel, after qualifying a psychiatrist as an expert, proceeds as follows:

Defense Counsel:

Q. Doctor, have you seen Tom Jones in your professional capacity?

A. Yes.

Q. Under what circumstances?

A. At your request I interviewed Mr. Jones and administered various psychological tests.

Q. On how many occasions did you consult with Mr. Jones?

A. Four separate occasions.

Q. On what dates did those consultations occur?

A. During various days in June and July of 1995.

Q. How many hours of consultation did you spend with Mr. Jones?

A. Twelve hours.

Q. What was the purpose of your examination?

A. I conducted psychiatric examinations of Mr. Jones to determine whether I could form an opinion as to his responsibility under the Insanity Defense Reform Act, 18 U.S.C. § 17 (1973, Supp. 1996) for certain criminal conduct occurring on March 3, 1995.

Q. As a result of your consultation with Mr. Jones, were you able to form an opinion as to whether Mr. Jones, on March 3, 1996, had a mental disease or defect?

A. Yes.

Q. What is that opinion?

A. On March 3, 1995, Mr. Jones was suffering from a mental defect.

Q. Is the mental defect from which the defendant was suffering on March 3, 1995, the result of any psychiatric or neurological disorder?

A. Yes.

Q. What is the nature of the mental defect from which the defendant was suffering on March 3, 1996?

A. The defendant was suffering from a psychotic depressive reaction.

Q. Do you have an opinion whether this mental defect caused the defendant to lack substantial capacity either to appreciate the criminality of his conduct or to conform his conduct to the requirements of the law?

A. Yes.

Q. What is that opinion?

A. It is my opinion that the defendant, as a result of the described mental defect, did not lack substantial capacity to appreciate the criminality of his conduct, but did lack substantial capacity to conform his conduct to the requirements of the law.

Q. What is the basis of your opinion?

A. My examination of the defendant, review of psychological test results, and his personal history.

Q. What are the reasons upon which you base your conclusion?

A. [The psychiatrist or psychologist should then relate all the reasons supporting his or her opinion.]

Comment

The American Law Institute (ALI) test expressed in the Insanity Defense Reform Act, 18 U.S.C. § 17 (1973 & Supp. 1996), is followed by federal courts in determining insanity. *See* United States v. Chandler, 393 F.2d 920 (4th Cir. 1968), and United States v. Gillis, 773 F.2d 549 (4th Cir. 1985). All of the federal circuit courts have utilized some variation of the ALI test. *See generally* United States v. Kimes, 246 F.3d 800, 806 (6th Cir. 2001), *cert. denied*, 122 S. Ct. 823 (2002); United States v. Vachon, 869 F.2d 653 (1st Cir. 1989); United States v. Pohlot, 827 F.2d 889 (3d Cir. 1987), *cert. denied*, 484 U.S. 1011 (1988); United States v. Cox, 826 F.2d 1518 (6th Cir. 1987), *cert. denied*, 484 U.S. 1028 (1988); United States v. Freeman, 804 F.2d 1574 (11th Cir. 1986); Wade v. United States, 426 F.2d 64 (9th Cir. 1970), *appeal after remand*, U.S. v. Wade, 489 F.2d 258 (9th Cir. 1973); United States v. Brawner, 471 F.2d 969 (D.C. Cir. 1972), *superseded by statute*, Shannon v. United States, 512 U.S. 573 (1994); Blake v. United States, 407 F.2d 908 (5th Cir. 1969) (en banc), modified *sub nom.* United States v. Lyons, 731 F.2d 243 (5th Cir.) (en banc), *cert. denied*, 469 U.S. 930 (1984); United States v. Shapiro, 383 F.2d 680 (7th Cir. 1967); Pope v. United States, 372 F.2d 710 (8th Cir. 1967), *vacated on other grounds*, 392 U.S. 651 (1968); United States v. Freeman, 357 F.2d 606 (2d Cir. 1966); Wion v. United States, 325 F.2d 420 (10th Cir. 1963), *cert. denied*, 377 U.S. 946 (1964); United States v. Agnello, 158 F. Supp. 2d 285, 286-87 (E.D.N.Y. 2001); United States v. Pendergraft, 120 F. Supp. 2d 1339 (M.D. Fla. 2000); United States v. Baxt, 74 F. Supp. 2d 436, 440 (D.N.J. 1999), *subsequent appeal*, 265 F.3d 1057 (3d Cir. 2001).

In federal court, the expert cannot be asked ". . . '[w]as the accused able to appreciate the nature and quality of his act or [w]as the accused able to appreciate the wrongfulness of his acts'?" However, the expert can be asked: "'Was the accused suffering from a mental disease or defect' or 'explain the characteristics of the mental disease and defect.'" MICHAEL H. GRAHAM, HANDBOOK OF FEDERAL EVIDENCE § 704.2 (3d ed. 1991). Although an expert cannot be asked whether a particular defendant knew what he was doing was wrong, counsel may ask generally whether an individual suffering from the mental illness would know what he was doing was wrong. *See* United States v. Brown, 32 F.3d 236 (7th Cir. 1994); United States v.

Thigpen, 4 F.3d 1573 (11th Cir. 1993), *cert. denied*, 512 U.S. 1238 (1994); United States v. Kristiansen, 901 F.2d 1463 (8th Cir. 1990).

J. OPINION OF APPRAISER TO ESTABLISH FAIR MARKET VALUE OF REAL ESTATE

In a condemnation case, defendant, Bernard Sabian, disputes the Government's opinion about the fair market value of his property. On behalf of Mr. Sabian, counsel calls a real estate appraiser, Henry Hallock, to express his opinion about the fair market value of the landowner's property:

Defense Counsel:

Q. Mr. Hallock, are you familiar with the property located at 1635 Oak Street in Perryville, Maryland?

A. Yes, I am.

Q. Did you recently perform an appraisal of that property at my request?

A. Yes, I did.

Q. Let me show you what has been marked for identification as Defendant's Exhibit No. 19, and ask whether you can identify this document?

A. Yes. This is my appraisal of that property.

Q. When did you perform this appraisal?

A. I completed it on June 4, 1995.

Q. What was the purpose of the appraisal?

A. To arrive at the fair market value of the property.

Q. What is meant by fair market value?

A. The highest price estimated, in terms of money that a buyer would be warranted in paying and a seller justified in accepting, provided that both parties were fully informed, acting intelligently and voluntarily and, further, that all rights and benefits inherent in or attributable to the property would be included in the transfer.

Q. Tell us what was the first thing you did when you commenced your appraisal, Mr. Hallock?

A. I visited the Land Records Office and reviewed the description of the property, the size and boundaries of the property involved; I reviewed assessment data from the County's Assessment Office; I reviewed the deeds for any unusual provisions; and I looked at maps at the Zoning Department.

Q. What was your next step?

A. I visited the property, observed the boundaries, and investigated the surrounding properties to determine their uses, types of buildings, and whether the neighborhood was improving or declining.

Q. Please give a description of the property, including its location and size.

A. The property consists of four acres with a home.

Q. To what use was the property being put?

A. It was and is the residence of Mr. and Mrs. Bernard Sabian.

Q. After you examined the property, did you determine what, in your opinion, based upon a reasonable degree of certainty, is the highest and best use of that property?

A. Yes.

Q. And what is the highest and best use?

A. Residential.

Q. Did you determine what in your opinion is the fair market value of that property?

A. Yes.

Q. What methods did you use in arriving at your opinion as to the fair market value?

A. I used what is known as the market data approach, the cost approach, and the income approach.

Q. Would you describe briefly what is meant by the market data approach?

A. This approach involves consideration of a number of recent sales of comparable properties to determine the sales prices. They are adjusted up or down with regard to location, size, and shape of improvements and land, zoning, and topography to reflect the differences between those properties and the one owned by Mr. Sabian, and on that basis I determined the value of his property.

Q. Please describe what you mean by the cost approach?

A. This approach considers what it would cost to reproduce the structure or replace it with a building of equivalent utility, less an allowance for depreciation and obsolescence. I then add the value of the land to this figure to obtain a value for the entire property.

Q. And now, tell us what is meant by the income approach method of appraising?

A. I evaluate the rental value of property and apply this to determine the fair market value of the property. I take the gross rental income less a vacancy allowance to determine adjusted gross income, and then deduct the expenses incurred by the property owner to arrive at a net income figure. The net income figure is then capitalized at the current market rate to ascertain the value through the income approach.

Q. Did you rely equally on all of these approaches in your report and opinion, sir?

A. No. I relied primarily on the market data approach and used the cost approach as a check against that result. I did not use the income approach to form my opinion, although I discussed this approach in my report.

Q. Why did you rely primarily on the market data approach?

A. The market data approach is usually the most reliable one for properties for which there is an active market. In this case, a three-bedroom home in a suburban location, there was an active market for this type of property, so the market data approach was the best approach to use in this instance.

Q. Mr. Hallock, what comparable sales did you ascertain that relate to your opinion of the fair market value of Mr. Sabian's property?

A. I located four comparable sales. The first was the home seven blocks away owned by Mr. and Mrs. Jasper. The house was sold six months prior to my report for $150,000. It is a home site almost identical to the property in question. Three other home sites were within a square mile and also sold for $200,000, $175,000 and $145,000, respectively. These comparable sales are listed in my report.

Q. Why did you use these four specific properties in appraising Mr. Sabian's property?

A. Each of these comparable properties was sold on the open market at the comparable time of the valuation date. Also, these comparable sales involved properties similar to Mr. Sabian's property.

Q. How did you ascertain these comparable sales?

A. Through public records and interviews with the homeowners of these properties. I also consulted the Lusk Sales Reports, which is a weekly report service, and the Central Maryland Multiple Listing Service of the Real Estate Board, which provides a monthly wrap-up of all properties that have transferred through the real estate agents' hands.

Q. Now, tell us, did you form an opinion based upon a reasonable degree of certainty as to the fair market value of Mr. Sabian's home at the time of your valuation?

A. Yes.

Q. And what is that opinion?

A. My opinion is that the home is worth $250,000.

Q. What is the basis of your opinion?

A. My observation of the property, my review of the data we discussed, and the selection of the market data approach, which offers the most reliable method for determining value in this case.

Q. What are the reasons upon which you base your conclusion?

A. Two of the three appraisal methods were considered, with the third approach—the income approach—not being used, because this was not an income-producing property. The cost approach depends on segregated valuations of land and improvements. The two segments are then combined to give an estimate of total value. The market data approach considers sales of similar style residential units, as total entities, currently taking place within the market area of the subject property. In this case, because the sales data are very recent and a very active market prevails, I selected the market data approach as the most accurate and reliable means to estimate the fair market value of the subject property.

Defense Counsel: We offer in evidence Mr. Hallock's appraisal.

Comment

Broad discretion is vested in the trial court to determine if a witness qualifies to express an opinion on the value of real estate. It is essential, however, that the witness demonstrate an understanding of the meaning of market value. *See generally In re* MDL-731-Tax Refund Litig. of Organizers and Promoters of Investment Plans, 989 F.2d 1290 (2d Cir.), *cert. denied*, 510 U.S. 964 (1993); United States v. L.E. Cooke Co., 991 F.2d 336 (6th Cir. 1993); Frymire-Brinati v. KPMG Peat Marwick, 2 F.3d 183 (7th Cir. 1993); United States v. 68.94 Acres of Land, 918 F.2d 389 (3d Cir. 1990); United States v. 10,031.98 Acres of Land, 850 F.2d 634 (10th Cir.

1988); United States v. 0.161 Acres of Land, 837 F.2d 1036 (11th Cir. 1988); United States v. 329.73 Acres of Land, 666 F.2d 281 (5th Cir. 1982); United States v. 75.13 Acres of Land, 693 F.2d 813 (8th Cir. 1982); United States v. 10.48 Acres of Land, 621 F.2d 338 (9th Cir. 1980); United States v. Whitehurst, 337 F.2d 765 (4th Cir. 1964); Riley v. District of Columbia Redev. Land Agency, 246 F.2d 641 (D.C. Cir. 1957); United States v. 100.01 Acres of Land, 2002 U.S. Dist. LEXIS 8133, at *5-*6 (W.D. Va. May 7, 2002); Vector Pipeline, L.P. v. 68.55 Acres of Land, 157 F. Supp. 2d 949, 956 (N.D. Ill. 2001).

Although slight variation may exist in the definition of fair market value, in condemnation cases under federal law, the expert's opinion must be in accordance with the general principles enunciated by the United States Supreme Court. Under Federal Rule of Civil Procedure 71A, an individual whose land is condemned may request a trial on the issue of just compensation. The United States Supreme Court, in Olson v. United States, 292 U.S. 246, 255 (1934), held that:

> [j]ust compensation includes all elements of value that inhere in the property, but it does not exceed market value fairly determined. The sum required to be paid the owner does not depend upon the uses to which he has devoted his land but is to be arrived at upon just consideration of all the uses for which it is suitable. The highest and most profitable use for which the property is adaptable and needed or likely to be needed in the reasonably near future is to be considered, not necessarily as the measure of value, but to the full extent that the prospect of demand for such use affects the market value while the property is privately held.

See United States v. 158.24 Acres of Land, 696 F.2d 559 (8th Cir. 1982).

K. INTRODUCTION OF NOVEL SCIENTIFIC EVIDENCE IN FEDERAL COURT

Plaintiff seeks to have DNA fingerprinting analysis admitted in federal court. Defense counsel objects. The court conducts a full evidentiary hearing on the matter pursuant to the so-called *Daubert* test. Plaintiff's counsel qualifies an expert in the field and proceeds.

Plaintiff's Counsel:

Q. Doctor August, what is DNA?

A. DNA is a genetic blueprint carried by every cell in the human body. It triggers the development of cells and outlines defining genetic features.

Q. Is the DNA in every human being unique?

A. When taken as a whole, every human being has unique DNA, with the exception of identical twins.

Q. Can DNA be used as a tool to identify people, much like a fingerprint?

A. Yes, when subject to appropriate testing.

Q. How does that testing process work?

A. We use tests that break the DNA into a series of fragments that can be identified and charted. Probes are used to look at particular parts of the DNA that are usually different in different human beings. Once a significant number of probes has been done, the results from the probes can be matched against the DNA taken from a specific subject.

Q. If you have two DNA probe samples from two different people, will they necessarily be unique?

A. If you compare only one probe sample, then no, they will not necessarily be unique.

Q. Why not?

A. Every human being has unique DNA when you are comparing all of the DNA; however, a probe sample only compares a small portion of DNA. Any one particular probe sample might match anywhere from 10 to 90 percent of the population at large. As you do more and more probe samples of DNA, the number of persons that match all of the DNA probes becomes smaller and smaller.

Q. Can DNA testing prove conclusively that one person is the only match for a particular DNA?

A. No, the testing does not prove that one person is the only match; instead, it rules out most of the population to the extent that you can have a very small number of potential matches.

Q. How are those numbers of matches calculated?

A. Through statistical formulas.

Q. Are those statistical formulas that you used generally accepted in the scientific community?

A. Yes.

Q. Have those statistical formulas been subjected to peer review publication?

A. Yes, many times.

Q. And have guidelines been established for the use of these statistical formulas?

A. Yes.

Q. What are those guidelines?

A. Basically, DNA data should be interpreted using the statistical formulas most favorable to the defendant in a criminal case. In a civil case, the formulas should favor the party against whom the evidence is sought to be used.

Q. With regard to the tests involved in extracting the DNA samples, are these tests generally reliable when correctly administered?

A. Yes.

Q. Have these testing procedures been subject to peer review publication?

A. Yes, many times.

Q. Have reliability parameters been developed for these testing procedures?

A. Yes, they have.

Q. And what are those parameters?

A. They vary based on the number of probes taken and the quality or rareness of those probes. They can range from a low of one match in a million people to a high of one match in a billion people.

Q. Do set standards and controls exist for carrying out these tests?

A. Yes.

Q. Is the process by which you match a sample DNA to the control DNA generally reliable?

A. Yes. The odds of the matching procedure incorrectly matching two samples is about one in a million.

Q. Thank you, Doctor.

Plaintiff's Attorney: Your Honor, we request that the court find DNA fingerprint testing meets the factors set forth in the *Daubert* case, and that plaintiff be allowed to lay a foundation for admitting such evidence in this case.

The Court: The ruling will be reserved subject to cross-examination by defendant's counsel.

Comment

The admissibility of expert testimony including novel scientific evidence is governed in the federal courts by Federal Rule of Evidence 702. Such testimony is admitted when the expert testimony could assist the trier of fact in understanding the evidence or determining a fact in issue, and when the witness is properly qualified to give the testimony as an expert. Fed. R. Evid. 702; United States v. Fosher, 590 F.2d 381 (1st Cir. 1979); United States v. Carson, 702 F.2d 351 (2d Cir.), *cert. denied*, 462 U.S. 1108 (1983); Hines v. Consol. Rail Corp., 926 F.2d 262 (3d Cir. 1991); Kopf v. Skyrm, 993 F.2d 374 (4th Cir. 1993); Sparks v. Gilley Trucking Co., 992 F.2d 50 (4th Cir. 1993); United States v. Fowler, 932 F.2d 306 (4th Cir. 1991); Persinger v. Norfolk & Western Ry., 920 F.2d 1185, 1188 (4th Cir. 1990); United States v. Webb, 625 F.2d 709 (5th Cir. 1980); Mannino v. Int'l Mfg. Co., 650 F.2d 846 (6th Cir. 1981); United States v. Watson, 587 F.2d 365 (7th Cir. 1978), *cert. denied*, 439 U.S. 1132 (1979); Holmgren v. Massey-Ferguson, Inc., 516 F.2d 856 (8th Cir. 1975); United States v. Christophe, 833 F.2d 1296 (9th Cir. 1987); Wheeler v. John Deere Co., 935 F.2d 1090 (10th Cir. 1991); United States v. Burchfield, 719 F.2d 356 (11th Cir. 1983); Coleman v. Parkline Corp., 844 F.2d 863 (D.C. Cir. 1988); United States v. Langan, 263 F.3d 613, 621 (6th Cir. 2001) (use of expert witness with respect to eyewitness identification); United States v. Smithers, 212 F.3d 306, 314 (6th Cir. 2000) (same); United States v. Mathis, 264 F.3d 321, 340 (3d Cir. 2001), *cert. denied*, 122 S. Ct. 1211 (2002) (same); Stewart v. Rowan Cos., 2002 U.S. Dist. LEXIS 4135, at *7 (E.D. La. Mar. 7, 2002) (qualified expert witness not strictly confined to area of practice but may testify regarding related applications); Ralston v. Smith & Nephew Richards, Inc., 275 F.3d 965, 970 (10th Cir. 2001) (same); Hardyman v. Norfolk & W. Ry., 243 F.3d 255, 260 (6th Cir. 2001) (validity of expert's theory must be shown; discusses differential etiology); Sullivan v. Ford Motor Co., 2000 U.S. Dist. LEXIS 4114, at *13 (S.D.N.Y. Mar. 31, 2000); United States v. Barile, 2002 U.S. App. LEXIS 7149, at *25 (4th Cir. Apr. 18, 2002); United States v. Hall, 165 F.3d 1095, 1102 (7th Cir.), *cert. denied*, 527 U.S. 1029 (1999); MICHAEL H. GRAHAM, HANDBOOK OF FEDERAL EVIDENCE § 702.1 (3d ed. 1991).

In the 1990s, a trilogy of decisions by the United States Supreme Court resulted in significant amendments to the Federal Rules of Evidence governing the admissibility of the opinions of experts including the admissibility of novel scientic evidence. *See* Kumho Tire Co. v. Carmichael, 526

U.S. 137 (1999); Joiner v. General Electric Co., 522 U.S. 136 (1997); Daubert v. Merrell Dow Pharms., Inc., 509 U.S. 579 (1993). Rule 702 now provides that proponents of expert opinion testimony must show: (1) the expert's testimony is based upon sufficient facts or data; (2) the testimony is the product of reliable principles and methods; and (3) "the witness has applied the principles and methods reliably to the facts of the case."

Until the United States Supreme Court decided *Daubert v. Merrell Dow Pharms., Inc.*, 509 U.S. 579 (1993), the federal courts followed the so-called *Frye* test in determining the admissibility of scientific evidence. The test established by *Frye v. United States*, 293 F. 1013 (D.C. Cir. 1923), provided that, before a scientific opinion could be received as evidence, the basis of the opinion had to be shown to be generally accepted as reliable within the expert's particular scientific field. However, in *Daubert*, the Supreme Court held that the *Frye* test was no longer valid, because the general acceptance test of *Frye* was incompatible with the liberal approach of the Federal Rules of Evidence in admitting opinion evidence of experts. In establishing the so-called *Daubert* test for the admissibility of scientific evidence, the Supreme Court listed the following factors to be considered for the presentation of an opinion relating to scientific evidence: first, whether the theory or technique has been tested; second, whether the theory or technique has been subject to peer review publication; third, the known or potential error rate, and whether standards and controls exist for the operation of the theory or technique; and fourth, whether the theory or technique is generally accepted in the scientific community. *See* Kumho Tire Co. v. Carmichael, 526 U.S. 137, 141 (1999) ("gatekeeping" obligation applies not only to "scientific" testimony but to all expert testimony); Downs v. Perstorp Components, Inc., 2002 U.S. App. LEXIS 382, *475 (6th Cir. Jan. 4, 2002) (chemical exposure); Dhillon v. Crown Controls Corp., 269 F.3d 865, 869 (7th Cir. 2001) (vehicle design; court notes 2000 amendment to Rule 702); Lauzon v. Senco Prods., 270 F.3d 687 (8th Cir. 2001) (sets out a collection of *Daubert* decisions in the Eighth Circuit); Oddi v. Ford Motor Company, 234 F.3d 136, 145-46 (3d Cir. 2000); Pride v. BIC Corp., 218 F.3d 566, 577-78 (6th Cir. 2000); Joiner v. General Elec. Co., 78 F.3d 524 (11th Cir. 1996), *cert. granted*, 520 U.S. 1114 (1997), *rev'd, remanded*, 522 U.S. 136 (1997), *on remand*, 134 F.3d 1457 (11th Cir. 1998); United States v. Dorsey, 45 F.3d 809 (4th Cir.), *cert. denied*, 515 U.S. 1168 (1995); United States v. Posado, 57 F.3d 428 (5th Cir. 1995); Gruca v. Alpha Therapeutic Corp., 51 F.3d 638 (7th Cir. 1995); Iacobelli Constr., Inc. v. County of Monroe, 32 F.3d 19 (2d Cir. 1994); *In re* Paoli

R.R. Yard P&B Litig., 35 F.3d 717 (3d Cir. 1994), *cert. denied*, 115 S. Ct. 1253 (1995); United States v. Davis, 40 F.3d 1069 (10th Cir. 1994), *cert. denied*, 514 U.S. 1088 (1995); United States v. Bonds, 12 F.3d 540 (6th Cir. 1993); United States v. Martinez, 3 F.3d 1191 (8th Cir. 1993), *cert. denied*, 114 S. Ct. 734 (1994); United States v. Amador-Galvan, 9 F.3d 1414 (9th Cir. 1993); Agri-Mark, Inc. v. Niro, Inc., 2002 U.S. Dist. LEXIS 1866, at 31-33 (D. Mass. Feb. 5, 2002); Maurizio v. Goldsmith, 2002 U.S. Dist. LEXIS 6032, at *9 (S.D.N.Y. Apr. 9, 2002; United States v. Salim, 189 F. Supp. 2d 93 (S.D.N.Y. 2002); United States v. Gricco, 2002 U.S. Dist. LEXIS 7564, at 3-5 (E.D. Pa. Apr. 26, 2002) (handwriting analysis); United States v. Santiago, 156 F. Supp. 2d 145, 147-48 (D. P.R. 2001) (stating that these four factors are not exclusive); Am. Family Ins. Group v. JVC Ams. Corp., 2001 U.S. Dist. LEXIS 8001, at *6 (D. Minn. Apr. 30, 2001); Sanner v. Bd. of Trade, 2001 U.S. Dist. LEXIS 15458, at *7 (N.D. Ill. Sept. 28, 2001) (district court has wide discretion in determining the competency of a witness as an expert and the relevancy of the testimony with respect to a particular subject); Hollander v. Sandoz Pharms. Corp., 95 F. Supp. 2d 1230, 1233 (W.D. Okla. 2000). Although the United States Supreme Court's decision in *Kumho Tire Co. v. Carmichael*, 526 U.S. 137 (1999) broadened the applicability of *Daubert* to all expert testimony, even beyond that relating to scientific testimony, Rule 702 does not codify all of the criteria enunciated in *Daubert* for evaluating the admissibility of expert testimony. Nevertheless, the rule clearly denotes that all expert testimony must be the product of reliable principles based on sufficient facts. A question arises whether Rule 702 requires a proponent of expert testimony to elicit on direct examination testimony from the expert that specifically addresses the criteria promulgated in the rule. In most instances this approach will not be necessary. Usually the expert's testimony will encompass the criteria, if not specifically, at least sufficiently to satisfy the court that the criteria of the rule have been satisfied. For example, when during the examination of the expert at trial the proponent asks, "What is the basis of that opinion?," the answer will include a recitation of facts sufficient to justify an opinion. The testimony will also encompass explanations relating to the reliability of the methods used to form the opinion and to the applicability of the opinion to the facts of the case. If there is any doubt, the proponent should pose specific questions to satisfy the rule, e.g., "What methods or principles did you use to form your opinion? Are these methods or principles accepted or recognized within the industry? Did you apply the methodology you adopted in a proper manner?" While, arguably, these questions go to the ultimate issue of admissibility, the answers they seek go to the heart of the criteria established by the rule to evaluate the admissibility of the testimony. In many instances, if doubt exists about the admissibility of the expert testimony, opposing counsel will most likely seek a so-called "*Daubert* hearing" prior to trial for purposes of obtaining a pretrial ruling to exclude the expert from giving testimony. Even if a *Daubert* hearing is not conducted, the court, acting as "gatekeeper" to assess reliability, can exclude the expert's testimony at trial. A cautious advocate will want to pay close attention to Rule 702 in conducting the direct examination of the expert.

In *Samuel v. Ford*, 96 F. Supp. 2d 491 (D. Md. 2000), Judge Paul Grimm, writing for the court, fashioned a *Daubert/Kumho Tire* "checklist," attached to the opinion as an appendix, that counsel should follow if seeking to challenge the admissibility of an expert's testimony at trial under *Daubert/Kumho Tire* standards. The checklist requires the following information: (1) The name of the expert whose opinion(s) is (are) challenged; (2) a brief summary of the opinion(s) challenged, including a reference to the source of the opinion (such as the FRCP 26(a)(2)(B) disclosure, deposition transcript, etc.); (3) a brief description of the methodology/reasoning used by the expert to reach the challenged opinion(s), including a reference to the source materials; (4) a brief explanation of the basis for the challenge to the reasoning/methodology used by the expert, including a reference to the source material for the challenge; (5) a discussion of the known or potential error rate associated with the methodology employed by the expert, if known; (6) a summary of the relevant peer review material, if available, with citation to the source; and (7) a discussion of whether the methods/principles used have been generally accepted within the relevant scientific or technical community, with citation to references. *Samuel*, 96 F. Supp. 2d at 504.

While all courts may not expect counsel to follow such a detailed checklist to present an evidentiary challenge to proffered expert testimony, it is a good reference tool, as it highlights the various components that must be considered in making a *Daubert/Kumho Tire* challenge. Further, it underscores that the facts related to the *Daubert/Kumho Tire* factors should be obtained during discovery. See also PAUL GRIMM, CHARLES FAX & PAUL MARK SANDLER, DISCOVERY PROBLEMS AND SOLUTIONS (ABA Litigation Section).

As distinguished from the federal courts, many state courts still follow the more strict *Frye* test in considering the admissibility of scientific evidence. *Consider* People v. Leahy, 882 P.2d 321 (Cal. 1994), where the California Supreme Court, in determining whether the results of a horizontal gaze nystagmus (HGN) field sobriety test were admissible, held that the *Kelly/Frye* test of admissibility, which had been modeled after the *Frye* test, had survived *Daubert*.

The application of the different state and federal tests for determining the admissibility of evidence, including scientific evidence, can produce conflicting results in factually similar cases. Such was the case in Arizona, where two cases involving the admissibility of DNA evidence produced different results at the state and federal levels. The Court of Appeals of Arizona found DNA evidence linking Mr. Hummert to a crime inadmissible under the *Frye* test in *Arizona v. Hummert*, 905 P.2d 493 (Ariz. 1994). That same month, in an Arizona case where DNA evidence was to be used similarly to link Mr. Chischilly to a crime, the federal Court of Appeals found DNA evidence admissible. United States v. Chischilly, 30 F.3d 1144 (9th Cir. 1994), *cert. denied*, 513 U.S. 1132 (1995); *see also* James Podgers, *Decisions Split on DNA Admissibility*, A.B.A.J., Dec. 1994, at 54.

For a discussion of the admissibility of DNA evidence under *Daubert* and *Frye*, *see* Barry C. Scheck, *DNA and Daubert*, 15 CARDOZO L. REV. 1959 (1994); Leonard J. Deftos, *Daubert & Frye: Compounding the Controversy Over the Forensic Use of DNA Testing*, 15 WHITTIER L. REV. 955 (1994).

L. DIRECT EXAMINATION OF A PHYSICIAN USING MEDICAL TEXT AS AUTHORITY

Dr. Larry Fox, a physician specializing in lung disease, is called to testify as a defense witness in a case involving a claim for asbestos-related disease. Counsel wishes to establish that CT scans are the only reliable method used to diagnose lung obstructions, a method the plaintiff's physician failed to utilize.

Counsel:

Q. Dr. Fox, are you familiar with diagnosing lung obstructions?

A. Yes. I have diagnosed lung obstructions, nearly one every day in my practice, for the last 13 years.

Q. How do physicians diagnose a lung obstruction?

A. By analysis of a CT scan, along with other more intrusive tests if necessary.

Q. Do you have an opinion based upon a reasonable degree of medical certainty whether the use of a CT scan is standard medical practice to diagnose a lung obstruction?

A. Yes.

Q. What is that opinion?

A. It is standard medical practice.

Q. What is the basis of your opinion?

A. I base my opinion on the education I have received, and upon Dr. Smythe's treatise, entitled Diagnosing Lung Obstructions.

Q. Is this a copy of Diagnosing Lung Obstructions?

A. Yes, it is.

Q. Do you recognize Dr. Smythe's treatise as authoritative in the field of diagnosing lung obstructions?

A. Yes, I do.

Q. Is Dr. Smythe's treatise used as a teaching textbook on lung obstructions in medical schools throughout this country?

A. Yes.

Q. Is Dr. Smythe a recognized authority on lung obstructions?

A. Yes.

Q. Doctor, on page 165, Dr. Smythe's treatise states that "only with a CT scan can a lung obstruction be properly detected." Do you agree with that statement, sir?

A. Yes, I do.

Q. If a doctor were to diagnose a lung obstruction without performing a CT scan, in your opinion, Doctor, would such a diagnosis be flawed?

A. Yes, sir, the diagnosis would be flawed and unreliable.

Q. Does your opinion conform with Dr. Smythe's writings?

A. Yes.

Comment

Federal practice, governed by Federal Rule of Evidence 803(18), provides that textbooks and treatises can be used as substantive evidence on direct examination of an expert, if the expert testifies that he or she relied on the treatise. *See* Costantino v. Herzog, 203 F.3d 164, 172 (2d Cir. 2000) (some periodicals are sufficiently esteemed to justify a presumption in favor of admitting the articles accepted for publication therein); Twin City Fire Ins. Co. v. Country Mut. Ins. Co., 23 F.3d 1175 (7th Cir. 1994); Meschino v. North American Drager, Inc., 841 F.2d 429 (1st Cir. 1988); Ward v. United States, 838 F.2d 182 (6th Cir. 1988); Schultz v. Rice, 809 F.2d 643 (10th Cir. 1986); Allen v. Safeco Ins. Co., 782 F.2d 1517, *aff'd in part, vacated in part on other grounds*, 793 F.2d 1195 (11th Cir. 1986); Ellis v. Int'l Playtex, Inc., 745 F.2d 292 (4th Cir. 1984); Tart v. McGann, 697 F.2d 75 (2d Cir. 1982); United States v. An Article of Drug, 661 F.2d 742 (9th Cir. 1981); Johnson v. William C. Ellis & Sons Iron Works, Inc., 609 F.2d 820 (5th Cir. 1980); Maggipinto v. Reichman, 607 F.2d 621 (3d Cir. 1979); Brown v. United States, 419 F.2d 337 (8th Cir. 1969); United States v. Horn, 185 F. Supp. 2d 530 (D. Md. 2002); Charles E. Hill & Assocs. v. Compuserve, Inc., 2000 U.S. Dist. LEXIS 14200, at *39-*40 (S.D. Ind. Aug. 24, 2000) (for such hearsay to be admissible, an expert must have relied on the statements and vouched for the reliability of the publication).

If a textbook or treatise is so admitted, the statements from the book may be read into evidence, but are not received as exhibits. The proper foundation for use of learned treatises as substantive evidence on direct examination includes establishing that the expert relied on the treatise or publication, and establishing that the witness recognizes the treatise as authoritative. An alternative approach is to ask the court to take judicial notice that the treatise is authoritative. *See* FEDERAL EVIDENCE PRACTICE GUIDE § 6.11[16] (Joseph M. McLaughlin ed., Matthew Bender 1990). Alternatively, a party may seek to have a textbook or treatise recognized only as the basis for an expert's opinion, and use of the book for this purpose does not require the same foundation. However, if a foundation is not laid, the treatise cannot be considered as substantive evidence. *See* section II A.3 for an example of cross-examination using authoritative treatises.

Character, Habit, and Custom

A. CHARACTER AS A MATERIAL PROPOSITION OR ESSENTIAL ELEMENT IN A CIVIL CASE

i. *Reputation*

Jill Spender instituted suit against All Spray Exterminating Company for negligent entrustment of an automobile to John Jones, an All Spray employee, who was involved in an automobile collision with the plaintiff. Counsel for defendant seeks to introduce evidence that the employee was a careful, courteous, and safe driver prior to being entrusted with his employer's car, because the issue is in dispute during the trial.

Defense Counsel:

Q. How long have you known John Jones?

A. For ten years.

Q. How close to John Jones do you live?

A. I am his next-door neighbor.

Q. What is your occupation, sir?

A. I am an Episcopal minister.

Q. How long have you been a minister?

A. For twenty-five years.

Q. Where, if you know, does Mr. Jones work?

A. At the school, three blocks from his home. He is now one of their custodians.

Q. Have you talked to people in the community about Mr. Jones?

A. Yes.

Q. Have you discussed with people in the community his driving an automobile?

A. Yes.

Q. Do you know whether or not as of January 2, 1995, Mr. Jones had a reputation in the community in which he lives and works with regard to his driving an automobile?

A. Yes, I do.

Q. Did he have such a reputation?

A. Yes, he did.

Q. What was that reputation?

A. He had a reputation for being a careful, courteous, and safe driver.

Comment

Character evidence means evidence concerning a person's nature or disposition. *See* Michael H. Graham, Handbook of Federal Evidence § 404.1 (3d ed. 1991). Federal Rule of Evidence 404 clearly provides that a person's character or trait of character is inadmissible to prove action in conformity with that character or trait. This policy is frequently referred to as the propensity rule. *See* 1A John Henry Wigmore, Wigmore on Evidence § 54.1 (Tillers rev. 1983 & Supp. 1991); *see also* 1 John W. Strong et al., McCormick on Evidence §§ 186-188 (4th ed. 1992). *See, e.g.,* Harriman v. Pullman Palace-Car Co., 85 F. 353 (8th Cir. 1898) (in defending civil negligence case, defendant porter was prohibited from showing that he was usually careful and attentive); *see also* Sparks v. Gilley Trucking Co., 992 F.2d 50 (4th Cir. 1993) (prior speeding tickets inadmissible to show defendant was speeding at time of accident). In *United States v. Hernandez*, 975 F.2d 1035 (4th Cir. 1992), the court explained that the propensity rule exists to prevent prejudice. *See also* United States v. Arbelaez-Agudelo, 2001 U.S. App. LEXIS 19490, at *9 (6th Cir. Aug. 27, 2001), *cert. denied*, 122 S. Ct. 1329 (2002) (Rule 404(b) not implicated when evidence of other crimes or wrongs is part of a continuing pattern of illegal activity); Okai v. Verfuth, 275 F.3d 606, 610 (7th Cir. 2001) (evidence of other crimes, wrongs, or acts admissible if offered for other purposes, such as motive, intent, plan, or opportunity); United States v. Duckett, 2000 U.S. App. LEXIS 23627, at *4 (4th Cir. Sept. 21, 2000) (Rule 404(b) is a rule of inclusion that allows all evidence of other crimes relevant to an issue in trial, except that which tends to prove only criminal disposition); Neuren v. Adduci, Mastriani, Meeks & Schill, 43 F.3d 1507 (D.C. Cir. 1995); Moorhead v. Mitsubishi Aircraft Int'l, Inc., 828 F.2d 278 (5th Cir. 1987); United States v. Dunn, 805 F.2d 1275 (6th Cir. 1986); Lataille v. Ponte, 754 F.2d 33 (1st Cir. 1985); McCluney v. Jos. Schlitz Brewing Co., 728 F.2d 924 (7th Cir. 1984); Hirst v. Gertzen, 676 F.2d 1252 (9th Cir. 1982); Commonwealth of Pennsylvania v. Porter, 659 F.2d 306 (3d Cir. 1981) (en banc), *cert. denied*, 458 U.S. 1121 (1982); United States v. Salisbury, 662 F.2d 738 (11th Cir. 1981), *cert. denied*, 457 U.S. 1107 (1982); Hackbart v. Cincinnati Bengals, Inc., 601 F.2d 516 (10th Cir.), *cert. denied*, 444 U.S. 931 (1979), modified *sub nom.* Perrin v. Anderson, 784 F.2d 1040 (10th Cir. 1986); St. Clair v. Eastern Air Lines, Inc., 279 F.2d 119 (2d Cir.), *cert. denied*, 364 U.S. 882 (1960); Lombardo v. Stone, 2002 U.S. Dist. LEXIS 1267, at *8-*9 (S.D.N.Y. Jan. 29, 2002).

Circumstantial use of character evidence, to imply that a person's character or trait tends to make it more probable that the person acted in conformity with that character or trait, is distinguishable from the permitted use of character evidence where character is in issue. *See* Fed. R. Evid. 405. Character is in issue when it is an essential element of a charge, claim, or defense in a civil or criminal case. When character is in issue, a person's possession of a particular trait or character is material to the resolution of the substantive rights and liabilities of the parties. The use of character evidence is always admissible when character is in issue.

Court decisions most often recognize the materiality of character evidence, that is, they recognize that character is in issue, where the focus of inquiry is essentially criminal. *See* Crumpton v. Confederation Life Ins. Co., 672 F.2d 1248 (5th Cir.), *reh'g denied*, 679 F.2d 250 (5th Cir. 1982) (in civil action on insurance policy for accidental death, character evidence as to peacefulness of decedent was admissible); *see also* Perrin v. Anderson, 784 F.2d 1040 (10th Cir. 1986). *Consider In re* Aircrash in Bali, 684 F.2d 1301 (9th Cir. 1982), *appeal after remand*, 871 F.2d 812 (9th Cir.), *cert. denied*, Pan-American World Airways, Inc. v. Causey, 493 U.S. 917 (1989); Breeding v. Massey, 378 F.2d 171 (8th Cir. 1967); Skultin v. Bushnell, 82 F. Supp. 2d 1258, 1260 (D. Utah 2000); 2 JACK B. WEINSTEIN ET AL., WEINSTEIN'S EVIDENCE § 404-130 to 404-132 (1995); MICHAEL H. GRAHAM, HANDBOOK OF FEDERAL EVIDENCE § 405.2 (3d ed. 1991). However, character also can be at issue in civil cases, for example, as illustrated in this pattern, or in cases of negligent entrustment or defamation. *See, e.g., In re* Aircrash in Bali, 684 F.2d 1301 (9th Cir. 1982) (holding that training records of pilot were admissible to show that airline had notice of pilot's incompetence and was therefore negligent); Weider v. Hoffman, 238 F. Supp. 437 (M.D. Pa. 1965) (holding that testimony concerning character of plaintiff in libel action was admissible as part of defendant's defense of truth); *see also* 1 JOHN W. STRONG ET AL., MCCORMICK ON EVIDENCE § 187 (4th ed. 1992).

Evidence of a character trait of an accused or of the victim of a crime is allowed under limited circumstances. *See* Fed. R. Evid. 404. Although the language of Federal Rule of Evidence 404(a) applies only to criminal cases, when the main issues of a civil case are criminal in nature, such as in civil assault, a defendant may use evidence of character as the basis for an inference that he did not commit the acts in question. Perrin v. Anderson, 784 F.2d 1040 (10th Cir. 1986); Crumpton v. Confederation Life Ins. Co., 672 F.2d 1248 (5th Cir. 1982). *Consider In re* Aircrash in Bali, 684

F.2d 1301 (9th Cir. 1982), *appeal after remand*, 871 F.2d 812 (9th Cir.), *cert. denied*, Pan-American World Airways, Inc. v. Causey, 493 U.S. 917 (1989); Breeding v. Massey, 378 F.2d 171 (8th Cir. 1967). State practice may not be the same. Prior to the adoption of the state evidence code in Maryland, case law permitted such use. *See* Bugg v. Brown, 246 A.2d 235 (Md. 1968).

The practice of admitting evidence of character in these types of civil actions that involve a criminal issue, however, is a minority position. *See* 1 JOHN W. STRONG ET AL., MCCORMICK ON EVIDENCE § 192 (4th ed. 1992); 22 CHARLES A. WRIGHT & KENNETH W. GRAHAM, JR., FEDERAL PRACTICE AND PROCEDURE: EVIDENCE § 5236 (1978 & Supp. 1996). Federal Rule of Evidence 405 provides that the method of proving character includes reputation and opinion. A witness testifying about reputation or offering an opinion cannot testify about specific prior acts. *See* Fed. R. Evid. 405; United States v. Marrero, 904 F.2d 251 (5th Cir.), *cert. denied*, 498 U.S. 1000 (1990). *See also* United States v. Talamante, 981 F.2d 1153 (10th Cir. 1992), *cert. denied*, 507 U.S. 1041 (1993); United States v. Camejo, 929 F.2d 610 (11th Cir.), *cert. denied*, 502 U.S. 880 (1991); United States v. Gravely, 840 F.2d 1156 (4th Cir. 1988).

Of course, on cross-examination a reputation witness can be probed about relevant specific instances for purposes of impeachment. *See* Fed. R. Evid. 608(b); United States v. Boone, 279 F.3d 163, 174-75 (3d Cir. 2002); United States v. Aronds, 2000 U.S. App. LEXIS 4145, at *30 (6th Cir. Mar. 14, 2000) (if direct testimony addresses community reputation, inquiry made be made on cross-examination about conduct, or even charges, that might have come to the attention of the relevant community; however, cross-examiner must possess good-faith belief that the described events are of a type "likely to have become a matter of general knowledge, currency, or reputation in the community"), *citing* United States v. Brugier, 161 F.3d 1145, 1150 (8th Cir. 1998); United States v. McHorse, 179 F.3d 889, 901 (10th Cir.), *cert. denied*, 528 U.S. 944 (1999); United States v. Pacione, 950 F.2d 1348 (7th Cir. 1991), *cert. denied*, 505 U.S. 1229 (1992); United States v. Coleman, 805 F.2d 474 (3d Cir. 1986). For example, if a witness expresses a favorable opinion on direct examination about a defendant, counsel on cross can ask the witness "have you heard" of a particular instance of conduct relevant to the character trait in question, and if so, "would that alter your opinion?" However, it would be improper to ask the character witness whether his or her opinion would change if the witness assumed that the defendant actually committed the act with which the defendant is charged. United States v. Mason, 993 F.2d 406 (4th Cir. 1993); United States v. Siers, 873 F.2d 747 (4th Cir. 1989), *cert. denied,* 506 U.S. 1086 (1993); *see also* United States v. Guzman, 167 F.3d 1350, 1352 (11th Cir. 1999); United States v. Wilson, 983 F.2d 221 (11th Cir. 1993); United States v. Velasquez, 980 F.2d 1275 (9th Cir. 1992), *cert. denied,* 508 U.S. 979 (1993); United States v. Oshatz, 912 F.2d 534 (2d Cir. 1990), *cert. denied,* 500 U.S. 910 (1991); United States v. Bartan, 888 F.2d 1220 (8th Cir. 1989); United States v. Page, 808 F.2d 723 (10th Cir.), *cert. denied,* 482 U.S. 918 (1987); United States v. McGuire, 744 F.2d 1197 (6th Cir. 1984), *cert. denied,* 471 U.S. 1004 (1985); United States v. Williams, 738 F.2d 172 (7th Cir. 1984); United States v. Curtis, 644 F.2d 263 (3d Cir. 1981), *cert. denied,* 459 U.S. 1018 (1982); United States v. Candelaria-Gonzalez, 547 F.2d 291 (5th Cir. 1977); United States v. Chan, 2002 U.S. Dist. LEXIS 1221, at *5 (S.D.N.Y. Jan. 25, 2002). *But see* United States v. White, 887 F.2d 267 (D.C. Cir. 1989) (holding that guilt-assuming hypotheticals may be asked of witnesses expressing a personal opinion as to a defendant's character, but not to witnesses testifying as to the defendant's reputation in the community).

Nevertheless, in cases where character is an essential issue, as in this pattern, proof of specific instances is admissible on direct examination. Fed. R. Evid. 405(b); United States v. Smith, 230 F.3d 300, 307 (7th Cir. 2000), *cert. denied,* 531 U.S. 1176 (2001) (in the limited instance when a person's character is an essential element of a charge, claim, or defense, proof also can be made by specific instances of conduct); United States v. Marrero, 904 F.2d 251 (5th Cir.), *cert. denied,* 498 U.S. 1000 (1990); United States v. Masters, 622 F.2d 83 (4th Cir. 1980).

When counsel seeks to establish character through evidence of reputation, he or she should appreciate that, under some state rules of evidence, a character witness in state court is required to confine his or her testimony to the individual's reputation in the community in which the individual resided. Opinions about the individual's reputation at the individual's place of business are inadmissible. *See* 22 CHARLES A. WRIGHT & KENNETH W. GRAHAM, JR., FEDERAL PRACTICE AND PROCEDURE: EVIDENCE § 5264 (1978 & Supp. 1996). Under the federal rules, however, a character witness is allowed to opine on reputation where the individual works. Blackburn v. UPS, Inc., 179 F.3d 81, 99 (3d Cir. 1999); United States v. Oliver, 492 F.2d 943 (8th Cir. 1974), *appeal after remand,* 525 F.2d 731 (8th Cir. 1975), *cert. denied,* 424 U.S. 973 (1976); United States v. Mandel, 591 F.2d 1347 (4th Cir. 1979), *aff'd on reh'g en banc,* 602 F.2d 653 (4th

Cir. 1979), *cert. denied*, 455 U.S. 961 (1980). There is a general movement to allow testimony concerning an individual's reputation at work, as well as the individual's community reputation. *See* 1 Stephen A. Saltzburg et al., Federal Rules of Evidence Manual 446-47 (6th ed. 1994 & Supp. February 1996).

The witness must demonstrate familiarity with the defendant's reputation and competence to testify about it. The testimony, furthermore, must relate to the accused's reputation at the time of the acts charged and to character traits pertinent to the offense in question. *See* 2 Jack B. Weinstein et al., Weinstein's Evidence §§ 405-19 to 405-21 (1995), and cases cited therein.

A person's reputation is the community's view or estimate of that person. Michael H. Graham, Handbook of Federal Evidence § 404.1 (3d ed. 1991). Professor Graham points out that the failure to distinguish between character and reputation causes confusion. This confusion is exacerbated often, because reputation is one method of proving character. *Id.* Counsel should appreciate that, on cross-examination, circumstantial evidence of character is admissible to impeach or support other evidence of a witness's character for truthfulness. Fed. R. Evid. 607, 608, 609. *See* Michael H. Graham, Handbook of Federal Evidence § 404.2 (3d ed. 1991); *infra* chapter 7.B-D.

Federal Rule of Evidence 608 provides that, if a witness's character has been attacked for truthfulness by means of reputation or opinion testimony, the character of that witness can be supported on redirect examination by reputation or opinion evidence. Specific instances are not provable. *See infra* chapter 7.A.iv.

Habit and custom, as distinguished from character, should also be considered. Federal Rule of Evidence 406 provides for the admission of evidence of habit and custom. *See infra* chapter 7.E-G.

ii. *Opinion*

Same facts as stated in previous pattern, except counsel for defendant seeks to introduce opinion evidence that the employee was known as a careful, courteous, and safe driver prior to being entrusted with the employer's car.

Defense Counsel:

Q. How long have you known John Jones?

A. For ten years.

Q. How close to John Jones do you live?

A. I am his next-door neighbor.

Q. What is your occupation, sir?

A. I am an Episcopal minister.

Q. How long have you been a minister?

A. For twenty-five years.

Q. Where, if you know, does Mr. Jones work?

A. At the school, three blocks from his home. He is one of their custodians.

Q. Have you ever had occasion to drive with John Jones?

A. Yes, I have.

Q. On more than one occasion?

A. Yes, I have driven with him many, many times.

Q. Do you have an opinion as to whether or not he was a careful, courteous, and safe driver of an automobile as of January 2, 1996?

A. Yes, I do.

Q. What is that opinion?

A. I think he is an excellent driver, and he always has been.

Comment

See Fed. R. Evid. 405. When character is in issue or is an essential element of a claim or defense, it can be proved by opinion, reputation, or by specific instances. When character is not in issue and is sought to be proved, counsel must use the method of opinion or reputation. Fed. R. Evid. 405; *supra* chapter 7.A.i-ii; *see also* United States v. Talamante, 981 F.2d 1153 (10th Cir. 1992), *cert. denied*, 507 U.S. 1041 (1993); United States v. Camejo, 929 F.2d 610 (11th Cir.), *cert. denied*, 502 U.S. 880 (1991); 1 STEPHEN A. SALTZBURG ET AL., FEDERAL RULES OF EVIDENCE MANUAL 448-49 (6th ed. 1994 & Supp. February 1996).

This pattern illustrates the opinion method. The court can conclude, as a matter of discretion, that the character witness lacks a sufficient basis to render an opinion. United States v. McMurray, 20 F.3d 831 (8th Cir. 1994); United States v. Dotson, 799 F.2d 189 (5th Cir. 1986); United States v. Nedza, 880 F.2d 896 (7th Cir.), *cert. denied*, 493 U.S. 938 (1989).

iii. *Opinion with Specific Instances*

Same facts as stated in previous pattern, but counsel relies on opinions and specific facts to illustrate the opinion.

Defense Counsel:

Q. How long have you known John Jones?

A. For ten years.

Q. How close to John Jones do you live?

A. I am his next-door neighbor.

Q. What is your occupation, sir?

A. I am an Episcopal minister.

Q. How long have you been a minister?

A. For twenty-five years.

Q. Where, if you know, does Mr. Jones work?

A. At the school, three blocks from his home. He is one of their custodians.

Q. Have you ever had occasion to drive with him?

A. Yes, I have.

Q. On more than one occasion?

A. Yes, I have driven with him many times.

Q. Do you have an opinion as to whether he is a careful, courteous, and reliable driver of an automobile?

A. Yes, I do.

Q. What is that opinion?

A. I think he is an excellent driver, and he always has been.

Q. Can you tell us of any particular instances when you have driven with him?

A. Well, one example that comes to mind was when he gave me a ride to pick up my automobile from the shop when it was being repaired.

Q. Can you tell us what you observed about his driving at that time?

A. He always stopped at stop signs. He didn't make those running-type stops that you often see, that is, where people slow down but do not come to a full stop. He came to a full stop. He would stop at all traffic lights; he never sped. There is one country road where the speed limit is only 30 miles per hour and almost everyone speeds, but Mr. Jones, I observed, maintained the speed limit.

Comment

See Fed. R. Evid. 405. In this pattern, if character were not in issue, testimony about specific instances would not be proper on direct examination. *Cf.* United States v. Keiser, 57 F.3d 847 (9th Cir.) (for specific instances to be admissible, relevant question is whether an element of the charge or claim involves a character trait), *cert. denied*, 516 U.S. 1029 (1995); Perrin v. Anderson, 784 F.2d 1040 (10th Cir. 1986) (specific incidents permitted only when rights of parties affected by existence of character trait).

iv. *Specific Instances*

Same facts stated in previous pattern, except counsel uses only specific acts to demonstrate character.

Defense Counsel:

Q. Have you ever had occasion to drive with Mr. Jones?

A. Yes, I have.

Q. Can you tell us of any particular instances when you have driven with him?

A. I recall an occasion when he gave me a ride to pick up my automobile from the shop.

Q. What did you observe about his driving at that time?

A. He always stopped at stop signs. He didn't make those running-type stops that you often see, that is, where people slow down but do not come to a full stop. He came to a full stop. He would stop at all traffic lights; he never sped. There is one country road where the speed limit is only 30 miles per hour and almost everyone speeds, but Mr. Jones, I observed, maintained the speed limit.

Q. No further questions.

Comment

See Fed. R. Evid. 405. When character is in issue or is an essential element of a claim or defense, it can be proved by opinion, reputation, or specific instances. United States v. Marrero, 904 F.2d 251 (5th Cir.), 498 U.S. 1000 (1990). *See also* United States v. Morris, 2002 U.S. App. LEXIS 3870, at *10 (10th Cir. Mar. 12, 2002); United States v. Taken Alive, 262 F.3d 711, 714 (8th Cir. 2001); United States v. Smith, 230 F.3d 300, 307 (7th Cir. 2000), *cert. denied*, 531 U.S. 1176 (2001); United States v. Saenz, 1999 U.S. App. LEXIS 1080, at *2 (9th Cir. Jan. 22, 1999), *subsequent appeal*, 179 F.3d 686 (9th Cir. 1999); United States v. Keiser, 57 F.3d 847 (9th Cir. 1995), *cert. denied*, 516 U.S. 1029 (1995); United States v. Hill, 40 F.3d 164 (7th Cir. 1994), *cert. denied*, 514 U.S. 1029 (1995); United States v. Piche, 981 F.2d 706 (4th Cir. 1992), *cert. denied*, 508 U.S. 916 (1993);

United States v. Waloke, 962 F.2d 824 (8th Cir. 1992); Perrin v. Anderson, 784 F.2d 1040 (10th Cir. 1986); United States v. Wallach, 935 F.2d 445 (2d Cir. 1991), *on remand*, 788 F. Supp. 739 (S.D.N.Y.), *aff'd*, 979 F.2d 912 (2d Cir. 1992), *cert. denied*, 508 U.S. 939 (1993); United States v. Frost, 914 F.2d 756 (6th Cir. 1990).

B. CHARACTER OF ACCUSED—REPUTATION METHOD

John Witherspoon is indicted for a robbery allegedly committed on January 3, 1995. He calls a witness to testify to his good character, to support his contention that he did not commit the robbery. His attorney proceeds as follows:

Defense Counsel:

Q. How long have you known Mr. Witherspoon?
A. For ten years.
Q. How close to John Witherspoon do you live?
A. I am his next-door neighbor.
Q. What is your occupation, sir?
A. I am a physician.
Q. How long have you been a physician?
A. Twenty years.
Q. Have you met John Witherspoon either socially or professionally?
A. Yes, many times socially, but not professionally.
Q. Have you spoken to him or heard others speak about him in your community?
A. Yes.
Q. Do you know if he has a reputation in the community for truthfulness?
A. Yes.
Q. Are you acquainted with that reputation in the community for truth and veracity?
A. Yes, I am.
Q. Do you have an opinion as to that reputation?
A. Yes.
Q. What is your opinion concerning his reputation?
A. His reputation is excellent.
Q. Would you believe him under oath?
A. Absolutely.

* * *

If Witherspoon had been indicted for assault, defense counsel might pose the question as follows:

Q. Have you spoken about him or heard others speak about him in your community?

A. Yes.

Q. Do you know if he has a reputation in the community for being a peaceable and law-abiding citizen?

A. Yes, I do.

Q. Can you tell us what that reputation is?

A. He has a reputation for being peaceful, quiet, and law-abiding.

Comment

Federal Rule of Evidence 404(a)(1) allows evidence of a pertinent trait of the character of an accused to be offered by the accused for the purpose of proving that the accused did not commit the crime charged. United States v. Han, 230 F.3d 560, 564 (2d Cir. 2000); United States v. Maiben, 2000 U.S. App. LEXIS 15777, *2 (9th Cir. July 6, 2000) (once introduced, government can impeach with questions about past bad acts); United States v. Moore, 27 F.3d 969 (4th Cir.), *cert. denied*, 513 U.S. 979 (1994); United States v. Santana-Camacho, 931 F.2d 966 (1st Cir. 1991); United States v. Pujana-Mena, 949 F.2d 24 (2d Cir. 1991); United States v. Cortez, 935 F.2d 135 (8th Cir. 1991), *cert. denied*, 502 U.S. 1062 (1992); United States v. Barry, 814 F.2d 1400 (9th Cir. 1987); United States v. Troutman, 814 F.2d 1428 (10th Cir. 1987); Virgin Islands v. Grant, 775 F.2d 508 (3d Cir. 1985); United States v. Reed, 700 F.2d 638 (11th Cir. 1983); United States v. West, 670 F.2d 675 (7th Cir.), *cert. denied,* King v. United States, 457 U.S. 1124, *cert. denied,* Jeffers v. United States, 457 U.S. 1139 (1982); United States v. Jackson, 588 F.2d 1046 (5th Cir.), *cert. denied*, 442 U.S. 941 (1979); United States v. Cylkouski, 556 F.2d 799 (6th Cir. 1977); United States v. Lechoco, 542 F.2d 84 (D.C. Cir. 1976).The rules also permit the prosecutor to use character evidence to rebut similar evidence offered by the accused to prove a character trait in question. Fed. R. Evid. 404(a) (1); *see* United States v. Moore, 27 F.3d 969 (4th Cir.), *cert. denied*, 513 U.S. 979 (1994); United States v. Reed, 700 F.2d 638 (11th Cir. 1983); *but see* United States v. Hands, 184 F.3d 1322, 1328 (11th Cir. 1999) (government cannot bootstrap irrelevant evidence into trial by using it to impeach answers to irrelevant questions). In addition, when the accused offers character evidence about the victim, the prosecutor may offer similar character evidence about the accused. Fed. R. Evid 404(a) (1). The rules provide that character can be established by evidence of reputation or by opinion evidence. Fed. R. Evid. 405(a). However, Federal Rule of Evidence 405(b) provides that, if character or a trait of character of the accused is an essential element of the charge, counsel may prove character by specific instances. Since character is not an essential element of the charge of robbery or assault in this pattern, proof of character by specific instances is prohibited.

When counsel seeks to establish character through evidence of reputation, he or she should appreciate that, prior to the adoption of state rules of evidence, a character witness in state court was required to confine his or her testimony to the individual's reputation in the community in which the individual resided. *See* 22 CHARLES A. WRIGHT & KENNETH W. GRAHAM, JR., FEDERAL PRACTICE AND PROCEDURE: EVIDENCE § 5264 (1978 & Supp. 1996). Under the federal rules, a character witness is allowed to opine on reputation where the individual works, in addition to the community where the individual resides. Blackburn v. UPS, Inc., 179 F.3d 81, 99 (3d Cir. 1999); United States v. Mandel, 591 F.2d 1347 (4th Cir. 1979), *aff'd on reh'g en banc*, 602 F.2d 653 (4th Cir. 1979), *cert. denied*, 455 U.S. 961 (1980); United States v. Oliver, 492 F.2d 943 (8th Cir. 1974), *appeal after remand*, 525 F.2d 731 (8th Cir. 1975), *cert. denied*, 424 U.S. 973 (1976).

The witness must demonstrate familiarity with the defendant's reputation and competence to testify about it. The testimony, furthermore, must relate to the accused's reputation at the time of the acts charged, and to character traits pertinent to the offense in question. *See* 2 JACK B. WEINSTEIN ET AL., WEINSTEIN'S EVIDENCE §§ 405-19 to 405-21 (1995), and cases cited therein; *see also* 22 CHARLES A. WRIGHT & KENNETH W. GRAHAM, JR., FEDERAL PRACTICE AND PROCEDURE: EVIDENCE § 5264 (1978 & Supp. 1996).

Although the language of Federal Rule of Evidence 404(a) applies only to criminal cases, when the main issues of a civil case are criminal in nature, such as in civil assault, a defendant may use evidence of character as the basis for an inference that he did not commit the acts in question. Perrin v. Anderson, 784 F.2d 1040 (10th Cir. 1986).

This pattern was cited with approval in MICHAEL H. GRAHAM, EVIDENCE: TEXT, RULES, ILLUSTRATIONS & PROBLEMS 421 (2d ed. 1988).

C. CHARACTER OF ACCUSED—OPINION METHOD

John Witherspoon is indicted for robbery. He calls a witness to testify to his good character to prove he could not have committed the robbery. His attorney proceeds as follows:

Defense Counsel:

Q. How long have you known John Witherspoon?

A. For ten years.

Q. How close to John Witherspoon do you live?

A. I am his next-door neighbor.

Q. What is your occupation, sir?

A. I am a physician.

Q. How long have you been a physician?

A. For ten years.

Q. Have you had any occasion to socialize or see John Witherspoon on occasions prior to this morning?

A. Yes, many, many times.

Q. Do you have an opinion as to whether or not Mr. Witherspoon is honest and truthful, law-abiding and peaceful [depending on crime charged]?

A. Yes, I do.

Q. And what is that opinion?

A. My opinion is that he is a very truthful and honest individual [or peaceful and law-abiding].

Q. Would you believe him under oath?

A. Yes, I would.

Comment

See supra chapter 7.A.ii-iii; United States v. McDonald, 688 F.2d 224 (4th Cir. 1982), *cert. denied*, 459 U.S. 1103 (1983) (psychiatric character testimony); Virgin Islands v. Petersen, 553 F.2d 324 (3d Cir. 1977) (opinion testimony, like reputation testimony, is based on the witness's observation of the defendant's conduct over a period of time). In *Petersen*, the court instructed that the best means to elicit opinion testimony is simply to inquire directly about the witness's opinion of the character trait in question. Of course, if counsel is using the opinion method of proving character, the witness can offer an opinion even if the witness is unfamiliar with the defendant's reputation. *See* United States v. Polsinelli, 649 F.2d 793

(10th Cir. 1981). Although a witness must have an adequate basis to testify about an individual's reputation or to give an opinion of the individual's character, this does not permit the witness to describe specific instances. Fed. R. Evid. 405.

This pattern was cited with approval in MICHAEL H. GRAHAM, EVIDENCE: TEXT, RULES, ILLUSTRATIONS & PROBLEMS 422 (2d ed. 1988).

D. EVIDENCE OF GOOD CHARACTER AND CONDUCT OF A WITNESS

During the course of a murder trial, defendant calls an alibi witness, who testifies that defendant was with him playing cards at the time when the State claims defendant was participating in the bank robbery in which the victim was killed. On cross-examination, the Government attacks the witness's truthfulness by obtaining an admission from him that he was convicted of forgery nine years ago, when he was 21 years old. On rebuttal, defendant calls the leader of a youth group of which the alibi witness was a member from the ages of 18 to 28, to support the credibility of the alibi witness. He elicits the following testimony:

Defense Counsel:

Q. Mr. Smith, tell us your education?

A. I'm a college graduate, University of Maryland, and majored in sociology.

Q. What is your present occupation?

A. I am the youth leader of the Rolling Mills Recreation Center.

Q. What is the Rolling Mills Recreation Center?

A. It is an organization funded by the community of Rolling Mills, which serves as a focal point for young people from the ages of 13 to 30 to participate in sports activities and community affairs.

Q. How is the recreation center organized?

A. We have a director, which I have been serving as for the past eight years. Before that, I was the assistant director. We also have positions of assistant director, secretary, and treasurer.

Q. How are the people selected to fill these positions?

A. The manager appoints the people to these positions.

Q. Do you know John Smith, who resides at 212 Rolling Mills Road?

A. Yes, I do.

Q. How do you know him?

A. John Smith has been a member of the recreation center since 1987, and I have had occasion to work with him and supervise him and watch him grow up.

Q. Did you have occasion to observe him when he participated in various sports activities?

A. Yes, I did. I also had the opportunity to help teach him to play basketball and baseball and to swim.

Q. Do you have an opinion as to whether or not Mr. Smith is a truthful person?

A. Yes, I do.

Q. Can you tell us what that opinion is?

A. I think he's one of the most truthful, honorable young men I have ever met.

Comment

Federal Rule of Evidence 608 permits the credibility of a witness to be supported by reputation or opinion evidence, provided that the evidence refers only to the witness's character for truthfulness or untruthfulness, and provided further that the witness's character has been previously attacked. *See* United States v. Balsam, 203 F.3d 72, 87, n.18 (1st Cir.), *cert. denied*, 530 U.S. 1250 (2000) (Rule 608(b) does not provide for admission of physical evidence, such as a tape recording); United States v. Hashisaki, 1999 U.S. App. LEXIS 30139, at *5 (9th Cir. Nov. 17, 1999), *cert. denied*, 529 U.S. 1043 (2000) (testimony regarding a person's job performance does not implicate the person's character for truthfulness and is not admissible under Rule 608); United States v. McMurray, 20 F.3d 831 (8th Cir. 1994); United States v. Williams, 986 F.2d 86 (4th Cir.), *cert. denied*, 509 U.S. 911 (1993); United States v. Dring, 930 F.2d 687 (9th Cir. 1991), *cert. denied*, 506 U.S. 836 (1992) (trial court has discretion to determine what constitutes attack on witness's character for being truthful); United States v. Bowie, 892 F.2d 1494 (10th Cir. 1990); United States v. McNeill, 887 F.2d 448 (3d Cir. 1989), *cert. denied*, 493 U.S. 1087 (1990); United States v. Candoli, 870 F.2d 496 (9th Cir. 1989); United States v. Hilton, 772 F.2d 783 (11th Cir. 1985); Stokes v. Delcambre, 710 F.2d 1120 (5th Cir. 1983); United States v. Angelini, 678 F.2d 380 (1st Cir. 1982); Beard v. Mitchell, 604 F.2d 485 (7th Cir. 1979); United States v. Medical Therapy Sciences, Inc., 583 F.2d 36 (2d Cir. 1978), *cert. denied*, 439 U.S. 1130 (1979); United States v. Cylkouski, 556 F.2d 799 (6th Cir. 1977). *Consider* United States v. Truslow, 530 F.2d

257 (4th Cir. 1975), for a discussion of the right of defense counsel to show the bad reputation of a prosecution witness for truth and veracity by asking a defense witness whether he was familiar with the general reputation of the prosecution witness for truth and veracity.

In rendering opinion testimony on character, the witness may state a reasonable basis for his or her testimony, but may not testify about specific instances. Although Federal Rule of Evidence 608 does not specifically use the term "reasonable basis," the basis for reputation or opinion evidence as to character usually involves the witness's having heard the reputation discussed by others or having been involved directly in discussions of the reputation. *See* MICHAEL H. GRAHAM, HANDBOOK OF FEDERAL EVIDENCE § 608.3 (3d ed. 1991); *cf.* United States v. Thomas, 768 F.2d 611 (5th Cir. 1985) (upholding a trial court's refusal to admit a polygraphist's testimony as to the truthfulness of the defendant/witness, because such testimony fell outside of the meaning of "opinion" evidence in Rule 608). Frequently, a follow-up question is asked after the witness renders his or her opinion: "Would you believe him or her under oath?" *See* United States v. McMurray, 20 F.3d 831 (8th Cir. 1994); United States v. Bright, 588 F.2d 504 (5th Cir.), *cert. denied*, 440 U.S. 972 (1979); United States v. Bambulas, 471 F.2d 501 (7th Cir. 1972).

A curious distinction exists between federal and some state practices with regard to a character witness being able to testify about whether another witness testified truthfully. Maryland Rule 5-608(a) (3) (A) prohibits such testimony. *United States v. Davis*, 639 F.2d 239 (5th Cir. 1981), expresses a contrary view.

E. HABIT, USUAL METHOD OF PRACTICE

Mrs. Smith institutes an employment discrimination suit, pursuant to 42 U.S.C. § 2000(e), et seq., against Raisin, Inc., claiming sex discrimination. She testifies that during the course of her hiring interview the company's agent asked her whether or not she could lift a weight over 50 pounds, and that she was also asked questions concerning her marital status, whether she had children, whether she was divorced, and whether she received child support. Defendant's agent has no specific recollection of interviewing the plaintiff, and cannot remember specifically that he did not ask the questions plaintiff alleges. He does know, however, that it was his usual practice not to ask questions of that nature when interviewing any applicants, female or male, and he is asked to so testify.

Defense Counsel:

Q. Mr. Jones, how long were you department director for Raisin, Inc., in the food sales division?

A. Twelve years.

Q. Was one of the things you did as director the hiring of personnel for the division?

A. Yes, it was.

Q. Would you outline your procedure in recruiting applicants to fill any vacant positions in 1995?

A. We would first advertise in the newspaper and send notification to recruitment offices at local schools and employment agencies. After we received the responses, we would send application forms to the individuals who responded. After we received the completed application forms, we would interview the applicants.

Q. In 1995, did you advertise a position in the food sales division of Raisin, Inc.'s Baltimore division?

A. Yes.

Q. Did you receive responses to those ads?

A. Yes.

Q. Did you forward application forms to those who responded?

A. Yes, we did.

Q. Did you conduct any interviews that year?

A. Absolutely.

Q. How many interviews did you conduct, if you remember?

A. Approximately 200 interviews.

Q. Do you remember conducting an interview with the plaintiff in this case, Renee Smith?

A. I'm sorry. I do not have any recollection of meeting her, although my notes definitely reflect that I did interview her.

Q. Do you remember what happened during your interview?

A. I'm sorry. I do not remember.

Q. Do you recall whether or not you asked her any specific questions?

A. I do not.

Q. In addition to the 200 interviews that you conducted for the position that Mrs. Smith applied for, how many other interviews have you conducted as a representative of Raisin, Inc.?

A. At least 1,500 interviews.

Q. Did you ever ask a question during any interview concerning a female applicant's ability to lift over a particular number of pounds, or did you ever ask whether a female applicant was married, divorced, or receiving child support or alimony?

A. Absolutely not. It was not my practice to ask any questions of that type.

Q. How can you be so sure?

A. Because at the many seminars that I attended on how to conduct interviews within the company, we were instructed never to ask questions of that type.

Q. When did you attend those seminars?

A. Twice a year. From 1980 up to this very time. We have seminars that deal with interview techniques.

Comment

Proof of habit is better received than proof of character. Federal Rule of Evidence 406 provides that evidence of the habit of a person or the routine practice of an organization, whether corroborated or not and regardless of the presence of eyewitnesses, is relevant to prove that the conduct of the person or organization on a particular occasion was in conformity with the habit or routine practice. United States v. Troutman, 814 F.2d 1428 (10th Cir. 1987) (habit is person's regular practice of meeting a particular kind of situation with a specific type of conduct, such as going down a particular stairway two stairs at a time, or giving a hand-signal for a left turn, or alighting from railway cars while they are moving; the doing of the habitual acts may become semi-automatic) (citing advisory committee notes); United States v. Angwin, 271 F.3d 786, 798-801 (9th Cir. 2001), *cert. denied*, 122 S. Ct. 1385 (2002) (Rule 406 is an exception to the general exclusion of character evidence so courts are somewhat cautious in admitting it); United States v. Newman, 982 F.2d 665 (1st Cir. 1992), *cert. denied*, 510 U.S. 812 (1993); United States Football League v. National Football League, 842 F.2d 1335 (2d Cir. 1988); Simplex, Inc. v. Diversified Energy Systems, Inc., 847 F.2d 1290 (7th Cir. 1988) (court considers three factors in deciding whether certain conduct constitutes habit: (1) the degree to which the conduct is reflexive or semi-automatic as opposed to volitional; (2) the specificity or particularity of the conduct; and (3) the regularity or numerosity of the examples of the conduct); General Inv. Corp. v. United States, 823 F.2d 337 (9th Cir. 1987); Loughan v. Firestone

Tire & Rubber Co., 749 F.2d 1519 (11th Cir. 1985) (explores standards for determining when behavior pattern emerges into habit); Keltner v. Ford Motor Co., 748 F.2d 1265 (8th Cir. 1984); Commonwealth of Pennsylvania v. Porter, 659 F.2d 306 (3d Cir. 1981), *cert. denied*, 458 U.S. 1121 (1982); Meyer v. United States, 638 F.2d 155 (10th Cir. 1980); Reyes v. Missouri P. R.R., 589 F.2d 791 (5th Cir. 1979); Wilson v. Volkswagen of Am., Inc., 561 F.2d 494 (4th Cir. 1977), *cert. denied*, 434 U.S. 1020 (1978); United States v. Callahan, 551 F.2d 733 (6th Cir. 1977), *appeal after remand*, 579 F.2d 398 (6th Cir. 1978); Levin v. United States, 338 F.2d 265 (D.C. Cir. 1964), *cert. denied*, 379 U.S. 999 (1965); Okehi v. Security Bank, 198 F.R.D. 388, 406 (M.D. Ga. 2001); United States v. Santos, 65 F. Supp. 2d 802, 821 (E.D. Ill. 1999) (requirement that party establish the degree of specificity and frequency of uniform response and to show more than a mere tendency to act in a given manner helps prevent attempts to "sneak in" inadmissible character evidence under Rule 404, i.e., evidence used to establish a party's propensity to act in conformity with her general character, as habit), *subsequent appeal, remanded*, 201 F.2d 953 (7th Cir. 2000). The method of proving habit, that is, reputation, opinion, or specific instances, is within the discretion of the trial judge. *See* 2 JACK B. WEINSTEIN ET AL., WEINSTEIN'S EVIDENCE § 406-22 (1995). Evidence of habit is more readily received than that of character because the uniformity of one's response to habit is far greater than the consistency with which one's conduct conforms to character. *See* JOHN W. STRONG ET AL., MCCORMICK ON EVIDENCE §§ 350-351 (4th ed. 1992). *See also* Meyer v. United States, 638 F.2d 155 (10th Cir. 1980).

This pattern could also be viewed as testimony supporting "usual method of practice," which is frequently admitted for purposes of showing a person's standard of care. Although in some instances "usual method of practice" is indistinguishable from habit, these are two areas of conduct that are separate and distinct. A third separate concept is known as "custom and usage." This concept refers to a habitual or customary practice among certain groups of people, for example, trades or neighborhoods. *See infra* chapter 7.G. However, the federal rules explicitly combine habit or routine practice in business under one rule and make no separate provision for "usual method of practice," although the doctrine is recognized. *See also* Columbia Nitrogen Corp. v. Royster Co., 451 F.2d 3 (4th Cir. 1971); U.C.C. §§ 1-205, 2-208.

F. ROUTINE PRACTICE (CUSTOM) IN BUSINESS

John Baines institutes suit against his landlord for negligence in failing to repair a porch, which collapsed and caused plaintiff's son serious injury. To show knowledge on the part of the landlord that the porch was in need of repair, Mr. Baines's attorney introduces documents of the Department of Housing reflecting that the porch was inspected by a housing inspector, that the inspector indicated on his report that the porch was in need of repair, and that after the report was completed by the housing inspector it was mailed to the landlord.

Plaintiff's Counsel:

Q. Mr. Richards, please tell us your occupation?

A. Regional manager of the Worcester Housing Authority.

Q. I show you Exhibit 32 and ask you if you are familiar with it?

A. Yes, this is a housing report used by our inspectors when they visit homes to conduct housing inspections.

Q. What premises are reflected in this report?

A. 16 Omaha Street.

Q. Do you recognize the signature at the bottom of the report?

A. Yes, it is Inspector Thomas's signature.

Q. Where is Inspector Thomas today, if you know?

A. He died last year.

Q. Directing your attention to Item 16 on the report, do you see the item "porch"?

A. Yes.

Q. What else do you see with regard to that item?

A. I note that the column "needs repair" is checked.

Q. How long have you been affiliated with the Housing Authority?

A. Five years.

Q. During your five years with the Housing Authority, have you become familiar with the routine practice [custom] with regard to the inspection of houses by the Department?

A. Yes, I have.

Q. During the year 1994, was there a routine practice or custom concerning the inspection of houses?

A. Yes.

Q. What was that routine practice [custom]?

A. That year, each landlord in the southeast section of the city received a notice from our Department advising that within sixty
days one of our inspectors would visit his rental property for purposes of conducting a general, overall inspection.

Q. What did this inspection consist of?

A. The inspectors went to the premises and generally reviewed the
plumbing, heating, and related facilities, as well as checked struc-
tural conditions, and in general looked for unsafe or unhealthy
conditions within the premises.

Q. What routine practice or custom, if any, would the inspector follow with regard to reporting defects?

A. He would indicate on his report that the particular improvement
or repair was necessary.

Q. Does the Department have a routine practice or custom with regard to processing the reports taken or made by the housing inspectors of the Authority?

A. Yes.

Q. What is that practice?

A. After the housing inspector completes his report, he files a copy
with us in the central office. The central office then makes five
additional copies for placement in the file and one is forwarded by
mail to the landlord.

Q. Do your agency's records reflect whether Mr. Herbert, the landlord in this case, received a copy of Mr. Thomas's report?

A. They do not.

Q. Why not?

A. Because of a fire that destroyed our records for that time.

Q. How was the routine that you described established?

A. The supervisor of the Department promulgated this policy at least
six years ago and it appears in the policy manual of the Department.

Q. How is the routine enforced?

A. By supervisory checks and administrative seminars, which all appropriate individuals attend.

Q. Is the routine practice and custom of the Housing Authority adhered to in every case?

A. Yes, to the best of my knowledge it is.

Comment

Federal Rule of Evidence 406 treats routine practice of a business exactly as it does evidence of habit. *See also* Wetherill v. University of Chicago, 570 F. Supp. 1124 (N.D. Ill. 1983). In that case, the court admitted testimony concerning the University's routine practice of obtaining consent from participants in experiments. These participants sued for damages they allegedly sustained while participating in the experiments. *In re* East Coast Brokers & Packers, Inc., 961 F.2d 1543 (11th Cir. 1992). *See also* Mobil Exploration and Producing U.S., Inc. v. Cajun Constr. Servs., Inc., 45 F.3d 96 (5th Cir. 1995); United States v. Rangel-Arreola, 991 F.2d 1519 (10th Cir. 1993); Rosenburg v. Lincoln Am. Life Ins. Co., 883 F.2d 1328 (7th Cir. 1989); United States Football League v. National Football League, 842 F.2d 1335 (2d Cir. 1988); Maynard v. Sayles, 817 F.2d 50 (8th Cir.), *vacated*, 831 F.2d 173 (1987) (en banc); O'Brien v. Papa Gino's of Am., Inc., 780 F.2d 1067 (1st Cir. 1986); Mathes v. The Clipper Fleet, 774 F.2d 980 (9th Cir. 1985); G.M. Brod & Co. v. U.S. Home Corp., 759 F.2d 1526 (11th Cir. 1985); Commonwealth of Pennsylvania v. Porter, 659 F.2d 306 (3d Cir. 1981) (en banc), *cert. denied*, 458 U.S. 1121 (1982); United States v. Callahan, 551 F.2d 733 (6th Cir. 1977), *appeal after remand*, 579 F.2d 398 (6th Cir. 1978); Wiles v. Nationwide Life Ins. Co., 334 F.2d 296 (4th Cir. 1964); ECDC Envtl., L.C. v. New York Marine & Gen'l Ins. Co., 1999 U.S. Dist. LEXIS 9836, at *38 (S.D.N.Y. June 30, 1999); *see also* Weil v. Seltzer, 873 F.2d 1453 (D.C. Cir. 1989).

G. CUSTOM AND USAGE

JBX, a partnership, purchased a large shipment of film from Columbia Film Company for the purpose of preparing a feature film. When numerous actors breached their contracts with JBX, the partnership sought to return the film and obtain a refund. The film company declined. The partnership instituted suit, calling an expert witness to testify that the contract between the parties, when construed in light of usage of the trade and course of dealings between the parties, imposed a duty on the film company to accept the return of the film and to refund the partnership's payment allocable to the film returned.

Plaintiff's Counsel:

(John Smith, having been qualified as a film expert, testified as follows.)

Q. Is there a custom, practice, or usage within the trade and industry of film merchandising with regard to the sale of film to be used in the production of full-length motion pictures?

A. Yes.

Q. Are you familiar with that custom, practice, or usage?

A. Yes.

Q. What is the custom, practice, or usage with regard to refunds when film footage is not used?

A. Frequently the film industry overestimates the amount of film necessary to shoot various scenes planned to be incorporated within full-length feature films. Film companies, therefore, traditionally accept the return of the film quite readily, and agree to refund the price of the returned film to a motion picture company.

Q. Do you have any personal knowledge as to whether or not defendant Columbia Film Company habitually observes this custom of accepting the return of unused film and refunding the purchase price?

A. Yes, I do.

Q. What do you know about that?

A. They do observe that custom. I know for a fact that they have observed it with Paramount Pictures and Metro Goldwyn Mayer on dozens of occasions.

Comment

Evidence of custom and usage is frequently admitted in cases dealing with contracts. *See* Hugo Boss Fashions Inc. v. Federal Ins. Co., 252 F.3d 608, 617 (2d Cir. 2001); Carey Canada, Inc. v. Columbia Cas. Co., 940 F.2d 1548 (D.C. Cir. 1991); H&W Indus., Inc. v. Occidental Chem. Corp., 911 F.2d 1118 (5th Cir. 1990); Walk-In Medical Centers, Inc. v. Breuer Capital Corp., 818 F.2d 260 (2d Cir. 1987); A.J. Cunningham Packing Corp. v. Florence Beef Co., 785 F.2d 348 (1st Cir. 1986); *In re* Pearson Bros. Co., 787 F.2d 1157 (7th Cir. 1986); Kern Oil & Refining Co. v. Tenneco Oil Co., 792 F.2d 1380 (9th Cir. 1986), *cert. denied*, 480 U.S. 906 (1987); G.M. Brod & Co., Inc. v. U.S. Home Corp., 759 F.2d 1526 (11th Cir. 1985); Ralph's Distrib. Co. v. AMF, Inc., 667 F.2d 670 (8th

Cir. 1981); Brunswick Box Co. v. Coutinho, Caro & Co., 617 F.2d 355 (4th Cir. 1980); Sunbury Textile Mills, Inc. v. Commissioner of Internal Revenue, 585 F.2d 1190 (3d Cir. 1978); Major v. Bishop, 462 F.2d 1277 (10th Cir. 1972); *In re* Worldcorp, Inc., 252 B.R. 890, 896 (Bankr. D. Del. 2000) Trent Partners & Assocs. v. Digital Equip. Corp., 120 F. Supp. 2d 84, 99 (D. Mass. 1999); Allapattah Servs. v. Exxon Corp., 61 F. Supp. 2d 1300, 1304 (S.D. Fla. 1999).

General Interest 8

A. IMMUNIZING THE WITNESS

During a wrongful death case, plaintiff's eyewitness to the collision is on the witness stand. The witness is expected to testify that she saw defendant run the red light. Previously during a deposition, the witness had testified that she had doubts about whether the light was yellow or red. Counsel wants to take the sting out of cross-examination by eliciting the witness's prior testimony on direct examination and having her explain it before cross-examination.

Plaintiff's Counsel:

Q. Did you see the collision?

A. Yes.

Q. Tell us exactly what you saw occur.

A. Mr. Smith ran the red light and collided with the car operated by the late Mrs. Duncan.

Q. Are you sure the light was red?

A. Yes.

Q. Did you ever testify differently in the past about what color you believed the light to be?

Defense Counsel: Objection. Counsel is about to impeach her own witness.

The Court: Overruled.

A. Yes.

Q. When?

A. Last year in a deposition in this case I testified that I could not remember if the light were yellow or red.

Q. Do you remember now?

A. Yes, the light was definitely red.

Q. Why did you testify differently in the deposition?

A. At the time of the deposition, I was experiencing cluster migraine headaches. I was taking certain medicines that affected my ability to remember.

Q. Do you have any doubt now about what color the light was at the time in question.

A. No, I do not. It was red.

Q. Thank you. No further questions.

Comment

Although at common law a party could not ordinarily impeach her own witness, modern practice adopts a different approach. Federal Rule of Evidence 607 and many state evidence codes now permit the credibility of a witness to be attacked by any party calling that witness.

The opportunity to impeach one's own witness offers counsel the ability to call a witness for favorable testimony. Then counsel can elicit the unfavorable testimony in a less harmful way than by simply turning the witness over for cross-examination. Taking the sting out of what could be a lethal cross-examination is a strategic technique well worth considering. See United States v. Rivera-Medina, 845 F.2d 12 (1st Cir. 1988); United States v. Marroquin, 885 F.1240 (5th Cir. 1989). *See also* SALTZBURG, MARTIN & CAPRA, FEDERAL RULES OF EVIDENCE MANUAL, Vol. 3 (8th Edition, LexisNexis 2000) 607.

The extent to which counsel can rehabilitate her witness after introducing the harmful evidence is a matter of discretion with the court. Thus, the questions to the witness about whether the witness is now sure that the light was red, although not improper, may be objected to on the basis of "asked and answered."

B. PRESENT SENSE IMPRESSION AND EXCITED UTTERANCE

Sam Shopper has sued the Green Grocery Store in negligence for injuries he sustained in a slip and fall at the store. He has called Wendy Williams as a witness to testify as to certain out-of-court statements she heard that tend to prove the existence of a dangerous condition on the premises and that the Green Grocery Store had prior knowledge of the condition.

Plaintiff's Attorney:

Q. Where were you at the time Mr. Shopper fell, Mrs. Williams?

A. I was in the dairy section of the store, looking for yogurt.

Q. What, if anything, do you recall?

A. Well, as I pushed my shopping cart toward where the yogurt is displayed, I passed a woman and her young daughter who were also shopping in the dairy section. A second or two later, I heard a young girl's voice—it must have been the daughter—say, "Mommy, look! There's milk all over the floor!"

Q. What happened after that?

A. The next thing I know I heard a smack, like the palm of your hand against concrete, and then I heard a man screaming. I turned and saw a man, who I later found out was Mr. Shopper, writhing in pain on the floor.

Q. What happened after that?

A. I went over to see if Mr. Shopper was injured, and a store manager came over as well.

Q. Did anyone else attend to Mr. Shopper?

A. Yes, a young woman came over and she had her cell phone with her. She called 911 and asked for an ambulance.

Q. How long did you stay with Mr. Shopper?

A. For as long as it took for the paramedics to arrive—probably no more than 10 or 15 minutes.

Q. What, if anything, do you recall happening when the paramedics arrived?

A. Mr. Shopper looked like he was in a lot of pain. The woman who called 911 was holding his hand and holding his hat, which I guess had come off in the fall. When the paramedics loaded him onto the stretcher, the woman said, "I can't believe nobody cleaned that floor. I saw milk on it over a half an hour ago."

Comment

The Federal Rules of Evidence codify the different, but closely related, common law hearsay exceptions for present sense impressions and excited utterance. According to the rules, the former applies to a "statement describing or explaining an event or condition made while actually perceiving the event or condition, or immediately thereafter," Rule 803(1), and the latter applies to a "statement relating to a startling event or condition made while the declarant was under the stress of excitement caused by the event or condition." Rule 803(2). *See* United States v. Obayagbona, 627 F. Supp. 329 (E.D.N.Y. 1985) (excited utterances and present sense impressions overlap, though based on somewhat different theories).

Each exception has a "time" element which must be satisfied before the proffered statement may be admitted. Present sense impression carries the more restrictive temporal measurement, with the declarant having to make the statement at the exact time he or she is perceiving the event, or "immediately thereafter." The advisory committee note to Rule 803 speaks of event-statement contemporaneity, with only a "slight lapse" permitted between the two. E.g., United States v. Parker, 936 F.2d 950 (7th Cir. 1991) (underlying rationale of present sense impression is that substantial contemporaneity of event and statement minimizes unreliability due to defective recollection or conscious fabrication); Pau v. Yosemite Park and Curry Co., 928 F.2d 880 (9th Cir. 1991) (statement made about accident two days after occurrence held not admissible under present sense impression exception); United States v. Campbell, 782 F. Supp. 1258 (N. D. Ill. 1991) (statement subject to 803(1) must describe or explain the event prompting it; declarant must have perceived the event described; and the description must be substantially contemporaneous with the event). *But see* United States v. Blakey, 607 F.2d 779 (7th Cir. 1979) (there is no per se rule indicating what time interval is too long under 803(1)).

By contrast, an excited utterance need not be made contemporaneously with the happening of a startling event, as long as the declarant made it at a time when he or she remained under the stress or excitement caused by it. McCurdy v. Greyhound Corp., 346 F.2d 224 (3d Cir. 1965) ("excited utterance" admissible as part of the "res gestae" is made by a participant in the event during a period when he was, for any reason, incapable of reasoned reflection about the occurrence); Murphy Auto Parts Co., Inc. v. Ball, 249 F.2d 508 (D.C. Cir. 1957) (existence of an exciting event and an utterance prompted by the event without time to reflect; "i.e., dominated by the excitement of the event" are required for admissibility). There is no specific "cut-off" point. Rather, courts will look to the totality of the circumstances to determine if the statement was made at a time when the declarant was so under the influence of the shock and excitement produced by the event as to hinder the declarant's ability to reflect on the incident. United States v. Shell, 633 F.2d 77 (8th Cir. 1980) (lapse of time between startling event and the out-of-court statement, although relevant, is not dispositive; it is simply a factor trial court must weigh when considering admissibility); Morgan v. Foretich, 846 F.2d 941 (4th Cir. 1988) (when deciding whether declarant was under stress of event at time of utterance, court will look to (1) the lapse of time between the event and the statement, (2) the age of the declarant, (3) physical and mental state of declarant, (4) characteristics of the event, and (5) the subject matter of the statement); Pau v. Yosemite Park and Curry Co., 928 F.2d 880 (9th Cir. 1991) (court did not abuse discretion denying admissibility on excited utterance exception; record does not clearly indicate decedent was under stress of accident when statement allegedly made). Also, the startling event need not be an unexpected event, such as an accident or a criminal act, as long as it affects the declarant's ability to reflect upon the statement. United States v. Moore, 791 F.2d 566 (7th Cir. 1986) (startling event need not be totally unexpected happening, as long as it has startling effect upon the declarant).

The advisory committee note, in acknowledging that the two exceptions overlap, recognized that the "most significant practical difference" between the two is in the allowable time lapse between the event and the statement.

Another common foundational requirement for the two exceptions is the relatedness of the statement to the event. To qualify as a present sense impression, the statement must "describe or explain" the event or condition, Rule 803(1); United States v. Campbell, 782 F. Supp. 1258 (N.D. Ill. 1991), whereas an excited utterance must merely "relate to" the startling event or condition, a standard which encompasses a much broader category of statements. Rule 803(2); United States v. Moore, 791 F.2d 566 (7th Cir. 1986).

C. DYING DECLARATION

John Wilson, M.D., treated Daniel Davis in the emergency room at Community Hospital after Mr. Davis's vehicle left the roadway and struck a utility pole, gravely injuring him. Mr. Davis's Estate has sued the Great Dane Bus Company as a result of the accident, and has called Dr. Wilson to testify at trial regarding statements Mr. Davis made in the emergency room.

Plaintiff's Attorney:

Q. Dr. Wilson, did you treat Mr. Davis on May 5th?

A. Yes I did.

Q. What was his condition when you treated him?

A. Mr. Davis was suffering from massive internal bleeding and was slipping into shock.

Q. Were you ever able to stabilize him?

A. Unfortunately not. The trauma to Mr. Davis's abdomen was so great that it was impossible to find and stop all of the bleeding. We realized after not too long that we would not be able to save Mr. Davis.

Q. What, if anything, did Mr. Davis say in the emergency room?

A. He said that he was cold, and that he was going to die.

Q. When Mr. Davis made that statement, how did he sound?

A. He said it, like, in a resigned fashion, and sounded sad.

Q. What if anything else did Mr. Davis say?

A. He said that a Great Dane bus had killed him. He said the bus crossed the center line and forced him off the road.

Comment

Dying declarations are an exception to the hearsay rule, and are governed by Federal Rule of Evidence 804(2), which states:

> The following are not excluded by the hearsay rule if the declarant is not available as a witness: In a prosecution for homicide or in a civil action or proceeding, a statement made by a declarant while believing that the declarant's death was imminent, concerning the cause or circumstances of what the declarant believed to be his death.

At common law, the exception was only applicable to homicide prosecutions; the federal rules have expanded it to now include civil proceedings.

Courts look to the state of the declarant's mind at the time the statement was made. It is not enough that a declarant fear or believe her illness may end in death. There "must be a 'settled hopeless expectation' that death is near at hand, and what is said must be spoken in the hush of its impending presence." Shepard v. United States, 290 U.S. 96, 100 (1933). See People v. Nieves, 492 N.E.2d 109, 113 (N.Y. 1986) (Support for the dying declaration exception to the hearsay rule is now generally based in the alleged psychological effect that awareness of impending death has on the declarant, as such knowledge is presumed to remove from the mind all motivation and inclination to lie.) If it can be reasonably inferred from the state of the wound or the state of the illness that the dying person was aware of his danger, then the requirement of impending death is met. State v. Quintana, 644 P. 2d 531, 534 (N.M. 1982).

D. SUBSEQUENT REMEDIAL MEASURES

The plaintiff, driver of an automobile, collided with a truck on State Highway 64. He was westbound and the truck was eastbound. They met head-on. Both the plaintiff and the truck driver were unconscious after the impact and did not recall how the accident happened, and so there was no direct evidence of the cause of it. At a bridge on Highway 64, there was a dangerous narrowing of the highway from 24 feet to 18 feet. Plaintiff sued not the State but rather a highway construction contractor with which the State had a contract to widen the section of Highway 64 on which the plaintiff was traveling. The defendant contractor argued that the dangerous condition existed on a portion of the highway excluded from the construction contract and, therefore, that the contractor had no duty to post a warning sign. On cross-examination of a representative of the defendant contractor, who had denied on direct that the contractor controlled the section of the highway where the accident occurred, plaintiff's attorney asks him about subsequent remedial measures taken after the accident.

Plaintiff's Counsel:

Q. After the accident, did your company install any warning signs or devices in the portion of the highway where the accident occurred?

Defense Attorney: Objection.

The Court: What's the basis of the objection?

Defense Attorney: The basis of the objection is that under Federal Rule of Evidence 407, remedial measures taken after an accident are not admissible to prove negligence, culpable conduct, or a need for a warning or instruction.

The Court: Overruled. Evidence of subsequent remedial measures as proof of an admission of fault is excluded. Nevertheless, exclusion is called for only when the evidence of subsequent remedial measures is offered as proof of negligence or culpable conduct. The rule does not require the exclusion of evidence of subsequent measures when offered for another purpose, such as proving ownership, control or feasibility of precautionary measures, if controverted, or for impeachment. Here, evidence that the defendant put out warning signs after the accident is admissible to show that the defendant contractor was in control of the site.

Comment

Federal Rule of Evidence 407 excludes evidence of subsequent remedial measures as proof of an admission of fault. As the advisory committee note to Rule 407 explains, the rule rests on two grounds. First, the conduct is not in fact an admission, since the conduct is equally consistent with injury by mere accident or through contributory negligence. As Barron Bramwell put it, the rule rejects the notion that "because the world gets wiser as it gets older, therefore it was foolish before." Hart v. Lancashire & Yorkshire Ry. Co., 21 L.P.R. N.S.261, 263 (1869). The second ground for exclusion rests on a social policy of "encouraging people to take, or at least not discouraging them from taking, steps in furtherance of added safety." Advisory committee note to Rule 407. The courts have applied the principle embodied in Rule 407 to exclude evidence of subsequent repairs, installation of safety devices, changes in company rules, and discharge of employees. Advisory committee note to Rule 407.

There are exceptions to the rule of exclusion. Exclusion is required only when the evidence of subsequent remedial measures is offered as proof of negligence or other culpable conduct. The rule of exclusion prevents the inference that fault is admitted by engaging in subsequent repairs. Other purposes are, however, allowable, including ownership or control; existence of duty; feasibility of precautionary measures, if controverted; and impeachment. *Id.*

The example above is drawn from *Powers v. J. B. Michael & Co.,* 329 F.2d 674 (6th Cir. 1964), an action against a road contractor for negligent failure to put out warning signs. There, the court allowed testimony that the defendant subsequently put out signs to show that the portion of the road in question was under the defendant's control.

The requirement that the other purpose "be controverted" calls for automatic exclusion of the subsequent repairs evidence "unless a genuine issue be present" and allows the opposing party to lay the groundwork for exclusion by making an admission. Otherwise, the factors of undue prejudice, confusion of issues, misleading the jury, and waste of time remain for consideration under Federal Rule of Evidence 403. Advisory committee note to Rule 407.

The 1997 amendments to Rule 407 made two changes in the rule. First, the amendment clarifies that the rule applies only to changes made after the occurrence that produced the damages giving rise to the action. Evidence of measures taken by the defendant prior to the "event" causing "injury or harm" are not excluded even if they occurred after the manufacture or design of the product.

Rule 407 was also amended to provide that evidence of subsequent remedial measures may not be used to prove "a defect in a product or its design, or that a warning or instruction should have accompanied a product." This amendment adopts the view of a majority of the federal circuits that have interpreted Rule 407 to apply to products liability actions. Advisory committee notes to the 1997 Amendments to Rule 407.

E. INITIAL EXAMINATION OF A CHILD

James Watson, a 5½-year-old boy, witnessed a vehicle matching the description of one driven by a criminal defendant leaving the scene of a homicide at the approximate time of the homicide. The prosecution has called young James to testify at the murder trial in an attempt to place the defendant at the scene of the crime.

Prosecutor:

Q. Jimmy, how old are you today?

A. Five and a half.

Q. When will you be six?

A. November 29th.

Q. Jimmy, do you know the difference between telling the truth and telling a lie?

A. Yeah.

Q. Is it o.k. to tell a lie?

A. No.

Q. What happens if you tell a lie, Jimmy?

A. My Mom and Dad said I will be in trouble. I will get a punishment.

Q. Did your Mom and Dad tell you to tell the truth today?

A. Yes.

Q. When that man over there asked you to raise your hand, do you know what he was asking you to do?

A. To tell the truth.

Q. And do you promise to tell the truth in court today, Jimmy?

A. Uh huh.

Q. Where do you live, Jimmy?

A. With Mom and Dad.

Q. Do you live in a house?

A. Yes.

Q. Do you know your address?

A. Yeah, it's 15 Springfield Road.

Q. Jimmy, are you in school?

A. Kindergarten.

Q. What is the name of your kindergarten?

A. It's called Fairview School.

Q. How do you get to school in the morning?

A. I ride the school bus.

Q. Where does the school bus pick you up?

A. It comes right in front of my house.

Q. What time does it come to pick you up?

A. After breakfast. I look out the window.

Q. Do you remember the morning the police cars came to the house across your street?

A. Yes.

Q. Do you remember what the weather was like the morning the police cars came to the house across the street?

A. It was raining.

Q. Were you looking out the window before the police cars came?

A. Yeah. I saw a big green truck.

Q. Where did you see the truck?

A. It was in the driveway across the street.

Q. Did you see the truck go anywhere?

A. I saw it drive down our street really fast. It made a lot of noise.

Comment

In 1895, in *Wheeler v. United States,* the United States Supreme Court enunciated what remain today as the guiding principles by which a trial judge decides whether or not a child is competent to testify. In *Wheeler,* the trial court permitted the 5½-year-old son of the murder victim to testify against the defendant, which the defendant claimed was error. Writing for the Court, Justice Brewer held:

> That the boy was not by reason of his youth, as a matter of law, absolutely disqualified as a witness is clear. While no one should think of calling as a witness an infant only two or three years old, there is no precise age which determines the question of competency. This depends on the capacity and the intelligence of the child, his appreciation of the difference between truth and falsehood, as well as of his duty to tell the former. The decision of this question

rests primarily with the trial judge, who sees the proposed witness, notices his manner, his apparent possession or lack of intelligence, and may resort to an examination which will tend to disclose his capacity and intelligence, as well as his understanding of the obligation of an oath. As many of these matters cannot be photographed into the record, the decision of the trial judge will not be disturbed on review, unless from that which is preserved it is clear that it was erroneous.

Wheeler v. United States, 159 U.S. 523, 524-25, 16 S. Ct. 93, 40 L. Ed. 244 (1895).

This century-old decision remains in effect today. Thus, a child witness will be permitted to testify if the trial judge is satisfied that he or she comprehends and appreciates the duty to tell the truth, and abides by that duty, and also that the child has demonstrated sufficient capacity for observing, remembering, and describing the facts relevant to the case. In establishing this foundation, as well as further along in the child's testimony, it is permissible for counsel to employ leading questions on direct examination. Although Federal Rule of Evidence 611(c) prohibits the use of leading questions on direct examination, the 1972 committee notes to subdivision (c) acknowledge that the examination of a child witness is a recognized exception.

F. LIFT OF STAY EXAMINATION

Richard M. Goldberg of Shapiro Sher Guinot & Sandler represents XYZ Bank, which made a loan to Mr. Roger Jones for the purchase of a Jeep. The Bank took a lien upon the Jeep to secure payment of the loan obligation. At the inception of the loan and for 12 months thereafter, Mr. Jones made payments on the loan in accordance with the agreement. Then Mr. Jones filed a Chapter 7 bankruptcy petition and ceased making all payments to the Bank.

The Bank has asked Goldberg to obtain relief from the automatic stay of section 362 of the Bankruptcy Code, so that the Bank may exercise its nonbankruptcy law rights in the Jeep, such as repossession and public or private sale.[1] The automatic stay precludes the exercise of such rights absent an

---

1. Any deficiency amounts remaining due will likely be discharged in bankruptcy, absent Mr. Smith having perpetrated a fraud on the Bank, which would require a separate adversary proceeding by the Bank against Mr. Smith.

order of the bankruptcy court, and specifically precludes any act to obtain possession of property of the bankruptcy estate or to exercise control over property of the bankruptcy estate. The Jeep is property of the bankruptcy estate.

The Bank calls Mr. John Smith, its consumer loan officer, to the stand:

Q. Please state your name.
A. John Smith.
Q. Where do you live?
A. 12 South Green Street, Baltimore, Maryland.
Q. What is your occupation?
A. I am the consumer loan officer for XYZ Bank
Q. What are your responsibilities in that position?
A. I receive, review and approve consumer loan applications and monitor such loans once made. Also, in the event of a default, I take all necessary steps to collect the defaulted loans and recover any collateral securing such loans.
Q. Does the Bank keep books and records in the ordinary course of business?
A. Yes
Q. Are entries made into the books and records in the ordinary course of business?
A. Yes
Q. Is it the ordinary course of business for XYZ Bank to make entries into its books and records?
A. Yes.
Q. Are you familiar with the account of Roger Jones?
A. Yes.
Q. What type of transaction did Mr. Jones enter into with XYZ Bank?
A. The Bank made a loan to Mr. Jones for his purchase of a Jeep. In connection with that loan, the Bank obtained a lien upon the Jeep.
Q. Did you review the books and records before coming to court to-day?
A. Yes.
Q. Other than providing the books and records to me for purposes of court today, have they remained under your dominion and control?
A. Yes.

Q. I would like to hand you a document which has been pre-marked as Movant's Exhibit 1 for identification. Would you please review this document?

Q. Can you identify the document?

A. Yes.

Q. What is it?

A. It is a Note and Security Agreement from Roger Jones to XYZ Bank.

Q. Have you seen this document before?

A. Yes.

Q. Who signed the documents?

A. Mr. Jones.

(Authentication of Note and Security Agreement, enter into evidence.)

Q. What are Mr. Jones's obligations under the Note?

A. He is to make monthly payments in the amount of $450 for a term of five years.

Q. What is the status of Mr. Jones's payments under the Note?

A. Default. Mr. Jones paid his note payments for twelve months, but has not made a single payment in the five months since he filed bankruptcy.

Q. Mr. Smith, I would like to hand you a document pre-marked as Movant's Exhibit 2. Please review that document. Can you identify this document?

A. Yes. It is a Loan Payoff Statement for Mr. Jones's loan.

(Authenticate document as business record; enter into evidence.)

Q. Pursuant to the Loan Payoff Statement, how much does Mr. Jones currently owe under the Loan?

A. $19,000 plus an additional $1,500 in outstanding interest and late fees.

Q. As part of the transaction with Mr. Jones, what, if any, collateral did the Bank take a lien upon?

A. Pursuant to the Note and Security Agreement, Mr. Jones granted XYZ Bank a security interest in the 1995 Jeep Cherokee, VIN # 1J4G278Y3VC61723. (Exhibit—Security interest filing statement or title to vehicle depending upon local law for perfection of security interest in a vehicle.)

Q. Is the Jeep depreciating in value?

A. Yes. All cars other than collectors' items depreciate in value, and this is not a collectors' item.

Q. What is the current value of the Jeep?

A. $12,500 at retail; $10,500 at wholesale.

Q. How do you know that?

A. Based on the value listed in the Kelly Blue Book. It is commonly used in the industry as a guide for the valuation of used automobiles.

Comment:

To prevail, Goldberg must prove that there is (i) "cause," including that the Bank is not adequately protected by its collateral (in this case, the Jeep), or (ii) there is no equity in the property (again, the Jeep) and the property is not necessary to an effective reorganization. By this example, we are seeking relief on the latter ground, namely, that there is no equity in the Jeep (its value is less than the debt it secures) and it is not necessary to an effective reorganization (because this a Chapter 7 case, which is a liquidation case, there will be no opportunity for reorganization; this portion of the relief is saved for argument to the court).

Section 362 of the Bankruptcy Code governs relief from the stay. A decision to lift the stay under section 362 is a matter within the discretion of the court. *In re* Robbins, 964 F.2d 342, 345 (4th Cir. 1992). Pursuant to section 362, the court may lift the stay "for cause." 11 U.S.C. § 362. The Fourth Circuit set forth several factors to consider when determining whether to lift the stay to allow state court litigation to proceed: "The factors that courts consider in deciding whether to lift the automatic stay include (1) whether the issues in the pending litigation involve only state law, so the expertise of the bankruptcy court is unnecessary, (2) whether modifying the stay will promote judicial economy and whether there would be greater interference with the bankruptcy case if the stay were not lifted because matters would have to be litigated in the bankruptcy court, and (3) whether the estate can be protected properly by a requirement that creditor seek enforcement of any judgment through the bankruptcy court." *In re* Robbins, 964 F.2d 342, 345 (4th Cir. 1992).

In re Kaplan Breslaw Ash, LLC, 264 B.R. 309 (Bankr. S.D.N.Y. 2001) (secured creditor seeking relief from the stay to exercise its rights in collateral, based upon debtor's alleged lack of equity therein, must show (1) amount of claim, (2) that claim is secured by valid, perfected lien in property of the estate, and (3) that debtor lacks equity in property).

In re Rogers, 239 B.R. 883 (Bankr. E.D. Tex. 1999) (To establish prima facie case of cause for relief from stay due to lack of adequate protection for its interests, movant must initially demonstrate that it holds claim, which is secured by valid, perfected lien upon estate property, and that decline in value of collateral is either occurring or threatened, against which creditor is precluded from protecting its interests due to existence of automatic stay; once movant presents such a prima facie case, burden shifts to debtor to prove that collateral is not declining in value or that the secured creditor is adequately protected.).

Part 2

Cross-Examination and Redirect

Prior Inconsistent Statement; Use of Textbooks

9

A. EXTRINSIC EVIDENCE OF PRIOR INCONSISTENT ORAL STATEMENTS

During a federal court trial for malicious prosecution, plaintiff, a disc jockey, claims that defendant radio station improperly prosecuted him for stealing records from the station. Plaintiff contends that, as program director of the station, he was entitled to take as many duplicate records as he desired. The station coordinator testified that plaintiff was never appointed program director.

Counsel for plaintiff seeks to impeach the station coordinator by means of a prior inconsistent oral statement:

Plaintiff's Counsel:

Q. Mrs. Smith, you were the station coordinator of WZBQ Radio Station in the year 1994, is that correct?

A. Yes.

Q. What were your responsibilities as station coordinator?

A. I was in charge of making all personnel appointments and coordinating these personnel.

Q. Was there a position of program director in 1994?

A. Yes.

Q. Would it be accurate to say that the plaintiff, John Reeves, was that director?

A. No, he was not.

Q. You did not appoint him director in the spring of 1994?

A. Absolutely not.

* * *

(John Brown, a witness, being first duly sworn, is called to the stand.)

Plaintiff's Counsel:

Q. Mr. Brown, what was your position at WZBQ Radio Station in 1994?

A. Disc jockey.

Q. Who was your immediate supervisor?

A. The program director.

Q. Who was that program director in the spring of 1994?

A. John Reeves.

Q. Do you know the circumstances under which John Reeves became that program director?

A. During a meeting of all staff personnel in May 1994, the station coordinator, Carol Smith, announced that John Reeves was appointed program director.

Q. No further questions.

Comment

Federal Rule of Evidence 613 modifies the rule with regard to the use of prior inconsistent oral statements for impeachment purposes. The traditional approach required that the witness be confronted on the stand while under cross-examination as to whether he or she made the supposed inconsistent statement, and be provided with the substance of the statement, as well as the time, place, and person to whom it was made. Federal Rule of Evidence 613, however, eliminates the requirement that the witness be afforded this opportunity. *See* Fed. R. Evid. 613, advisory committee's note. *Consider* United States v. Marks, 816 F.2d 1207 (7th Cir. 1987) (trial court retains discretion to require disclosure prior to questioning).

Impeachment by prior inconsistent oral or written statement requires that: (a) the statement be inconsistent; (b) the inconsistency relate to a matter of sufficient relevancy; (c) there be compliance with the rule requiring disclosure of the prior statement to opposing counsel upon request and an opportunity for explanation, for denial, and for interrogation by the opposing party; and (d) the court instruct the jury as to the purpose of the inconsistent statement. Firemen's Fund Ins. Co. v. Thien, 8 F.3d 1307 (8th Cir. 1993); United States v. Rogers, 549 F.2d 490 (8th Cir. 1976), *cert. denied*, 431 U.S. 918 (1977). *See also* United States v. Larry Reed & Sons P'ship, 280 F.3d 1212, 1215 (8th Cir. 2002); Conte v. Gen'l Housewares Corp., 215 F.3d 628, 638 (6th Cir. 2000); United States v. Winchenbach, 197 F.3d 548, 557-59 (1st Cir. 1999) (explains dichotomy between Rule 613(b) and Rule 608(b)), *magistrate's recomm'n*, 2000 U.S. Dist. LEXIS 9219 (D. Me. June 30, 2000); United States v. Turner, 189 F. 3d 712, 718 (8th Cir. 1999) (prior inconsistent statement can be admissible for impeachment but not for the truth of the matter contained therein); United States v. Causey, 834 F.2d 1277 (6th Cir. 1987), *cert. denied*, 486 U.S. 1034 (1988); United States v. Grubbs, 776 F.2d 1281 (5th Cir. 1985); Bell v. City of Milwaukee, 746 F.2d 1205 (7th Cir. 1984), *limited by* Niehus v. Liberia, 973 F.2d 526 (7th Cir. 1992); United States v. Miller, 664 F.2d 94 (5th Cir. 1981), *cert. denied*, 459 U.S. 854 (1982); United States v. Stahl, 616 F.2d 30 (2d Cir. 1980); United States v.

Palumbo, 639 F.2d 123 (3d Cir.), *cert. denied*, 454 U.S. 819 (1981); United States v. Ling, 581 F.2d 1118 (4th Cir. 1978); Cathron v. Jones, 190 F. Supp. 2d 990 (E.D. Mich. 2002), United States v. Gonzalez, 142 F. Supp. 2d 1052, 1059 (N.D. Ill. 2001). *See generally* 2 JOHN W. STRONG ET AL., MCCORMICK ON EVIDENCE § 34, at 113 (4th ed. 1992) (discussing the degree of inconsistency required).

The instruction given by the court is important. The statement can be admissible for impeachment purposes only or as substantive proof, depending on the nature of the statement. Significantly, Federal Rule of Evidence 801(d)(1)(A) exempts from the hearsay rule a prior statement of a declarant who testifies at trial and is subject to cross-examination about the statement, if the prior statement is inconsistent and was given under oath, subject to the penalty of perjury, at a trial, hearing, or other proceeding, or in a deposition. These types of prior inconsistent statements are admissible as substantive proof in the case. *Cf.* Fed. R. Evid. 801(d)(1). Counsel should also bear in mind that treatment of a prior inconsistent statement on cross-examination is distinguished from treatment of a statement of a party opponent. The statement of a party opponent is also treated as substantive evidence, but it is governed by Federal Rule of Evidence 801(d)(2). Introduction of the statement of a party opponent under Federal Rule of Evidence 801(d)(2) does not require any foundation on cross-examination. *See generally* 2 JOHN W. STRONG ET AL., MCCORMICK ON EVIDENCE § 254, at 141-42 (4th ed. 1992).

The test for determining inconsistency to permit impeachment is somewhat elastic. *See* MICHAEL H. GRAHAM, HANDBOOK OF FEDERAL EVIDENCE § 613.3 (3d ed. 1991 & Supp. 1995). Inconsistency exists if the witness states that he or she does not remember making the prior statement. Under that circumstance, the making of the statement can be proved by extrinsic evidence, e.g., another witness. United States v. Billue, 994 F.2d 1562 (11th Cir. 1993), *cert. denied*, 510 U.S. 1099 (1994); *accord* United States v. Cline, 570 F.2d 731 (8th Cir. 1978); United States v. Sisto, 534 F.2d 616 (5th Cir. 1976); Williamson v. United States, 310 F.2d 192 (9th Cir. 1962); United States v. Gibson, 84 F. Supp. 2d 784, 789 (S.D. W. Va.), *aff'd*, 92 F. Supp. 2d 562 (S.D. W. Va.), *aff'd*, 238 F.3d 416 (4th Cir. 2000), *reprinted in full*, 2000 U.S. App. LEXIS 29495 (4th Cir. Nov. 17, 2000). *But see* United States v. Devine, 934 F.2d 1325 (5th Cir. 1991), *cert. denied*, 502 U.S. 929, 502 U.S. 1047, 502 U.S. 1064, 502 U.S. 1065, 502 U.S. 1092, 502 U.S. 1104 (1992) (holding that the testimony of the witness that he did not remember making a prior statement did not constitute an inconsistent statement, and was therefore properly excluded as hearsay); *accord* United States v. Palumbo, 639 F.2d 123 (3d Cir.), *cert. denied*, 454 U.S. 819 (1981). However, if the witness admits making the prior inconsistent statement, the prevailing view is that counsel may not introduce extrinsic evidence to impeach. Michael H. Graham, Handbook of Federal Evidence § 613.3 (3d ed. 1991 & Supp. 1995); John W. Strong et al., McCormick on Evidence § 37, at 48 (4th ed. 1992). Counsel may impeach with a prior inconsistent oral statement, even if that statement is reduced to writing. *See* Jankins v. TDC Mgmt. Corp., 21 F.3d 436 (D.C. Cir. 1994).

Although Queen Caroline's Rule is abolished by court rule, strategic cross-examinations nevertheless establish traditional foundations to spring the trap. For example, in this pattern, counsel could have gone further to establish a foundation by inquiring: "In your capacity as director, you called many meetings of your staff. From time to time you made important announcements filling new positions at these meetings. You talked to your staff during these meetings about John Reeves. Didn't you announce at one of your staff meetings that you were appointing John Reeves to the position of program director?" Striking the balance between establishing enough foundation to lay the trap and too much so as to reveal the trap goes to the heart of the skill of the cross-examiner. This skill is innate and also acquired.

Federal Rule of Evidence 613(b) governs the use of extrinsic evidence of prior inconsistent statements. Extrinsic evidence refers to evidence presented by other witnesses or by documentary evidence not authenticated by the witness who is on the stand and who made the prior inconsistent statement. Thus, impeaching by a prior inconsistent statement that the witness authenticates is not impeaching by extrinsic evidence. Federal Rule of Evidence 613(b) requires that extrinsic evidence of a prior inconsistent statement by a witness is not admissible unless the witness is afforded an opportunity to explain or deny the statement. *See* United States v. Sutton, 41 F.3d 1257 (8th Cir. 1994), *cert. denied*, 514 U.S. 1072 (1995); United States v. Hudson, 970 F.2d 948 (1st Cir. 1992); United States v. Bonnett, 877 F.2d 1450 (10th Cir. 1989); United States v. Holt, 817 F.2d 1264 (7th Cir. 1987); Wammock v. Celotex Corp., 793 F.2d 1518 (11th Cir. 1986), *substituted opinion*, 835 F.2d 818 (11th Cir. 1987); United States v. Cutler, 676 F.2d 1245 (9th Cir. 1982); United States v. Lay, 644 F.2d 1087 (5th Cir.), *cert. denied*, 454 U.S. 869 (1981); Hilyer v. Howat Concrete Co.,

Inc., 578 F.2d 422 (D.C. Cir. 1978). *Cf.* Udemba v. Nicoli, 237 F.3d 8, 18 (1st Cir. 2001); United States v. Young, 248 F.3d 260, 267-68 (4th Cir.), *cert. denied*, 533 U.S. 961 (2001); United States v. Winchenbach, 197 F.3d 548, 557 (1st Cir. 1999); United States v. Smith, 13 Fed. R. Evid. Serv. 1258 (4th Cir. 1983). This opportunity need not be provided by counsel conducting the cross-examination, but may be left to counsel conducting redirect. MICHAEL H. GRAHAM, HANDBOOK OF FEDERAL EVIDENCE § 613.3 (3d ed. 1991 & Supp. 1995).

As a tactical device, counsel may wish to read Rule 613(b) to the court, after the extrinsic evidence is presented, and "remind his adversary that the witness has the right to resume the stand to explain or deny the extrinsic evidence." A problem is posed when the witness, who is impeached by extrinsic evidence, becomes unavailable to explain the inconsistency. In this situation, the court may exercise discretion to disallow the prior statement. *See* Wammock v. Celotex Corp., 793 F.2d 1518 (11th Cir. 1986), *substituted opinion*, 835 F.2d 818 (11th Cir. 1987). If counsel for the proponent anticipates this problem, he or she might use the traditional method of confronting the witness or might introduce the extrinsic evidence prior to laying the foundation for the inconsistent statement. *See* United States v. Bibbs, 564 F.2d 1165 (5th Cir. 1977), *cert. denied*, 435 U.S. 1007 (1978); Wammock v. Celotex Corp., 793 F.2d 1518 (11th Cir. 1986), *substituted opinion*, 835 F.2d 818 (11th Cir. 1987); United States v. Wilson, 490 F. Supp. 713 (E.D. Mich. 1980), *aff'd*, 639 F.2d 314 (6th Cir. 1981).

This latter approach was used in *United States v. Barrett*, 539 F.2d 244 (1st Cir. 1976), where it was held that the trial judge erred in preventing a second witness from testifying as to the prior inconsistent statement of a first witness. The first witness had not been questioned about the statement on cross-examination prior to the testimony of the second witness. According to the circuit court's view of the record, however, after the impeaching testimony there would still have been an opportunity for the first witness to explain or deny the contradictory statement. A witness clearly can be impeached by extrinsic proof, even if counsel does not question the witness about the matter. *See* United States v. Glascoe, 12 Fed. R. Evid. Serv. 1586 (4th Cir. 1983). *Cf.* United States v. Saget, 991 F.2d 702 (11th Cir.) (no impeachment with a third party's interpretation of a witness's prior oral statement unless the witness had adopted the third party's statement as his or her own), *cert. denied*, 510 U.S. 950 (1993), United States v. Barile, 2002 U.S. App. LEXIS 7149, at *18 (4th Cir. Apr. 18, 2002).

B. EXAMINATION OF WITNESS ON PRIOR INCONSISTENT WRITTEN STATEMENT

Same facts as stated in previous pattern, except counsel for plaintiff seeks to impeach the station coordinator with a prior inconsistent written statement in federal court.

Plaintiff's Counsel:

Q. Mrs. Smith, you were the station coordinator of WZBQ Radio Station in the spring of 1994, is that correct?

A. Yes.

Q. What were your responsibilities as station coordinator?

A. I was in charge of making all personnel appointments and coordinating the staff.

Q. Was there a position of program director at the station in 1994?

A. Yes.

Q. Who occupied that position?

A. It was vacant.

Q. Would it be accurate to say that the plaintiff, John Reeves, was the program director during the spring of 1994?

A. No, he was not.

Q. Did you appoint him program director in the spring of 1994?

A. No, I did not.

Q. Did you ever appoint him as program director of WZBQ?

A. No.

Q. Didn't you circulate a memorandum in the spring of 1994 announcing the appointment of Reeves to the position of program director?

A. No.

Q. Would the Clerk please mark this document. Mrs. Smith, I show you what has been marked Plaintiff's Exhibit 1 for identification and ask you to review the document and tell us whether or not your signature appears at the bottom?

A. Yes, it does.

Q. Did you prepare this document?

A. Yes, I did.

Q. What is the date at the top of the document?

A. May 1, 1994.

Q. Your Honor, we offer Plaintiff's Exhibit 1 for identification in evidence. Would you please read for us, Mrs. Smith, the first paragraph of Plaintiff's Exhibit 1?

A. "On this date, effective immediately, I appoint John Reeves as program director of WZBQ Radio Station. Please join with me in extending to him our congratulations."

Q. No further questions.

Comment

Federal Rule of Evidence 613 modifies the rule enunciated in Queen Caroline's Case, 2 Br.&B. 284, 129 Eng. Rep. 976 (1820), which required that the witness be shown his own prior written statement before counsel could cross-examine the witness about that statement.

Nevertheless, under the federal rule, disclosure to opposing counsel is required. This disclosure is designed to protect the witness from being misled by unwarranted insinuations that a statement has been made when, in fact, there has never been any such statement.

Under the federal rule, there is no rigid requirement that the foundation for impeachment include the four elements traditionally required for that purpose, i.e., whether the witness ever made a statement, whether it was made to a particular party, whether it was made at a particular time, and whether it was made at a particular place. The only foundation that is required under the federal rule is that the witness be given the opportunity at some time to explain or deny the prior statement. *See* United States v. Sutton, 41 F.3d 1257 (8th Cir. 1994), *cert. denied*, 514 U.S. 1072 (1995); United States v. Hudson, 970 F.2d 948 (1st Cir. 1992); United States v. Bonnett, 877 F.2d 1450 (10th Cir. 1989); United States v. Holt, 817 F.2d 1264 (7th Cir. 1987); Wammock v. Celotex Corp., 793 F.2d 1518 (11th Cir. 1986), *substituted opinion*, 835 F.2d 818 (11th Cir. 1987); United States v. Cutler, 676 F.2d 1245 (9th Cir. 1982); United States v. Lay, 644 F.2d 1087 (5th Cir. 1981); Hilyer v. Howat Concrete Co., Inc., 578 F.2d 422 (D.C. Cir. 1978).

Cf. United States v. Young, 248 F.3d 260, 267 (4th Cir.), *cert. denied*, 533 U.S. 961 (2001); Udemba v. Nicoli, 237 F.3d 8, 18 (1st Cir. 2001); United States v. Chee, 1999 U.S. App. LEXIS 8406, at *15-*16 (10th Cir. May 3, 1999), *cert. denied*, 528 U.S. 909 (1999); United States v. Smith, 13 Fed. R. Evid. Serv. 1258 (4th Cir. 1983); Jones v. City of New York,

2002 U.S. Dist. LEXIS 2052, at *11 (S.D.N.Y. Feb. 11, 2002); Behler v. Hanlon, 199 F.R.D. 553, 558-60 (D. Md. 2001) (discusses impeachment by contradiction—not explicitly set forth in Federal Rules—as well as by prior inconsistent statement). This opportunity need not be provided by counsel conducting the cross-examination, but may be left to counsel conducting redirect. MICHAEL H. GRAHAM, HANDBOOK OF FEDERAL EVIDENCE § 613.3 (3d ed. & Supp. 1995).

Impeachment by prior inconsistent oral or written statement requires that: (a) the statement be inconsistent; (b) the inconsistency relate to a matter of sufficient relevancy; (c) there be compliance with the rule requiring disclosure of the prior statement to opposing counsel upon request, as well as an opportunity for explanation, denial, and interrogation by the opposing party; and (d) the court must instruct the jury as to the purpose of the inconsistent statement. Firemen's Fund Ins. Co. v. Thien, 8 F.3d 1307 (8th Cir. 1993); United States v. Rogers, 549 F.2d 490 (8th Cir. 1976), *cert. denied*, 431 U.S. 918 (1977). *See also* United States v. Larry Reed & Sons P'ship, 280 F.3d 1212, 1215 (8th Cir. 2002); Conte v. Gen'l Housewares Corp., 215 F.3d 628, 638 (6th Cir. 2000); United States v. Winchenbach, 197 F.3d 548, 557-59 (1st Cir. 1999) (explains dichotomy between Rule 613(b) and Rule 608(b)), *magistrate's recomm'n*, 2000 U.S. Dist. LEXIS 9219 (D. Me. June 30, 2000); United States v. Turner, 189 F. 3d 712, 718 (8th Cir. 1999) (prior inconsistent statement can be admissible for impeachment but not for the truth of the matter contained therein); United States v. Causey, 834 F.2d 1277 (6th Cir. 1987); United States v. Grubbs, 776 F.2d 1281 (5th Cir. 1985); Bell v. City of Milwaukee, 746 F.2d 1205 (7th Cir. 1984); United States v. Palumbo, 639 F.2d 123 (3d Cir. 1981); United States v. Miller, 664 F.2d 94 (11th Cir. 1981), *cert. denied*, 459 U.S. 854 (1982); United States v. Stahl, 616 F.2d 30 (2d Cir. 1980); United States v. Ling, 581 F.2d 1118 (4th Cir. 1978); Cathron v. Jones, 190 F. Supp. 2d 990 (E.D. Mich. 2002); United States v. Gonzalez, 142 F. Supp. 2d 1052, 1059 (N.D. Ill. 2001). *See generally* JOHN W. STRONG ET AL., MCCORMICK ON EVIDENCE § 34, at 119 (4th ed. 1992) (discussing the degree of inconsistency required).

The instruction given by the court is important. The statement can be admissible for impeachment purposes only, or as substantive proof, depending on the nature of the statement. Significantly, Federal Rule of Evidence 801(d) (1) (A) exempts from the hearsay rule a prior statement of a declarant who testifies at trial and is subject to cross-examination about the statement, if the prior statement is inconsistent and was given under oath, subject to the penalty of perjury, at a trial, hearing or other proceeding, or in a deposition. These types of prior inconsistent statements are admissible as substantive proof in the case. *Cf.* Fed. R. Evid. 801(d) (1). Counsel should also bear in mind that treatment of a prior inconsistent statement on cross-examination is distinguished from treatment of an admission of a party opponent. The admission is also treated as substantive evidence, but it is governed by Federal Rule of Evidence 801(d) (2). Introduction of the admission of a party opponent under Federal Rule of Evidence 801(d) (2) does not require any foundation on cross-examination, pursuant to Federal Rule of Evidence 613(b).

C. CROSS-EXAMINATION UTILIZING AUTHORITATIVE TREATISES AND TEXTBOOKS

Dr. Willoughby Frund, a psychiatrist, has testified in a manner contrary to an authoritative and standard text in the field of psychiatry. The cross-examiner wishes to impeach Dr. Frund's testimony, using the standard text, and proceeds as follows:

Counsel:

Q. Doctor, I show you the two-volume work captioned *Basic Psychiatry*, by Friedman, Lipwitz, and Jones. Would you agree that this work is recognized in the field of psychiatry as authoritative?

A. Yes.

Q. It is true, is it not, that this work is used in medical schools throughout the country as a text for instruction?

A. Yes.

Q. And the authors, Friedman, Lipwitz, and Jones, are recognized authorities in the field of psychiatry, is that not accurate?

A. Yes.

Q. And you have this work in your own medical library, do you not?

A. Yes.

Q. And from time to time you have occasion to refer to it, is that not correct?

A. Yes.

Q. Now, may I call your attention to the section on page 50, where the authors make this statement. (Statement is read.) Would you agree or disagree with that statement?

A. I would disagree.

Q. Are there any recognized authorities whose writings disagree with the statement of Doctors Friedman, Lipwitz, and Jones?

A. I don't recall any particular writing at this time.

Comment

Learned treatises are used in cross-examination in three situations. First, when an expert relies on specific material from a treatise to reinforce an opinion on direct. Second, when an expert admits to having relied upon general authorities, although not the particular material sought to be used for impeachment. Third, as in the pattern examination, when no reference is made to the particular textbook on direct examination, but the expert recognizes the particular materials as being authoritative. *See* Johnson v. William C. Ellis & Sons Iron Works, Inc., 609 F.2d 820 (5th Cir. 1980); Annotation, *Use of Medical or Other Scientific Treatises in Cross-Examination of Expert Witness*, 60 A.L.R.2D 77 (1958). *See also* Henry Wade Rogers, THE LAW OF EXPERT TESTIMONY 64 (3d ed. 1941).

The treatises themselves are not received as exhibits. *See* Fed. R. Evid. 803(18). *See also* United States v. Mangan, 575 F.2d 32 (2d Cir.), *cert. denied*, 439 U.S. 931 (1978).

Federal Rule of Evidence 803(18) provides that textbooks and treatises can be used as substantive evidence on direct examination of an expert, if the expert testifies that he or she relied on the treatise. The proper foundation for use of learned treatises as substantive evidence on direct examination includes: establishing that the expert relied on the treatise or publication, and establishing that the witness recognizes the treatise as authoritative. Caruolo v. John Crane, Inc., 226 F.3d 46, 54-55 (2d Cir. 2000); Costantino v. Herzog, 203 F.3d 164,168-70 (2d Cir. 2000) (videotape of accepted obstetrical procedures properly admitted as visual version of a learned treatise); United States v. Horn, 185 F. Supp. 2d 530, 556 (D. Md. 2002); Charles E. Hill & Assocs. v. Compuserve, Inc., 2000 U.S. Dist. LEXIS 14200, at *39-*40 (S.D. Ind. Aug. 24, 2000). An alternative approach is to ask the court to take judicial notice that the treatise is authoritative. *See* Fed. R. Evid. 201; United States v. Horn, 185 F. Supp. 2d 530, 556 (D. Md. 2002). Alternatively, a party may seek to have a textbook or treatise recognized only as the basis for an expert's opinion, and use of the book for this purpose does not require the same foundation. However, if a foundation is not laid, the treatise cannot be considered as substantive evidence. *See* section F.12 for an example of direct examination using authoritative treatises.

This pattern was cited with approval in LYNN MCLAIN, MARYLAND EVIDENCE: STATE AND FEDERAL § 607.5 n.2 (1987 & Supp. 1995).

D. CROSS-EXAMINATION OF A CHARACTER WITNESS

Defendant is accused of aggravated sexual assault on a baby-sitter for his children. On direct examination, defendant's counsel calls Reverend Jones, who testifies to the defendant's good character. Defendant's counsel establishes that Reverend Jones has knowledge of the defendant's good reputation in the community and of the defendant's reputation for having a peaceful nature.

Prosecuting Counsel:

Q. Reverend Jones, you testified that Danny Defendant has a good reputation in your community and that you have known the defendant to maintain a peaceful nature?

A. Yes.

Q. Are you aware that on June 28, 1995, January 23, 1995, and September 13, 1994, the police were called to Danny Defendant's home by his wife, who complained of being beaten by him?

A. No.

Q. Do you know that on March 30, 1989, Danny Defendant was arrested for assaulting a woman he was dating and spent 30 days in jail?

A. No.

Q. And have you ever seen this article, from page 1 of the Metro Section of the *Washington Post*, dated May 20, 1985, entitled "Danny Defendant Gets 30 Days for Assaulting Date"?

A. No, I have not.

Q. Reverend, if you had read this article, and if you had known of Mr. Defendant's previous run-ins with the law, would you still hold the belief that Mr. Defendant is a peaceful person with a good reputation?

A. Well, yes, I would.

Q. Reverend, weren't you incarcerated for three days in the County Jail in 1981 for committing perjury?

A. Yes, but I was let out when the trial ended, and the charges were dropped.

Comment

Federal Rule of Evidence 405 allows counsel on cross-examination to ask character witnesses about their knowledge of a defendant's specific acts. *See generally* Michelson v. United States, 335 U.S. 469 (1948). The Fourth Circuit has established the parameters of cross-examination of defense character witnesses as follows:

> Of course, the prosecutor is free upon cross-examination to in-
> quire of the defendant's reputation witnesses whether they have
> heard particular rumors about the defendant or have heard about
> specific instances of misconduct on his part, but such inquiries are
> for the purpose of revealing inconsistencies between what the wit-
> ness has heard and the conclusion about the defendant's reputa-
> tion which the witness expressed upon direct examination, and
> not for the purpose of proving the defendant's bad reputation.

United States v. Curry, 512 F.2d 1299, 1305 (4th Cir.), *cert. denied*, 423 U.S. 832 (1975). *See also* United States v. Boone, 279 F.3d 163, 174-75 (3d Cir. 2002); United States v. Aronds, 2000 U.S. App. LEXIS 4145, at *30 (6th Cir. Mar. 14, 2000) (if direct testimony addresses community reputation, inquiry may be made on cross-examination about conduct, or even charges, that might have come to the attention of the relevant community; however, cross-examiner must possess good-faith belief that the described events are of a type "likely to have become a matter of general knowledge, currency, or reputation in the community"), *citing* United States v. Brugier, 161 F.3d 1145, 1150 (8th Cir. 1998); United States v. McHorse, 179 F.3d 889, 901 (10th Cir.), *cert. denied*, 528 U.S. 944 (1999).

The trial court has the discretion to allow the Government to attempt to undermine a witness's credibility, in situations where the witness has given testimony of the defendant's good character. The Government may do so by asking if the witness has knowledge of the defendant's prior misconduct that is not consistent with the witness's direct testimony. United States v. Evans, 569 F.2d 209 (4th Cir.), *cert. denied*, 435 U.S. 975 (1978); United States v. Bright, 588 F.2d 504 (5th Cir.), *cert. denied*, 440 U.S. 972 (1979); Virgin Islands v. Roldan, 612 F.2d 775 (3d Cir. 1979), *cert. denied*, 446 U.S. 920 (1980). There is a tendency for these types of cross-exami-nation to impinge on Federal Rule of Evidence 403's standard that the probative value of the evidence should not be substantially outweighed by the danger of unfair prejudice. Therefore, important limitations are placed on judicial discretion in admitting inquiries concerning such prior misconduct. These limitations include the requirement of a threshold showing that the question is relevant to the character trait testified to by the witness on direct. This showing should be accomplished by a sidebar or proffer outside the hearing of the jury. The trial judge must determine that the probative value of the testimony will not be substantially outweighed by the danger of unfair prejudice. A cautionary instruction to the jury regarding the purpose of the evidence may be given. *See generally* United States v. Bailey, 505 F.2d 417 (D.C. Cir. 1974), *cert. denied*, 420 U.S. 961 (1975).

It is reversible error to permit a character witness to be asked on cross-examination if the witness's opinion of defendant would change if the defendant had committed the crime for which he is on trial. Such guilt-assuming hypotheticals should not be asked of character witnesses. United States v. Guzman, 167 F.3d 1350, 1352 (11th Cir. 1999); United States v. Damblu, 134 F.3d 490, 494-95 (2d Cir. 1998); United States v. Mason, 993 F.2d 406 (4th Cir. 1993); United States v. Chan, 2002 U.S. Dist. LEXIS 1221, at *5 (S.D.N.Y. Jan. 25, 2002).

Improper cross-examination of a character witness, especially in a criminal law context, can be highly prejudicial. Merely asking questions suggesting past criminal acts committed by an accused is improper. Michelson v. United States, 335 U.S. 469, 481 (1948); United States v. Senffner, 280 F.3d 755, 762-66 (7th Cir. 2002); United States v. Clark, 2001 U.S. App. LEXIS 27023, *7-*8 (6th Cir. Dec. 14, 2001), *cert. denied*, 2002 U.S. LEXIS 2415 (2002); United States v. Wilson, 244 F.3d 1208 (10th Cir.), *cert. denied*, 533 U.S. 962 (2001); United States v. Varoudakis, 233 F.3d 113, 118-19 (1st Cir. 2000); United States v. Schneider, 157 F. Supp. 2d 1044, 1069-70 (court stated that the prosecutorial misconduct that permeated the trial demanded more than "ritualistic verbal spanking"). When a character witness testifies regarding a specific character trait, cross-examination must be limited to those crimes or acts of the defendant that evidence bad character for that specific character trait. *See* United States v. Aronds, 2000 U.S. App. LEXIS 4145, at *29 (6th Cir. Mar. 14, 2000); United States v. Monteleone, 77 F.3d 1086 (8th Cir. 1996); United States v. Adair, 951 F.2d 316 (11th Cir. 1992); United States v. Bright, 588 F.2d 504 (5th Cir. 1979). For example, if a defendant is charged with embezzlement and calls character witnesses to testify to his good character for honesty, those witnesses should not be cross-examined about rumors of an illicit love affair. Such rumors, even if true, are not relevant to the character trait of honesty. Aaron v. United States, 397 F.2d 584 (5th Cir. 1968).

The character witness's prior criminal record and certain bad acts (whose commission would tend to establish the witness's lack of veracity or penchant for not telling the truth) are also admissible in impeaching the character witness. *See* United States v. Pennix, 313 F.2d 524 (4th Cir. 1963); Henderson v. United States, 202 F.2d 400 (6th Cir. 1953), *appeal after remand*, 218 F.2d 14 (6th Cir.), *cert. denied*, 349 U.S. 920 (1955); Campbell v. United States, 176 F.2d 45 (D.C. Cir. 1949).

Redirect 10

A. REHABILITATION, USE OF PRIOR CONSISTENT STATEMENT

During the course of a personal injury trial, defense counsel impeaches a witness for the plaintiff on the basis of fabricated testimony due to improper motive. The witness testified that he had been standing at the intersection and observed the defendant's motor vehicle strike the plaintiff. The thrust of defense counsel's attack is that the witness fabricated his testimony to aid the plaintiff, because the owner of the motor vehicle operated by the defendant was the C&P Telephone Company, where the witness is employed and against whom the witness has a grudge. The plaintiff's counsel rehabilitates the witness on redirect examination as follows:

Plaintiff's Counsel:

Q. Mr. Valentine, prior to this trial, have you ever given a statement concerning the accident?

A. Yes, sir, I have.

Q. When was that statement made?

A. On January 3, approximately 20 minutes after the accident.

Q. In what form was your statement given?

A. It was given to Officer James P. Senior, a police officer who investigated the accident.

Q. Can you identify this document?

A. Yes, this is the statement that I gave to the police officer.

Plaintiff's Counsel: I now offer in evidence Plaintiff's Exhibit No. 32. If the court please, may I read pertinent portions of this statement to the jury?

The Court: Yes, you may.

(Counsel reads to jury.)

Q. Mr. Valentine, when did you first learn that the owner of defendant's car was the C&P Telephone Company?

A. Today, during the course of my testimony.

Comment

Rehabilitative evidence consisting of prior consistent testimony is admissible in federal court pursuant to Federal Rule of Evidence 801d)(1)(B), when the testimony sought to be bolstered has first been impeached for truth and veracity. Mere contradiction of testimony is not enough. The

Federal Rules limit the use of prior consistent testimony to rebuttal of an express or implied charge of recent fabrication or improper influence or motive. *See* United States v. Burrell, 2002 U.S. App. LEXIS 8381, at *3 (2d Cir. May 1, 2002) (prior consistent statement made by cooperating witness at the time of his arrest was admissible under Rule 801(d) (1) (B) because defendant's opening statement argued that the witness had a motive to lie); Pecoraro v. Walls, 2002 U.S. App. LEXIS 618, at *13 (7 th Cir. Apr. 1, 2002); United States v. Argo, 2001 U.S. App. LEXIS 1658, at *14 (when defendant's counsel implies that a witness's testimony has been fabricated in exchange for a favorable plea agreement, a previous consistent statement made before the plea agreement was negotiated is admissible; a prior consistent statement is admissible only if it was made before the witness had a motive to lie), *cert. denied*, 122 S. Ct. 1192 (2002); United States v. Williams, 264 F.3d 561, 575 (5th Cir. 2001); United States v. Smith, 746 F.2d 1183 (6th Cir. 1984) (for prior-consistent-statement exception to apply, it is imperative that the consistent statement be admitted to rebut the charge of improper motive); United States v. Weil, 561 F.2d 1109 (4th Cir. 1977) (the prior consistent statement must predate the motive to fabricate). *Accord* United States v. Henderson, 717 F.2d 135 (4th Cir. 1983), *cert. denied*, 465 U.S. 1009 (1984).

The Supreme Court recently resolved the previously unsettled issue over whether, to be admissible, the prior consistent statement must have been made before the motive to fabricate existed. In *Tome v. United States*, 513 U.S. 150 (1995), the Court held that the prior consistent statement must have been made before the time of the charged recent fabrication or improper influence or motive. Federal Rule of Evidence 801 permits the prior consistent statement to be admitted as substantive evidence. *See* Phoenix Assocs. III v. Stone, 60 F.3d 95 (2d Cir. 1995); Engebretsen v. Fairchild Aircraft Corp., 21 F.3d 721 (6th Cir. 1994); United States v. White, 11 F.3d 1446 (8th Cir. 1993); United States v. Cherry, 938 F.2d 748 (7th Cir. 1991); United States v. Parry, 649 F.2d 292 (5th Cir. 1981); United States v. Dominguez, 604 F.2d 304 (4th Cir. 1979), *cert. denied*, 444 U.S. 1014 (1980); Grisanti v. Cioffi, 2001 U.S. Dist. LEXIS 14358, at *22 (D. Conn. June 14, 2001); United States v. Ealy, 2002 U.S. Dist. LEXIS 3255, at *15 (W.D. Va. Feb. 26, 2002). *See also* United States v. Simonelli, 237 F.3d 19, 26-29 (1st Cir.) (discusses and distinguishes *Tome* and addresses a question of first impression in the First Circuit; states that just because Rule 801 does not preclude admissibility does not establish that there is a basis for admissibility and "join[s] the majority view, well expressed by the Fourth Circuit . . . that 'where prior consistent statements are not offered for their truth but for the limited purpose of rehabilitation, . . . Rule 801(d) (1) (B) and its concomitant restrictions do not apply' . . . [but w]hen the prior statements are offered for credibility, the question is not governed by Rule 801"), *cert. denied*, 122 S. Ct. 54 (2001); Pursell v. Horn, 187 F. Supp. 2d 260, 344 (W.D. Pa. 2002) ("In Pennsylvania, prior consistent statements of a witness are not admissible as either substantive evidence or as corroborative evidence . . . [with] certain well-recognized exceptions . . . : prior declarations of a witness, which are consistent with his present testimony, may be admissible to corroborate his present testimony if it be alleged that the witness' present testimony is recently fabricated, or if it be claimed that the witness is testifying from corrupt motives[; and e]vidence of consonant statements, if admissible, are admissible only for the purpose of showing that that which the witness now testifies to has not been recently fabricated and not for the purpose of proving the truth of the present testimony.").

Part 3

Use of Discovery Devices in Trial

Depositions 11

A. IMPEACHMENT

An alleged witness to an accident is on the witness stand. The witness, June Smith, is the aunt of the infant, Mary Jones, who is the plaintiff in a suit for negligence against the landlord of June Smith's apartment. The infant plaintiff claims that the landlord negligently failed to repair a kitchen screen door. As a result of the landlord's negligence, the infant plaintiff, while playing in the kitchen, touched the screen door and fell off the second-story kitchen porch, suffering severe injuries. The witness is trying to show that the child touched the screen door, causing the door to fall, and that the door did not fall by other means or as a result of another child's activity. Cross-examination on behalf of the landlord proceeds in the following manner.

Defense Counsel:

Q. Is it your testimony that you saw the infant plaintiff touch the screen door and fall through the kitchen door onto the porch, and then from the porch onto the ground?

A. Yes.

Q. Miss Smith, do you recall that you were summoned to appear in my office over one year ago?

A. Yes.

Q. Do you remember coming to the office with an attorney?

A. Yes.

Q. Do you recall that we met in my library and that a court reporter was there who took down questions that I asked you and your answers to those questions?

A. Yes.

Q. The testimony that was taken down by the court reporter was taken down or recorded the same way as in this court, except there was no judge or jury present, is that correct?

A. Yes.

Q. And you were under oath then just as you are now?

A. Yes.

Q. The lawyer that accompanied you to my office for what was your deposition is the same lawyer who represents you now, is that correct?

A. Yes.

Q. When you finished testifying, your testimony was typed up by the court reporter word for word as you gave it and was submitted to you to read and to correct any mistakes, isn't that true?

A. Yes.

Q. Did you in fact read your deposition?

A. Yes.

Q. You did find mistakes in the transcript, did you not?

A. Yes.

Q. And you made notes of the corrections you felt had to be made, didn't you?

A. Yes.

Q. And then you signed your deposition as corrected by you before a Notary Public, isn't that true?

A. Yes.

Q. Miss Smith, I am now going to read to you beginning at Line 7 on Page 81 of the transcript of the testimony as typed by the court reporter and corrected by you:

> Q. Prior to the accident involving the infant plaintiff, where were you, Miss Smith?
>
> A. I was in the bedroom looking after my little boy.
>
> Q. When was the last time you had seen the infant plaintiff prior to the accident?
>
> A. After we had breakfast, she was playing with the other children staying with me, and I went to nurse my baby.
>
> Q. Am I correct in understanding that your testimony is that after breakfast you left the infant plaintiff with the other children and that you went into the bedroom to nurse the baby and that you did not see the infant plaintiff until after she had the accident?
>
> A. Yes.

Q. Now, Miss Smith, what I have just read was your testimony under oath on April 14, 1987, wasn't it?

A. I cannot remember what I said at that time, but I suppose that what you read is what I said, if that's what it says.

Q. Well, you are not suggesting that what I read was anything but your previous testimony, are you?

A. No.

Q. Now, is your testimony today correct under oath, or was your testimony correct as you gave it in April of 1987?

A. I don't know.

Comment

It is not always effective simply to ask the witness whether she recalls her deposition being taken on a previous occasion. Members of a jury may not know the significance of the deposition. Therefore, counsel should ask more detailed questions, as in this pattern, to illustrate the significance of the deposition and to emphasize the subsequent inconsistent trial testimony. *See generally* Coletti v. Cudd Pressure Control, 165 F.3d 767, 774 (10th Cir. 1999); Shearing v. Iolab Corp., 975 F.2d 1541 (Fed. Cir. 1992) (at trial, attempted impeachment of witnesses occurred when they had recollections that had not been mentioned in previous depositions); Aetna Cas. & Sur. Co. v. Guynes, 713 F.2d 1187 (5th Cir. 1983) (previous deposition testimony used to impeach trial witness testimony). *But see* New Mexico Sav. & Loan Ass'n v. United States Fid. & Guar. Co., 454 F.2d 328 (10th Cir. 1972) (party may not introduce deposition testimony as substantive evidence or to impeach when witness merely cannot remember facts to which the witness previously testified).

The last question, "Now, is your testimony today correct under oath, or was your testimony correct as you gave it in April of 1995?" is optional. Some prefer this type of question to dramatize the inconsistency during the testimony stage of the proceedings. Others prefer to end the examination with the inconsistency, without the final question, reserving opportunity in closing argument to emphasize and elaborate upon the significance of the inconsistency. Both approaches are used in varying situations.

The advantage of the first approach is that the heightened dramatization can have a significant influence on the jury during the course of testimony. The weakness in this approach is that the witness, when confronted with the proverbial question, "Are you lying now, or were you lying then?" is given the opportunity to explain away the inconsistency. *See* Fed. R. Evid. 613; Fed. R. Civ. P. 32(9).

Still another approach to impeachment using a transcript is to simply remind the witness she just testified that she saw the incident, but that in her deposition at a certain page and line she swore that she did not see the incident. *See*, for example, Herbert J. Stern, *Trying Cases to Win,*

Cross-Examination, Wiley Law Publications, John Wiley & Sons, Inc. (1993).

B. ADVERSE PARTY

Jones institutes suit against Weeks Exterminator Company on grounds of negligent entrustment of a company vehicle. Jones takes the deposition of the driver, Hannibal Smith, an employee of Weeks and also a defendant in the case. Smith was off on a frolic and not acting in the scope of his employment at the time of the accident. During the deposition, the driver testifies that his employer was aware of his poor driving record prior to entrusting him with the vehicle. Plaintiff does not wish to call the driver as a witness at trial, because the driver may attempt either to change his testimony or explain it away. However, plaintiff wishes to get the driver's clear admission into evidence and let defense counsel, if he wishes, call the driver as a defense witness. The following procedure is adopted by plaintiff's counsel:

The Court: Mr. Darrow, call your next witness, please.

Mr. Darrow: Your Honor, before we call our next witness, we would request permission to read in evidence a portion of the deposition of defendant Smith.

Weeks' Counsel: We would object because Hannibal Smith is present in court and available to testify, and also because Smith is adverse to my client on the issue of negligent entrustment and his deposition testimony on that issue cannot be admitted against my client.

The Court: The rules of procedure are clear. Plaintiff's counsel has the right to use the deposition of a party for any purpose. He can therefore read in evidence portions or all of the deposition of the driver, and this evidence can be considered as part of the plaintiff's case against both defendants. You, on the other hand, have the right to introduce any other part of the deposition that ought, in fairness, to be considered with those portions introduced by plaintiff's counsel. *See* Fed. R. Civ. P. 32 (a)(4).

Mr. Darrow: If the court please, I should read for the jury from page 38 of the defendant driver's deposition, line 3, which states as follows: "Mr. Weeks, president of the tire company, told me that I had too many accidents, and if I had another automobile accident, I would have to find another job, because he couldn't take the chance of being sued on my account."

Comment

Plaintiff's counsel used the deposition testimony of the driver as substantive evidence, rather than merely for impeachment. In this way, he put the burden, tactically, onto the defense attorney to clarify this point. If plaintiff's counsel questioned the president of the exterminating company, after the president testified and denied making the statement testified to by Mr. Smith, the deposition testimony could have been used for impeachment by prior inconsistent statement. *See* Fed. R. Civ. P. 32; Fey v. Walston & Co., Inc., 493 F.2d 1036 (7th Cir. 1974).

Another alternative available to plaintiff's counsel would be to call the president of the exterminating company or the driver as an adverse party. *See* Fed. R. Evid. 801(d)(2), which provides for the admission of a party opponent as non-hearsay. Alternatively, counsel can treat the admission as an exception to the hearsay rule. *See* Fed. R. Evid. 607. This rule provides that the credibility of a witness may be attacked by any party, including the party calling the witness.

If the person who made the damaging statement read from the driver's deposition is available for trial and was a lower-level supervisor who on deposition admitted making the same statement, that person's deposition also could be used as substantive evidence in the case, if the deposition testimony was inconsistent with the supervisor's trial testimony. Federal Rule of Evidence 801(d)(2) (admissions of party opponent) provides for the admissibility against a party of statements by the party's agent or employee. However, before the court can find that a statement is admissible as a statement made by the agent of a party-opponent, the court must determine that the declarant was in fact an agent of the party at the time the statement was made. Bourjaily v. United States, 483 U.S. 171 (1987). This case reflects the federal view of "bootstrapping" the statement itself in making the determination of whether the statement was made within the scope of employment. The federal view is that the statement is considered in determining the issue of scope of employment. *See also, e.g.*, Sea-Land Serv. v. Lozen Int'l, 285 F.3d 808 (9th Cir. 2002); Weston-Smith v. Cooley Dickinson Hosp., Inc., 282 F.3d 60, 66 (1st Cir. 2002); Albright v. Virtue, 273 F.3d 564, 569 (3d Cir. 2001); Yates v. Rexton, Inc., 267 F.3d 793, 802 (8th Cir. 2001).

C. WITNESS NOT AVAILABLE

Defense Counsel: Your Honor, at this point defendants would like to read in evidence the deposition of James McCullough. Mr. McCullough, whose deposition was taken last April, is now in Lewiston, Maine, a distance greater than 100 miles from this courthouse. We are prepared to present evidence to this effect, if that is necessary.

The Court: Is there any dispute as to the location of the witness?

Plaintiff's Counsel: No, Your Honor.

The Court: Very well, proceed.

Defense Counsel: Your Honor, I would ask that my co-counsel, Mr. Ames, take the witness stand. I will read the questions asked of Mr. McCullough during his deposition, and Mr. Ames will read Mr. McCullough's answers.

Defense Counsel: Your Honor, will you explain to the jury the nature and effect of a deposition?

The Court: Very well. (Court explains nature and effect of a deposition, how it is taken, the fact that it is evidence, the same as if McCullough were personally on the witness stand.)

(Counsel then reads the questions and co-counsel reads the answers.)

Comment

Federal Rule of Civil Procedure 32(a)(3)(B) provides that the witness is unavailable if beyond 100 miles from the place of trial. The reading of a deposition of a witness, or the use of a witness's deposition for any purpose, if that witness is unavailable, is permitted under Federal Rule of Civil Procedure 32(a)(3). *See* Tatman v. Collins, 938 F.2d 509 (4th Cir. 1991); Jauch v. Corley, 830 F.2d 47 (5th Cir. 1987). *Cf.* Battle v. Memorial Hosp., 228 F.3d 544, 551 (5th Cir. 2000) (nothing prevents the use of a discovery [as opposed to a trial] deposition at trial, particularly against the party who conducted it); Rosebud Sioux Tribe v. A & P Steel, Inc., 733 F.2d 509 (8th Cir.) (reading of deposition into evidence constituted an unfair manipulation of the rules of evidence when unavailability of witness was due to invocation of Fifth Amendment), *cert. denied*, 469 U.S. 1072 (1984); Chum Ltd. v. Lisowski, 2001 U.S. Dist. LEXIS 15423, at *2 (S.D.N.Y. Oct. 2, 2001), *j. entered*, 2002 U.S. Dist. LEXIS 2926 (S.D.N.Y. Apr. 18, 2002). Defendant's attorney calls his co-counsel to read the answers for the testimonial effect of having a live witness clearly and articulately respond, so as to maintain the jury's interest.

When a deposition of an unavailable witness is introduced in evidence and read to the jury, it is customary for counsel to request, and for the court to give, an explanatory comment to the jury.

Interrogatories 12

A. USE IN COURT

Plaintiff sues defendant for damages resulting from an automobile collision. Plaintiff claims $50,000 special damages. Before resting his case, defendant's counsel proceeds as follows:

> **Defendant's Counsel**: Your Honor, before defendants close their case, we would like to read in evidence No. 27 of defendant's interrogatories or questions to plaintiff and the answer to that question, which plaintiff gave under oath.
>
> **Plaintiff's Counsel:** We object. The plaintiff is available in court, and if defense counsel wishes to question or cross-examine plaintiff he has the opportunity to do so.
>
> **The Court:** Federal Rule of Civil Procedure 33(c) provides that the answers to interrogatories may be used for any purpose, to the extent permitted by the rules of evidence. Unless there is some relevancy objection, I am going to allow defendant's counsel to proceed.
>
> **Defendant's Counsel**: Thank you, Your Honor. Interrogatory, or Question 27: "Itemize the expenses paid or incurred by you as a result of the occurrence." The answer to that question was filed on April 23, 1978, and reads as follows: "1. Property damage—$5,000. 2. Medical bills—$6,000."

Comment

The use of interrogatories during trial follows a pattern similar to the use of depositions. *See* Fed. R. Civ. P. 33. *See also* Exum v. General Elec. Co., 819 F.2d 1158 (D.C. Cir. 1987). *But see* Frankel v. Burke's Excavating, Inc., 397 F.2d 167 (3d Cir. 1968) (refusal to allow party to read into evidence opposing party's answers to interrogatories not erroneous due to binding instructions given to jury).

B. IMPEACHMENT

Same facts as stated in previous pattern, except the plaintiff is testifying, and on cross-examination defense counsel proceeds as follows:

> **Defense Counsel:** Mr. Jones, you testified that your expenses, as a result of this occurrence, were in excess of $40,000, is that correct?
> A. Yes.

Q. Do you recall that you were served with interrogatories or a series of questions in this case?

A. Yes.

Q. Do you recall that you helped your counsel write answers to these interrogatories?

A. Yes.

Q. And you reviewed the answers before they were filed in court?

A. Yes.

Q. You wanted them to be correct before you swore to them, didn't you?

A. Yes.

Q. And you appeared before a Notary Public, did you not, and made oath or declared under penalty of perjury that the answers were true to the best of your information and belief?

A. Yes.

Q. When you reviewed those answers, your lawyer advised or explained to you the significance of these questions and how they were being answered, didn't he?

A. Yes.

Q. And did you, in fact, review the answers to these interrogatories in the light of your counsel's explanation and advice before the answers were filed in court?

A. Yes.

Comment

The use of interrogatories for impeachment is similar to the use of depositions for impeachment. *See* Fed. R. Civ. P. 33. *See also* Clark Equip. Co. v. Keller, 570 F.2d 778 (8th Cir.), *cert. denied*, 439 U.S. 825 (1978); Troutman v. S. Ry Co., 441 F.2d 586 (5th Cir.), *cert. denied*, 404 U.S. 871 (1971); United States Lines Co. v. King, 363 F.2d 658 (4th Cir. 1966). *But see* DeBenedetto v. Goodyear Tire & Rubber Co., 754 F.2d 512 (4th Cir. 1985) (refusal to allow jury to consider interrogatories for purposes of impeaching opposing party not in error, where interrogatories and requests for admissions considered irrelevant in light of the party's admissions at trial).

Index

A

absent witness 7
adverse party 231–32
   admission of a party opponent as
      non-hearsay 232
   Federal Rule of Evidence
      801(d)(2) 232
American Law Institute 144
anatomical model 82
   admissibility of 82
   as visual aids 83

B

best evidence rule 56–60
   original documents, preference 57
   previous pattern 60–62
business records 25
   computer printouts 27
   exception to the hearsay rule 27
   factual findings 31
   Federal Rule of Evidence 803(6)
      27, 28, 30
   Federal Rule of Evidence 803(8)
      30
   Federal Rules of Evidence 902(11)
      28
   hearsay declarations 30
   hearsay, second level of 29
   hospital records 27
   opinions, admissibility of 31
   police reports 27
   proper foundation for introduction
      as evidence 27
   "regular practice of that business"
      29
   summaries or compilations 27

C

character evidence
   allowed under limited circum-
      stances 163
   as a material proposition in a civil
      case 161–70
   as an essential element in a civil
      case 161–70
   circumstantial use of 163
   credibility of a witness 175
   Federal Rule of Evidence 406 178
   Federal Rule of Evidence 608 166
   good character and conduct of
      witness 174–76
   habit, usual method of practice
      176–79
   inadmissibility of 162
   materiality of 163
   opinion 166–67
   opinion with specific instances
      167–68
   proof of specific instances 165
   reputation 161
   specific instances 169
character evidence, accused
   Federal Rule of Evidence 404(a)(1)
      171
   opinion method 173–74
   reputation method 170–72
charts 83–86
   evidence vs. explanatory 86
   exclusion of 86
   pretrial review of data 85
   use of 84
computer animation 73–77
   aid to expert witnesses 75
   foundation for introduction 75
   prediction of future events 76

H

I